Microsoft®

Office® Professional 2013 Plain & Simple

Katherine Murray

Published with the authorization of Microsoft Corporation by:
O'Reilly Media, Inc.
1005 Gravenstein Highway North
Sebastopol, California 95472

ISBN: 978-0-7356-6932-1

1 2 3 4 5 6 7 8 9 TI 8 7 6 5 4 3

Printed and bound in Canada.

Microsoft Press books are available through booksellers and distributors worldwide. If you need support related to this book, email Microsoft Press Book Support at mspinput@microsoft.com. Please tell us what you think of this book at *http://www. microsoft.com/learning/booksurvey*.

Microsoft and the trademarks listed at *http://www.microsoft.com/about/legal/en/us/IntellectualProperty/Trademarks/EN-US. aspx* are trademarks of the Microsoft group of companies. All other marks are property of their respective owners.

The example companies, organizations, products, domain names, email addresses, logos, people, places, and events depicted herein are fictitious. No association with any real company, organization, product, domain name, email address, logo, person, place, or event is intended or should be inferred.

Acquisitions Editor: Kenyon Brown
Project and Developmental Editor: Katharine Dvorak
Production Editor: Melanie Yarbrough
Editorial Production: Octal Publishing
Technical Reviewers: Kristin Merritt, Vince Averello, Todd Meister, Andrew Vickers
Copyeditor: Bob Russell
Indexer: WordCo Indexing Services
Cover Design: Twist Creative • Seattle
Cover Composition: Zyg Group, LLC
Illustrator: S4 Carlisle Publishing Services

Contents

5   Creating and saving a Document in Word 2013 . . . . **65**

8 Creating long documents in Word 2013. 139

9 Creating and saving worksheets in Excel 2013 161

10   Formatting and enhancing an Excel 2013 worksheet **191**

13 Collaborating and finishing your presentation in PowerPoint 2013 253

Acknowledgments

Writing a book is always an adventure, and each project has unexpected twists and turns and high points as well as icky spiderwebs. Luckily I've been able to travel in the company of a number of talented people. Special thanks to:

- Kenyon Brown, senior editor, for wanting me to write this book (love it!) and for coming up with creative solutions as time grew short;

- Katharine Dvorak, project editor, for her excellent, persistent, and faithful development, management, and support all the way through;

- Bob Russell, copy editor, for his great editing skill and terrific sense of humor;

- Kristen Merritt, Vince Averello, Todd Meister, and Andrew Vickers, technical reviewers, for carefully testing the manuscript and offering suggestions that made tasks clearer and easier to understand;

- Melanie Yarbrough, production editor, for keeping all the production files flowing and being flexible and friendly as this project headed into the home stretch;

- Curtis Frye, Jim Boyce, and Andy Couch, who contributed content for tasks in the Excel, Outlook, and Access sections when deadlines were looming;

- And to Claudette Moore, my agent, as always, for everything.

About this book

1

Hello, and welcome to the next generation of Microsoft Office 2013! Whether you're all about touch on the tablet and smartphone or you prefer a more conventional mouse-and-keyboard approach to your favorite Office applications, Office 2013 has something to offer you.

Office 2013 is much different from anything we've seen before. This version makes the most of the color, movement, and integration that Windows 8 brings; it helps you to stay social by keeping you within a click of colleagues, friends, and family; and it gives you easy access to your files by saving them to the "cloud" so that you can get to your documents using any device that connects to the web. The idea is that you can work or play anywhere, anytime, with anyone you choose.

Sound intriguing? This book shows you how to get the most from these and many more features, helping you to master the basics quickly and focus on the things that matter most to you.

In this section:

- Plain talk about Office 2013
- The plain & simple approach
- What's new in Office 2013
- Which editions of Office 2013 are available?
- What you'll find in this book
- A few assumptions
- Before we begin

Plain talk about Office 2013

We live in a time of information overload. What we need isn't more information; rather, it's easier access to the clear information that's become vital. Whether you're hurrying to get something done, trying to iron out a glitch, or simply learning how to use a feature for the first time, you shouldn't need to read about every possible option under the sun just to complete a simple task. And, if there are easy-to-follow, colorful illustrations along the way to point out what you click on the screen or show you the order of steps to take, so much the better.

Microsoft Office Professional 2013 Plain & Simple is written in plain language; there's no "computerspeak" or technical jargon to get in the way of what you're trying to learn. Simple examples reflect the types of things you're likely to want to do with Office 2013, and the information provided is factual, to the point, and clear.

The Plain & Simple approach

If you're the type of person who likes to get the straight scoop on new tools and tasks, this is your book. One of the great things about the *Plain & Simple* series is that it helps you explore what you need to master the tasks that you're most interested in learning, using an easy-to-follow, visual format. The goal of *Microsoft Office Professional 2013 Plain & Simple* is to teach you all the basics quickly and efficiently so that you can get busy creating, sharing, and collaborating with others to create the projects that inspire you. You'll find friendly and focused steps, clear and colorful illustrations, and tips and notes along the way to help you get the most out of the program you're using without giving you a lot of information that you don't need.

Here are some of the key elements in this book that help you find and master what you need quickly:

- You can read the book in any order that makes sense to you. You can start in any section that explains what you want to learn.

- Screenshots show you at a glance where to find the features you need on your screen.

- Steps offer the quickest and best way to accomplish a particular task.

- Tips provide valuable information that go along with the task being covered.

- "See Also" notes tell you where in the book similar or complementary tasks are covered.

- "Try This!" exercises encourage you to try a technique yourself by using the steps in the section.

- Cautions warn you of potential problems or preventive measures you can take to avoid trouble down the road.

Microsoft Office Professional 2013 Plain & Simple is designed specifically to help you learn what you need to know about this latest version of the Microsoft Office suite.

What's new in Office 2013

Office 2013 is a big story set in the context of an even bigger one. Windows 8 arrived on the scene in the fall of 2012, promising to usher in a new era of technology by personalizing our computing experience and seamlessly connecting us to our data in new and ever-expanding ways. Office 2013, with its different editions, builds on the promise of Windows 8, offering a natural touch interface (which still works just as naturally with mouse and keyboard, too). You'll also find a modern, clean interface that does away with the frames of the window when you're working with an app in full screen.

Program designers focused on four key areas when they were renovating Office:

- **Build on the best of Windows 8, but also run on Windows 7.**   Office 2013 is now fully optimized for touch-operated devices, offering a clean, airy interface and easy-to-navigate ribbon and panes. You can use the Windows 8 touch keyboard—which is available in several styles—or your own keyboard to enter content quickly and accurately. You can *dock* your open applications so that you can have more than one window open on the Windows 8 screen at a time, and you can easily connect to devices, people, other apps, and more from within your Office apps. If you want to run Office 2013 on your Windows 7 computer, you'll find all the same features, including touch mode for Windows 7 touch devices.

- **Put Office in the cloud.**   Now, not only is there an edition of Office 2013 available solely in the cloud, but also the traditional desktop version of Office 2013 saves naturally to the cloud, where you can access and work on your files from anywhere, using any device that has access to the web. Office on Demand is a service available through Office 365 subscriptions with which you can stream Office on a computer; you don't need to have Office installed.

- **Keep it social.**   Social media was on the rise when Office 2010 first appeared on the scene, but today, it is a way of life. Office 2013 connects to social media services by which you can share and use photos and files, connect with your contacts, ask questions on social media sites, and more.

- **Enable new experiences.** Office 2013 includes new features that can improve your computing experience, whether you're reviewing new documents, taking notes that you want to review later, or giving a presentation at a large business meeting. For example, Microsoft Word includes a new Reading Mode that adjusts easily to the size of your screen, live layout functionality that reflows your document as you move objects on the page, and "peeks" that help you get the information you need without leaving your current view.

> **SEE ALSO**   You'll learn more about all of the new features in Office 2013 in Sections 5 through 21, where I cover topics and tasks related to the different Office applications.

Which editions of Office 2013 are available?

Technology continues to change the way we live and work, and Office 2013 editions reflect different working styles for different types of users. Here's a quick overview of the different editions.

If you're a big fan of cloud technology and love the idea of working on files from anywhere, using any device, you will like the subscription-based Office model available through Microsoft Office 365. There are several subscription plans available so that you can choose the one that fits what you want to accomplish with Office. Office 365 Home Premium is designed for home users and consumers who want to use Office on up to five computers and devices. Office apps include stalwart Microsoft products: Word, PowerPoint, Excel, Outlook, OneNote, Access, and Publisher. Other Office 365 subscriptions cater to small business and enterprise. In addition, a version of Office for Mac is available through Office 365. Office on Demand is also available through the Office 365 edition, which you can use to stream Office live so that you can work on computers that don't even have Office apps installed.

If you prefer the more conventional method of installing Office on your computer and using it as a stand-alone suite of programs (although you can still save your files to the cloud, if you choose), you can purchase and install Microsoft Office 2013. If you use a device with an ARM processor and Windows RT, your device will come equipped with Office on Windows RT. This edition includes Word, Excel, PowerPoint, and OneNote and is provided by the manufacturer. It's not something you can buy separately and install.

What you'll find in this book

You don't have to read the sections in *Microsoft Office Professional 2013 Plain & Simple* in any particular order; instead, simply jump in to the section that offers the answers you seek. You'll find that the book is organized to cover shared tasks and topics first. Later, sections focus on specific application tasks. For example, in Section 2, "Getting started with Office 2013," you learn the new features of the Office 2013 screen as well as how to use the ribbon, display minibars, switch to Full Screen Mode, and display the Backstage view.

In Section 3, "Office 2013 by touch, mouse, and keyboard," you find out how to navigate in Office 2013, no matter what type of device you're using and what your navigation preferences might be. Section 4, "Accomplishing Basic Tasks in Office 2013," offers the how-to's on all the basic common tasks you'll perform using the various apps. You'll find out how to do things like choosing backgrounds, opening apps, docking apps on the screen, changing the ribbon display, saving files to the cloud or your hard drive, tagging files, previewing and printing files, translating content, sharing files, exporting files, and getting help in Office 2013.

Section 5, "Creating and Saving a Document in Word 2013," begins the sections in which I focus on specific Office apps. In this section, you learn how to navigate the Word window, start a new document, add your own content, insert bookmarks and pictures, flow your text and use live layout, search and replace text, edit and format content, add tables and SmartArt diagrams, and insert text boxes and online video. Section 6, "Formatting Your Content in Word 2013," focuses on applying themes and styles to your document to help you achieve the professional look you're aiming for. You also learn to work with spacing, margins, and tabs in this section. Section 7, "Collaborating with Word 2013," teaches you what you need to know to share and work successfully with others on your Word documents. You'll find out how to track changes, add comments, collaborate in the cloud, and restrict editing in parts of your shared document. Section 8, "Creating Long Documents in Word 2013," rounds out the tutorial on Word by showing you how to add headers and footers, insert page numbers, create sections, add columns, insert footnotes and endnotes, add a table of contents, prepare a mailing, design a form, and customize long documents.

Section 9, "Creating and Saving Worksheets in Excel 2013," introduces you to Excel 2013 and gives you the lay of the land of the Excel window. You find out how to create a new worksheet, add worksheet data, insert pictures, add a chart, save and share a workbook, and export or collaborate on a worksheet. Section 10, "Formatting and Enhancing an Excel 2013 Worksheet," shows you how to apply a theme, format cells, add and delete columns and rows, hide and display information, work with multiple worksheets, create a data series, and set a print range. Section 11, "Analyzing Your Excel 2013 Data," presents what you need to know to analyze your worksheet data. You discover how to create and work with functions and formulas, create data tables, sort your data, create PowerView Reports, add sparklines, work with PivotTables, add slicers and a timeline, and change data relationships.

Section 12, "Creating a Presentation in PowerPoint 2013," teaches you about creating, editing, and formatting a presentation. You learn how to choose a slide layout, work with master slides, insert pictures and video, and add sound effects. Section 13, "Collaborating and Finishing Your Presentation in Power-Point 2013," shows you how to animate slide elements, add transitions, preview your presentation, time your delivery, add speaker notes and narration, and print the materials you need for the show.

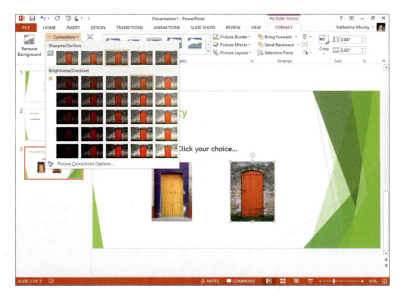

Section 14, "Managing and Sharing Notes in OneNote 2013," introduces you to digital note-taking by guiding you on a tour of the OneNote window and showing you how to create a notebook, open existing notebooks, create sections, add note pages, use page templates, manage pages and sections, file unfiled notes, insert side notes, add notes in audio or ink, clip notes from the web, and much more. Section 15, "Stay in Touch with

Outlook 2013," shows you how to launch Outlook, navigate the Outlook window, set up your email accounts, add contacts, set up teams and groups, read and respond to mail, use Quick Steps to manage your mail, flag mail for follow-up, tag and organize your mail, and add and manage RSS feeds. Section 16, "Keeping Your Calendar Current," spotlights all things scheduling, showing you how to display calendar views, share your calendar, create a team calendar, and publish your calendar online. You learn to create an appointment, invite participants, set recurrences, and schedule a team meeting. Section 17, "Managing People, Tasks, and Notes in Outlook 2013," wraps up the focus on Outlook by demonstrating how to view, organize, add, and find contacts; create, assign, and track tasks; and create, categorize, manage, and share your notes.

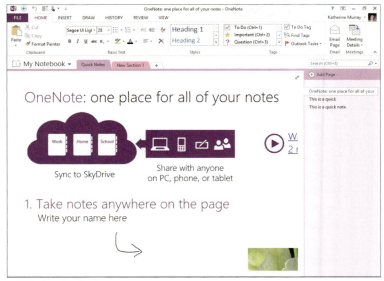

Section 18, "Make Contact Now with Lync 2013," introduces you to Lync 2013, Microsoft's online meeting and instant messaging tool that is included as part of Office 2013 ProPlus. This section shows you how to launch Lync, add contacts, send and respond to instant messages, chat in a chat room, and make phone, audio, and video calls. Section 19, "Creating Publications with Publisher 2013," shares how you can create your own publications—newsletters, flyers, brochures, invitations, and more—by using Publisher templates. Discover how to flow text, tweak images, add tables, create boilerplate content, stack and group objects, and finalize your publication.

Section 20, "Creating a Desktop Database with Access 2013," introduces you to Access, spotlights Access data templates, and goes through the basics of creating a simple database. What's more, Section 21, "Creating a Web App with Access 2013," shows how you how to design and produce your own web apps to collect and organize data from customers and colleagues.

A few assumptions

I wrote this book with a few assumptions in mind. First, I'm assuming that you've already installed Office 2013 on your computer and other devices. If you haven't yet installed Office 2013, you can install the software easily by purchasing and downloading it from *www.microsoftstore.com* or by installing it from the CD in the packaged software you purchased.

I'm also assuming that you're interested in the most popular Office 2013 applications: Word, Excel, PowerPoint, Outlook, OneNote, Access, Lync, and Publisher. You might be using either Office 365 Home and Family, Office 2013 ProPlus, or Office 2013.

Additionally, I've assumed that for the most part you're familiar with computer basics, that you know how to use your mouse, you're familiar with your computer, and that you've already connected your computer to the Internet and to your printer.

Before we begin

The primary goal of *Microsoft Office Professional 2013 Plain & Simple* is to help you learn the tasks you most want to accomplish in Office 2013. Hopefully, along the way you'll discover new features you're excited to try; learn how to connect to friends, family, and colleagues you haven't talked with in a while; and find out how great it can be to have the freedom and flexibility to work from anywhere, anytime, with anyone you choose.

Office 2013 makes it possible for you to work the way you choose and create the documents, worksheets, presentations, notebooks, messaging, and web apps you want. I hope you'll enjoy exploring all the possibilities in Office 2013 as much as I enjoyed writing this book for you.

The best way to learn is by doing, so let's get started using Office 2013.

Adapting task procedures for touchscreens

In this book, we provide instructions based on traditional keyboard and mouse input methods. If you're using Word, for example, on a touch-enabled device, you might be giving commands by tapping with your finger or with a stylus. If so, substitute a tapping action any time we instruct you to click a user interface element. Also note that when we tell you to enter information in Word, you can do so by typing on a keyboard, tapping in the entry field under discussion to display and use the onscreen keyboard, or even speaking aloud, depending on your computer setup and your personal preferences.

Getting started with Office 2013

2

This is the section in which you get to say hello to Office 2013. Whether you're using Office 2013 with Windows 8 or Windows 7, you'll find the new, clean interface, the roomier display, the flexibility of the ribbon, and the new minibars make it easier than ever to work with your Microsoft Office apps in the way that is most comfortable for you.

This section shows you how to launch Office 2013 and explore the look and feel of the program window. You'll also find out how to use the ribbon and learn how minibars offer the tools you need based on the context of what you're trying to accomplish. You'll also learn a bit about your Microsoft Account and discover its importance in providing a computing experience that travels easily with you from computer to browser to tablet to phone.

In this section:

- Launching Office 2013
- Adding Office 2013 to the Windows 8 desktop
- Exploring the look and feel of Office 2013
- Learning the Office 2013 screen
- Using the ribbon
- Displaying minibars
- Changing the ribbon display
- Going backstage

Launching Office 2013

If you're using Windows 8, you will notice right away how easy it is to launch an app on the Start screen. With just a single click, you can be working with the Office 2013 app of your choice.

If you're using Windows 7, you begin with the Start button in the lower-left corner of the Windows 7 desktop. When you choose All Programs you can navigate to the Microsoft Office 2013 folder and launch the application that you want to use.

Start Office apps from the Windows 8 Start screen

1 Scroll to the far-right end of the Start screen apps.

2 Click the Office 2013 app that you'd like to launch.

The app opens on the Windows 8 desktop.

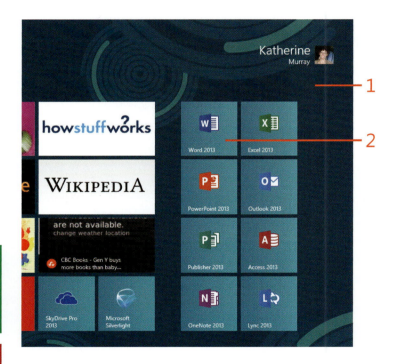

> ✓ **TIP** If you prefer to use the mouse, move it to the bottom edge of the Windows 8 Start screen and the scroll bar appears. Click toward the right end of the scroll bar to display apps currently off the right side of the screen and then click the app tile for the Office 2013 program you want to luanch.

> → **TRY THIS!** If you want to add Office app tiles to the Windows desktop taskbar, select the app tile by swiping down on it or right-clicking it, and then click Pin To Taskbar. The app icon appears in the Quick Launch area of the Windows desktop. You can then launch the app by clicking the icon on the desktop taskbar.

Launch Office 2013 in Windows 7

1 Click the Start button.

The Start menu appears.

2 Click All Programs.

3 Scroll through the programs list and click Microsoft Office 2013.

4 Click the Office 2013 program that you want to launch.

The program opens on your desktop.

Adding Office 2013 to the Windows 8 desktop

You initially launch the Office 2013 app you want to use from the Start screen, but it opens on the Windows desktop. If you prefer, you can pin your favorite Office 2013 apps to the Windows desktop so that you can launch the programs directly from there.

Add Office 2013 to the Windows 8 desktop

1 On the Windows 8 Start screen, scroll to the far right side of the Office app tiles.

2 Right-click or swipe down the Office 2013 app that you want to add to the desktop taskbar.

3 Click Pin To Taskbar.

4 Scroll to the left and click the Desktop app.

File Explorer appears.

5 In the taskbar, click the Office 2013 app icon to start it.

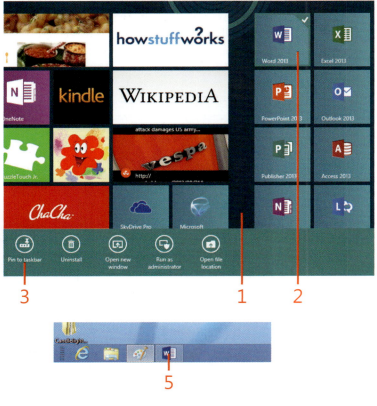

Exploring the look and feel of Office 2013

So, are you ready to dive in and have a good look around at Office 2013? One of the first things you'll notice about the design of Office 2013 is that it is clean and uncluttered. Some even call it *minimalist*. The idea is to make the tools so unobtrusive that they won't detract from the attention you really need to focus on your work. Plus, the new *modeless window* you see (or more accurately, you *don't* see) when the app is open fully on the screen gives you the maximum amount of space you can have as you work.

Some of the key tools you'll work with throughout your Office 2013 experience include the ribbon, which provides the majority of the tools and options you'll use no matter which app you're using; the Quick Access toolbar, which is like a customizable shortcut palette of tools you use often; the Microsoft Office Backstage view, in which you can manage your file, set program options, get help, and more; and minibars, which provide you with options related to the item you've selected in the file.

TRY THIS   If you prefer to keep your taskbar clean, you can create a desktop shortcut to the Office 2013 apps you want to launch from the Desktop, as well. Simply right-click the desktop, point to New, and then click Shortcut. In the Create Shortcut dialog box, click the Browse button. Navigate to the folder containing your program files. Click the icon of the app you want to add and then click Next. Type a name for the shortcut and then click Finish. The shortcut is added to your desktop, and you can launch the app by clicking it.

SEE ALSO   You can also easily hide and redisplay the ribbon at will by using the new Unpin The Ribbon tool (when the ribbon is suppressed, it displays as the Pin The Ribbon tool). You learn how to customize—and hide and display—the Office 2013 ribbon in Section 4, "Accomplishing basic tasks in Office 2013."

Learning the Office 2013 screen

- The **ribbon** contains groups of tools related to specific tasks you'll want to perform with the program.

- The **Quick Access toolbar** is customizable so that you can add often-used tools and find them easily.

- **Tabs** organize the tools on the ribbon according to function. Click the tab for which you want to display the tools related to that task.

- **Contextual tabs** appear only when an item is selected in the file, offering tools and options related to that object (which could be text, an image, a chart, an object, or another element).

- Clicking the File tab displays **the Backstage view** so that you can work with the file and set program options.

- **Help** displays the help window for the application you are using.

- **Minibar** controls display and hide small palettes of tools related to the selected item.

- **Ribbon Display Options** enables you to choose how much of the ribbon you want to see onscreen while you work.

- **View** controls change the way the file is displayed on the screen.

- The **status bar** gives you information about the current document. In the accompanying illustration, the status bar at the bottom of the Microsoft Word document shows the number of pages and words as well as the language in use.

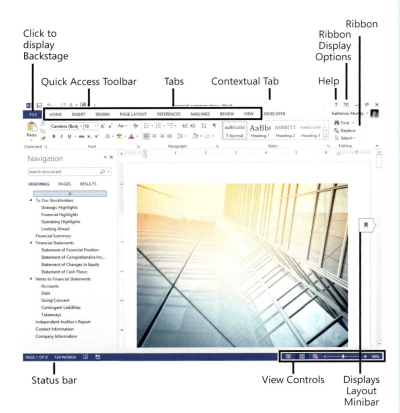

Click to display Backstage

Ribbon

Ribbon Display Options

Quick Access Toolbar   Tabs   Contextual Tab   Help

Status bar

View Controls   Displays Layout Minibar

Using the ribbon

On the ribbon, you'll find all the tools you need as you create, edit, enhance, and share your Office 2013 files. In addition to the standard tabs that you see by default in your current Office 2013 application, additional tabs called contextual tabs appear that present you with tools related to any object that you have selected. To choose the tool you want to use on the ribbon, you begin by selecting the tab you need and then clicking the specific tool you need. Some tools on the ribbon offer you additional options and display a menu when you click them. You can also display traditional dialog boxes for some groups of tools—for example, the Paragraph group on the Home tab—when you click the small dialog launcher in the lower-right corner of the tool group.

Use the ribbon

1 With the Office 2013 app open on the screen, click a tab to the right of the Home tab.

2 Click an option in any group that displays an arrow.

   Arrows indicate that additional options will appear when you click the tool.

3 Click the tool you want to select.

4 Click a dialog launcher to open a dialog box that contains additional options related to that group of tools on the ribbon.

5 In the dialog box that opens, choose the options and settings that you want.

6 Click OK to save your changes.

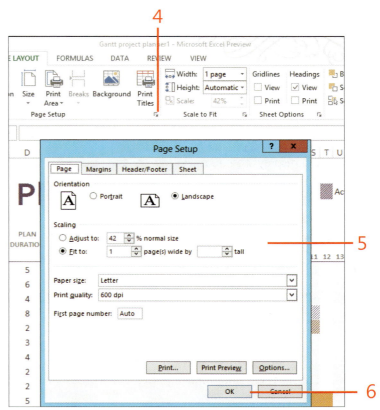

Displaying minibars

Minibars are a great new feature in Office 2013 that bring the tools you need to your work area based on the item you've selected on the page. For example, if you click an image, a minibar that contains image editing and formatting tools will appear. If you choose a table, the minibar will display tools you can use for editing, updating, and enhancing the table.

Display minibars

1 In your Office 2013 document, select some content, such as text, cells, or a picture.

2 Click the minibar icon near your selection.

3 If categories appear, click the one reflecting the task you want to accomplish.

4 Click your choice.

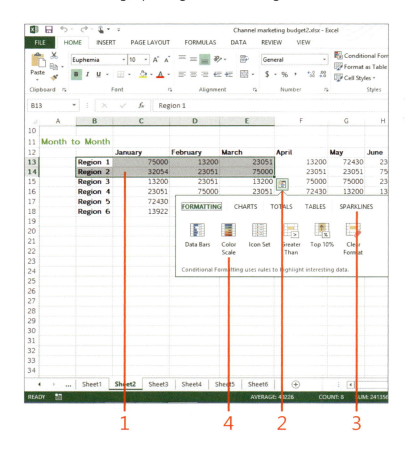

Changing the ribbon display

When Microsoft first introduced the ribbon, not everyone fell in love with it. Some users were concerned that it took up too much room on the screen; others found it clunky or cumbersome. With Office 2013, Microsoft offers new options that give you the ability to change the way the ribbon behaves. You can choose to auto-hide the ribbon so that it disappears when you're not using it, display only the tabs so that tools are visible only when you click the tab you need, or show tabs and commands, which keeps the ribbon on the screen at all times. By doing this, you can focus on your content without any distractions; you can return to normal ribbon display easily, with a single click.

Change ribbon options

1 In your Office 2013 app, click the Ribbon Display Options icon.

A list of options appears.

2 Click your choice. If you want the ribbon to disappear when not in use, choose Auto-Hide The Ribbon. To hide all but the ribbon tabs, choose Show Tabs. Or, to leave the ribbon as-is, leave the default option, Show Tabs And Commands, selected.

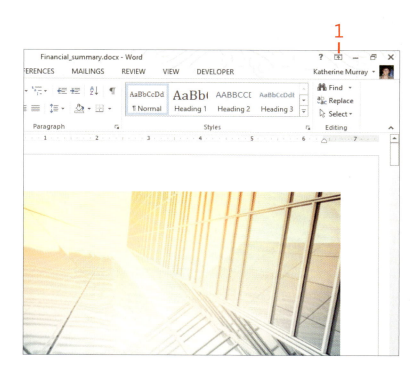

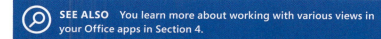

SEE ALSO You learn more about working with various views in your Office apps in Section 4.

TIP The Click Here For More Commands prompt appears only the first time you switch from Full Screen Mode back to the ribbon display. After that, you'll see an ellipsis (…) in place of the prompt.

Going backstage

Using the tools on an Office 2013 app ribbon, you can work with the content of your file in myriad ways. The only thing you can't do on it is manipulate the file itself. To do that, you need to click the File tab, which displays the Backstage view. Here, you'll find all the tools you need to work with files, such as opening an existing file, saving the current file, finding recent files, sharing the file, checking your account information, connecting to social media accounts, and much more.

Use the Backstage view

1 With your Office 2013 file open on the screen, click the File tab.

2 Choose what you want to do next with the file.

3 Review and update file properties.

4 Check the status of your Microsoft Account, connected services, and subscriptions.

5 Close the current file.

6 Display program options for this Office 2013 app.

7 Return to the document display.

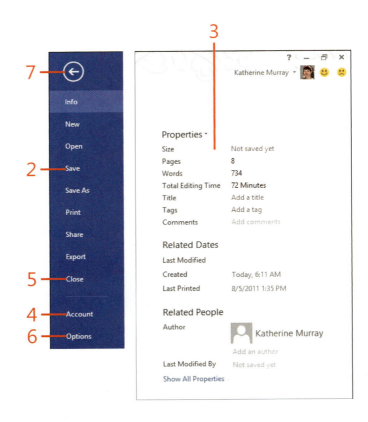

Office 2013 by touch, mouse, and keyboard

3

Some people are good desk-sitters. They can sit quietly at their desks all day, feet on the floor, back straight. That's not me. I twirl in my seat, sit on my legs, fidget, spin, and find lots of reasons to get up and search for something on the bookshelf, get more coffee, or go outside.

When developers were thinking about the ways people would be using the Microsoft Office applications, they tried to take all the many various types of users into account. People at their desktops were probably happy typing on physical keyboards and using mice. Folks on the train might still use a laptop, but these days, they could be using tablets and smartphones, too (which means navigating by touch). Considering the different ways and places people might want to use Office, program designers thought through the ways they would want to navigate using the different types of computers and devices. In this section, you'll learn about your choices for navigating Office 2013. You'll find out how to get around the old-fashioned way (using mouse and keyboard) and learn simple touch techniques for working with your documents, worksheets, presentations, and more.

In this section:

- Navigating Office 2013
- Pointing and clicking by using the mouse or trackpad
- Selecting and dragging text
- Right-clicking to access related options
- Using the scrollbar
- Navigating the ribbon with the keyboard
- Creating your own keyboard shortcuts
- Exploring touch techniques
- Turning on touch mode
- Single-tapping to select an item
- Tapping and holding an item
- Swiping the screen to view content
- Spreading and pinching to enlarge and reduce content

Navigating Office 2013

If you've used a previous version of Office, you are accustomed to pointing and clicking your way through the various programs in the suite. To display tools on the ribbon that you need to carry out a task, you click the tab that contains the relevant tools. To select text on the screen, you drag the mouse pointer (the cursor) over the text. To insert a paragraph in a document, you click the mouse where you want the text to appear and then type the content.

Simple, right? If this is your navigation style of preference, you'll be pleased to know that even though Office 2013 is optimized for touch, it was designed first and foremost to work well with your trusty mouse and keyboard. Nothing has been lost in translation here; all the familiar mouse and keyboard techniques with which you've become accustomed will work in Office 2013. In fact, the new minimalist design of the Office 2013 screen actually helps you find what you're looking for, thanks to the clean lines of the new look.

Some people prefer to use as many keyboard techniques as possible to select tools, add content, and navigate through their Office files. Office includes a number of keyboard shortcuts, and you can easily create your own if you have favorites that you want to add. You can press and hold the Alt key to display shortcut keys on the Office 2013 ribbon, and then simply press the key that appears over the tool you want to use. There are many other keyboard shortcuts, too, which you'll learn about in "Navigating the ribbon with the keyboard," later in this section.

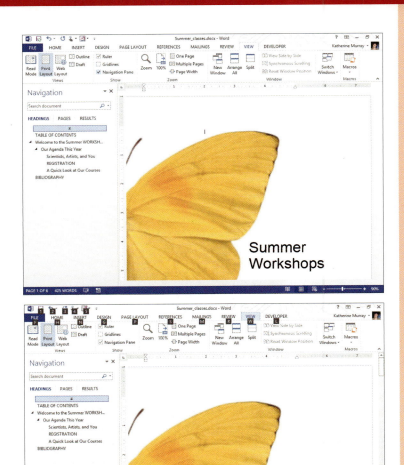

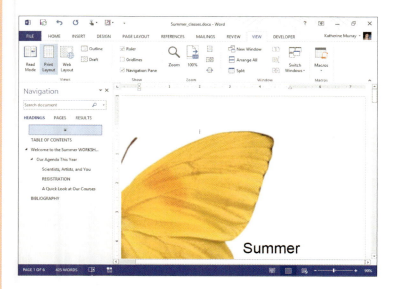

Office 2013 can travel with you just about anywhere you go, thanks to the availability of the program on your computer, tablet, phone, and in the cloud. So, you can use a laptop, a netbook, a tablet, or a smartphone and still be able to review files, add comments, and collaborate with others. You can use touch or mouse and keyboard techniques (or a combination of all three) whether you're sitting at your desk, lying on the couch, standing at a counter, waiting for a train, or perched on the bleachers at a soccer game.

The givens for navigating in Office 2013

- If you do a lot of typing, you'll get more done, faster and more accurately by using a real keyboard.

- If you are working with a file that requires precision—for example, your Microsoft PowerPoint presentation includes a number of small elements that you want to animate—you're better off using a mouse.

- If you're standing or need to check something quickly, touch enables you to open a file, flip through it, and find what you need fast.

- If you will be doing more reading than writing and more reviewing than reconfiguring, the touch interface is fast and fluid and can help you to scan the content easily without using buttons or clicks to do it.

Of course, Office 2013 also offers additional navigation choices. You can use your finger on your touch-enabled screen or device to navigate the ribbon in much the same way you used a mouse before. But touch offers you other features, as well: the ability to move quickly through pages, zoom the display in one step, and select items individually or in groups without a lot of clicks or complicated drags are just a few of them. One of the ways Office 2013 ensures that the touch interface works well for users who are trying to navigate a small touchscreen device is through the new Touch Mode feature. Touch Mode adds space around ribbon tools so that you can easily and accurately touch the tool you want to use (and not one of its neighbors, accidentally).

Pointing and clicking by using the mouse or trackpad

The chances are good that you use the mouse to do a lot of things on your computer—if, that is, your computer *has* a mouse. Traditionally, desktop computers come equipped with a mouse that you use along with your keyboard. Laptops don't include mice, but they do offer a pointing device such as a trackpad (usually built in to the area just in front of the keyboard) that you can use to move the pointer on the screen and click (or, alternately, tap).

One of the most common things you do with your mouse is point and click; you move the mouse pointer to a location on the screen and then click the left mouse button to select whatever is beneath the pointer—whether it's a tab on the ribbon, a tool that you want to use, or a picture that you want to brighten.

Point and click

1 Using your mouse or trackpad, move the mouse pointer to the item on the screen that you want to choose. For this example, on the ribbon, click the Insert tab to display the tools it contains.

2 Click the left mouse button. This displays the tools you need to insert elements in your Office document.

Selecting and dragging text

When you want to select information on the page, message, worksheet, or slide, you drag the mouse pointer over the information you want to select. This highlights the selected content on the screen. Once the data is selected, you can do all sorts of things with it: cut, copy, or move it; apply formatting settings to it; perform calculations with it; animate it; and much more, depending upon what you've selected and what app you're using.

Dragging to select text

1 Point to the beginning of the information you want to select and then press and hold the mouse button.

2 Drag to the end of the content you want to select.

The selected text or data is clearly highlighted. You can then choose a ribbon tool, select an option from the minibar, or cut or copy the selection, as you desire.

1

2

Right-clicking to access related options

In many places in Office 2013, when you right-click the mouse or trackpad button, a settings or options menu appears that presents commands relevant to the task at hand and the object you've selected. For example, if you right-click a block of text in Word, the menu that appears displays options with which you can cut, copy, and paste the text block. Additionally, you can set paragraph spacing, translate the block, add a link or comment, or look for synonyms and definitions.

Right-click for more options

1 Select the text or object with which you want to work by clicking it or selecting and dragging.

2 Right-click the selected text or object

3 Click the tool you want to use.

> ✓ **TIP** If you right-click an item on the page—such as a picture—and the settings menu doesn't appear, check to see whether there's a minibar button to the right of the element you selected. The new minibars in Office 2013 make available a set of tools related to the object you've selected, performing much the same function as the menus that you invoke by right-clicking.

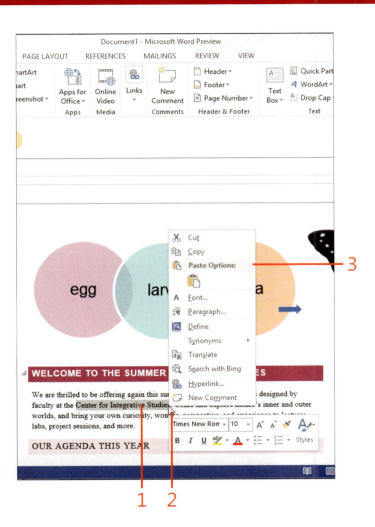

Using the scrollbar

Depending on the type of file you're working with and how much you've zoomed in to work with the content, you might see one or two scrollbars in your Office 2013 apps. Word 2013, for example, shows a vertical scroll bar along the right side of the document window, and Microsoft Excel shows two: a vertical scrollbar and a smaller horizontal scrollbar in the lower-right corner of the window. You use the scrollbar to move through your file and display aspects of the document that are currently not visible in the app window.

Scroll the screen

1 Click the scroll box on the vertical or horizontal scroll bar.

2 Drag the vertical scroll box down to display additional areas of the document.

   If your file shows a horizontal scroll bar, you can drag the scroll box to the right to see areas that are beyond the right edge of the window.

You can also drag the slides pane scroll box to scroll through slides

TIP When you drag the scroll box, the Office app you are using displays a pop-up window indicating where you are in the document. For example, in PowerPoint, you might see a message that says "Slide: 6 of 31" and lists the name of the current slide. Or, in a Word document, the message displays the page number and the title of the current section. You can use these messages to navigate directly to the section or page that you want to view.

Navigating the ribbon with the keyboard

If you prefer keeping your fingers on the keyboard as much as possible, Office 2013 provides keyboard shortcuts that you can use to find what you need on the ribbon instead of pointing and clicking the display.

Navigate the ribbon with the keyboard

1 Display the Office app you want to use.

2 Press and hold the Alt key. Letters and numbers appear on the tab names and the tools on the Quick Access toolbar.

3 While still pressing the Alt key, press the letter or number of the tab that you want to view.

4 When that tab appears, the shortcut keys appear on the new tab. Press the letter or letter combination to choose the tool that you want to use.

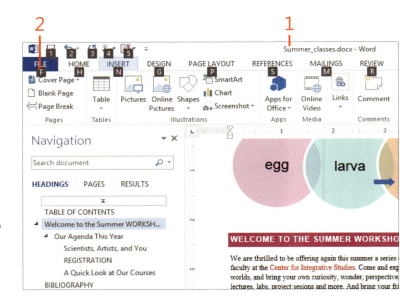

Additional keys for working with the ribbon	
To select the current tab by using the keyboard	Press F10
To move to other tabs on the ribbon	Press the Right Arrow key or the Left Arrow key
To hide and redisplay the ribbon	Press Ctrl+F1
To choose a tool on the selected tab	Press the Down Arrow key to move the highlight to a group and then press the Left Arrow key to move to the tool that you want to use

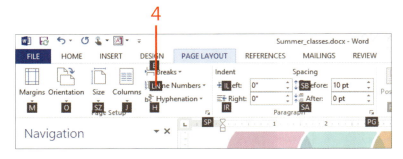

TIP You can press the Alt key on your physical keyboard or the Alt key on the Windows extended touch keyboard. Both display the shortcut keys on the ribbon that you can use to choose the tools that you need.

Using key combinations

Pressing a key combination is similar to pressing a shortcut key: simply type the characters in close succession, and the Office application will carry out the command or display the tool you selected.

Some key combinations display yet another list of options that you can select. For example, when you press Alt to display shortcut keys and then press P, the Page Layout tab appears. When you type LN to select Line Numbers, another list appears that offers choices (and their corresponding shortcut keys) you can use to choose the way in which you want the Line Numbers to appear.

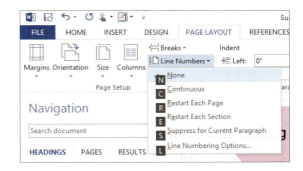

> ✔ **TIP**   If you're a big fan of keyboard shortcuts, you'll be pleased to know that there's a huge list of shortcuts you can use in each of the Office applications to carry out tasks. In this section, you learn about the shortcut keys you use for navigating documents, but in the sections that follow, you'll learn shortcut keys along with the mouse and touch techniques in sections on the specific tasks.

Creating your own keyboard shortcuts

Office 2013 offers a number of ready-made shortcuts that you can use in the various applications, but it's also a simple task to create your own. If you have certain key combinations you like to use regularly, you can teach Office 2013 those combinations and assign them to the tools of your choice. You start the process of customizing keyboard shortcuts by displaying the Microsoft Office Backstage view and opening the Options dialog box.

Create your own keyboard shortcuts

1 In Word 2013, click the File tab.

2 Click Options.

The Word Options dialog box opens.

3 Click Customize Ribbon.

4 Click Customize.

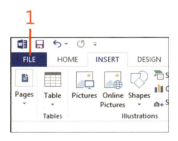

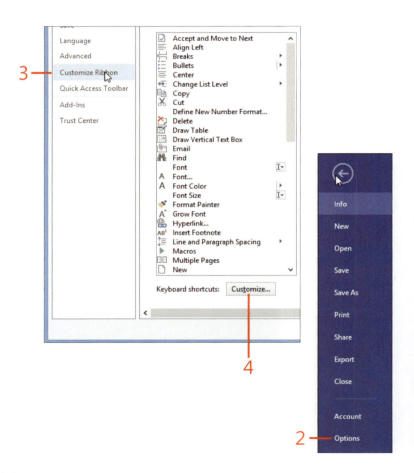

5 Click the category of the tool for which you'd like to create a shortcut key.

6 Click the command in the tab or group you want to use.

The current keys assigned to the command you select are displayed.

7 Click or type your new shortcut key.

8 Click to choose where you want to save the new key. You can choose to save the shortcut key to the Normal template (if you want it to be available in all your documents) or to the current documents that you have open.

9 Click Assign to save the new shortcut key.

10 Click Close to close the dialog box.

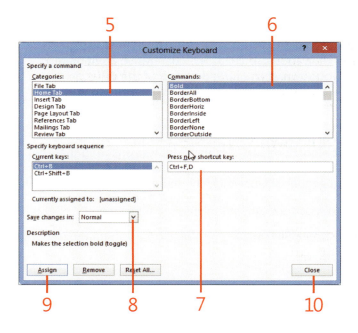

Exploring touch techniques

If you use a tablet, you will be pleased with the touch features built in to Office 2013. The changes you'll find aren't simply touch capability added on top of the program, but enhancements and improvements that make working with touch easier and more accurate.

The touch responsiveness of Office 2013 was one of the focal points of program designers, as was ensuring that the elements on the screen were large enough targets for most people to touch successfully. This led to a number of changes in the user interface that you'll notice if you're using touch, including the following:

- The new Touch Mode changes the appearance of the Office 2013 screen—including the ribbon, dialog boxes, and other interface elements—by adding space around the tools and elements, producing larger touch targets.

- The Quick Access toolbar is larger so that you can easily choose those tools with your fingertip.

- The height of the status bar has been increased.

- The formatting bar is expanded with more space.

- The handles on objects such as pictures and charts are larger, making them easier to select and manipulate.

TIP If you're mobile, how mobile are you? Do you use one hand or two to hold your device? Do you need to use your thumbs to navigate on the screen, or is one hand free to tap and swipe? If you're using Office 2013 on a touch device, you can choose the type of On-Screen Keyboard to use. You can display the On-Screen Keyboard on a Windows 8 touch device by tapping in a text box or by tapping the keyboard icon on the taskbar of the Windows 8 Desktop. With the keyboard displayed, you can choose from among several different styles.

Turning on touch mode

One of the new features that make Office 2013 touch-friendly is Touch Mode, which increases the amount of space between tools and options on the ribbon and in lists and dialog boxes. This makes it easy for you to tap the tools you want without inadvertently selecting the wrong item. Thanks to the addition of the Touch/Mouse Mode button in the Quick Access toolbar, you can easily switch between Touch and Mouse mode while you're working with Office on your touch-enabled device.

Turn on touch mode

1 Click the Touch/Mouse Mode tool in the Quick Access toolbar.

2 Click Touch Mode.

The spacing of tools on the ribbon changes to allow more room for selecting tools and options using touch.

3 To return to normal mode, click the Touch/Mouse Mode tool again and choose Mouse from the list.

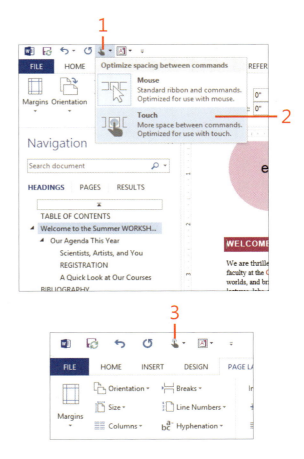

Single-tapping to select an item

What could be easier than a single tap? If you've ever tapped someone on the shoulder, pushed the button on an ATM, or dialed a cell phone, you know that this action is as natural to you as breathing.

Single-tap the screen

1 Tap the tab on the ribbon that you want to view.

2 Tap the tool that you want to select, once, quickly.

Office 2013 responds to the touch by selecting the tool, which might complete an action, display a dialog box, or show options related to that tool.

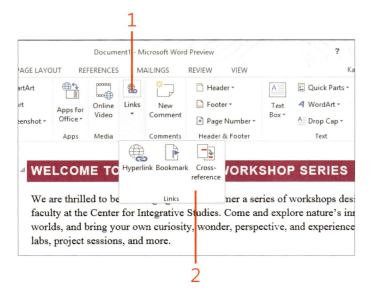

Tapping and holding an item

The tap-and-hold technique on touch devices is similar to right-clicking when you're using the mouse or trackpad. When you tap and hold your finger on an item, Windows 8 interprets that gesture as you wanting to know more about the item. When you release the touch, an options list or the On-Screen Keyboard appears so that you can take further action.

Tap and hold

1 Tap and hold your finger on the screen element that you want to select. This might include a word, a title, a tool, an object, or another screen element.

A square appears at the point where you touched.

2 Release your touch. If you tapped text, the text is selected and the On-Screen Keyboard appears. If you tapped a tool, an options list appears giving you choices with which you can manipulate that element.

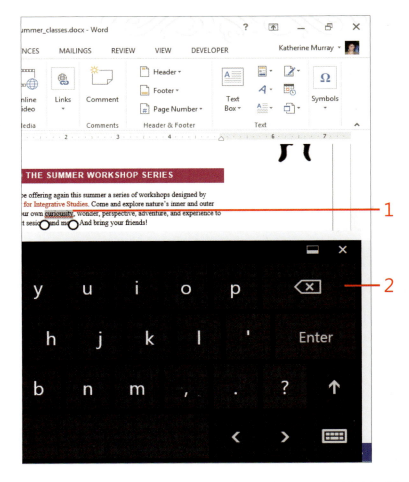

Choose your keyboard

The On-Screen keyboard appears automatically whenever you tap an area of the screen in which you can add information. You can choose from a number of keyboards so that you can enter text or values in the way that is most comfortable for you.

You can find the keyboard selection tool in the lower-right corner of the keyboard. Tap it and a popup bar of keyboard choices appears. You can choose from a standard keyboard, a thumbs keyboard, a handwriting palette, or an extended keyboard that includes the Windows key, Alt keys, and Ctrl keys.

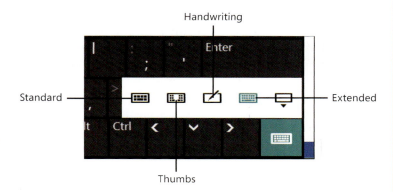

Handwriting

Standard

Extended

Thumbs

Swiping the screen to view content

Swiping the screen right and left is a similar gesture to the one you use to turn the page of a traditional, hold-in-your-hands book. To display content that's beyond the right edge of your screen, swipe your display to the left; to display content that's beyond the left edge of your screen, swipe the display to the right.

Swipe the screen

1 Display the file that you want to use.

2 Swipe upward from the bottom of the screen to scroll content into view.

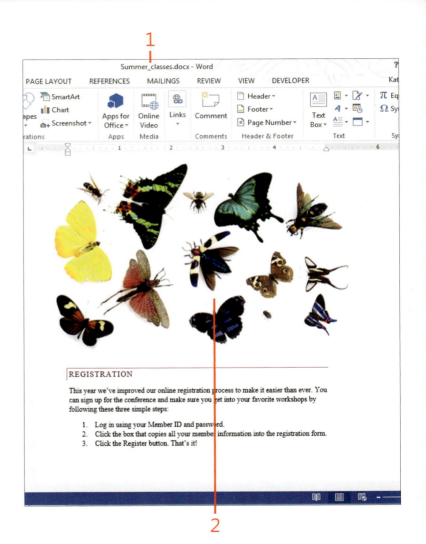

Spreading and pinching to enlarge and reduce content

If you use a smartphone, you are familiar with this gesture, as well. On touch devices, you can easily enlarge or reduce the size of the display by spreading your thumb and finger apart or by pinching them together, respectively.

Zoom in and out

1 To enlarge the content display of your file, position your fingers on the screen at the point on which you want to zoom in and spread them apart.

2 To reduce the display of the content in your file (zoom out), put two fingers on the screen and move them toward one another in a pinching motion.

The screen reduces as you move your fingers on the screen.

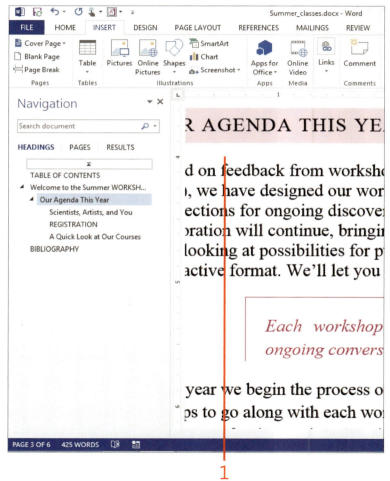

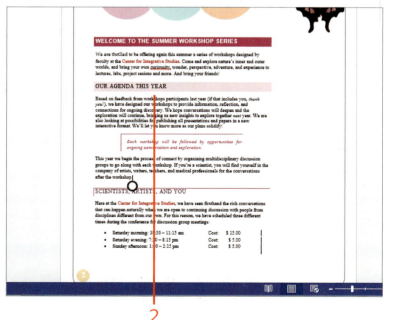

Accomplishing basic tasks in Office 2013

4

One of the great things about working with a suite of programs such as Microsoft Office is that there are a fair number of tasks you'll perform that will be the same from app to app, ensuring an intuitive and familiar feel. Basic tasks such as opening, creating, saving, sharing, protecting, and closing a file follow the same basic process, so once you learn the steps for one app, you can use those same steps for the same process in other apps. This section introduces you to many of the tasks you'll need to know, no matter which app you are using in Office 2013.

In this section:

- Launching apps
- Choosing an Office background
- Adding services
- Managing your Office 2013 account
- Setting program options
- Getting help
- Moving among open apps
- Docking apps
- Adding Office apps to the Windows 8 taskbar
- Using app jump lists
- Opening, saving, and closing files
- Exporting files
- Previewing and printing files
- Changing view controls
- Protecting and sharing files
- Sending files via email

Launching apps

Once you've installed Office 2013 on your Windows 8 computer, whether you've installed it from a DVD or downloaded and installed Office 2013 from Office 365, you'll find the app tiles on the far right side of the Windows 8 Start screen. When you launch the Office app you want to use by clicking it, the program opens on your Windows 8 desktop.

Launch an app

1 Display the Windows 8 Start screen and scroll to the far right.

2 Click the Office app that you want to launch.

   The program opens on your Windows 8 desktop.

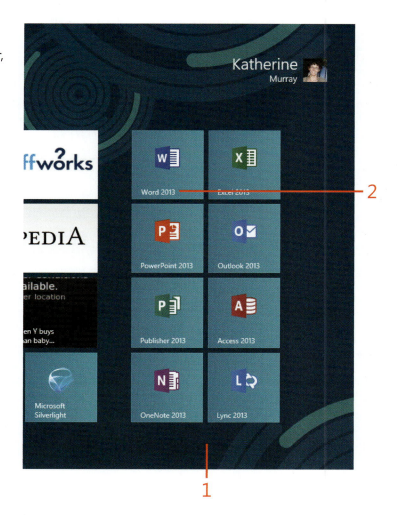

Choosing an Office background and theme

The new Office Background addition is one of those gosh-you-didn't-have-to-do-that items in Office 2013 that offers a fun way to personalize your Office experience. You can choose from a set of ready-made background designs that just add a little personality to your Office apps. Don't worry—the backgrounds don't take up a lot of room or dramatically change the color

of your screen; they just add a subtle design in the upper-right corner of your app window. You can also choose from one of three basic themes for Office 2013: white (default), light gray, and dark gray. These different themes give you options that change the overall appearance of your Office apps so you can choose the setting that is easiest on your eyes.

Choose a background

1 With the program of your choice open on the screen, click the File tab to display the Microsoft Office Backstage view.

2 Click Account.

3 Click the Office Background arrow.

4 From the scroll list, choose the background style that you want.

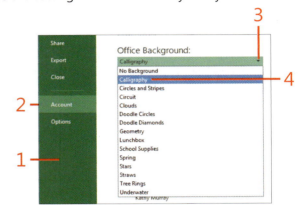

Select an Office theme

1 In Backstage view, choose Account.

2 Click the Office Theme arrow.

3 Click the theme you want to use with Office 2013.

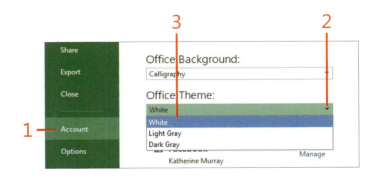

Adding services

Connection is a big story in Office 2013. Now, you can easily connect Office 2013 to your favorite web services. The great thing about this idea is that by adding services, you can work seamlessly with sites you're already using. For example, if you've stored thousands of photos in Flickr, you can access those photos and use them in your Microsoft Word 2013 documents or your Microsoft PowerPoint 2013 presentations simply by adding Flickr to your Connected Services. That saves you the trouble of downloading the photos to your device and then adding them to your Word document. Nice, right? You can also add other popular social media accounts, such as Facebook, SkyDrive, LinkedIn, Twitter, and YouTube.

Add services

1 Open the Office app that you want to use and click the File tab to display the Backstage view.

2 Click Account.

3 In the Connected Services area, review the services.

4 Click Add A Service.

A pop-up window appears, giving you the option to add a service with which you can incorporate images and videos or to specify to save your documents in the cloud.

5 Point to the option you want; the available services appear to the right of the choice.

6 Click the service you want to add. Office 2013 adds the service to your Account page.

> **✓ TIP** Are you wondering how Office 2013 knows about the services to which you're a subscriber? If you connected the People app or the Photos app in Windows 8, Office 2013 is also able to "see" those connections as part of the app sharing features in Windows 8. This ultimately saves you time and trouble and gives you easy access to files you have stored in various places on line. You can control the permissions you grant these other sites so that you're only sharing the amount and type of information you want to share.

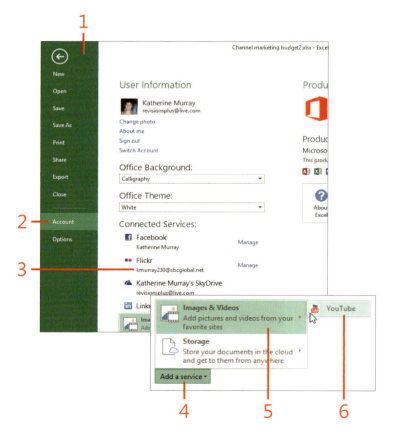

Changing services

You can later remove or manage the services you added to Office 2013. Point to the service you want to change and notice the link provided on the right. Some services offer the choice to remove the service, whereas others display Manage.

Removing a service that displays Remove as a link is a simple matter: just click Remove. Office then asks you to confirm the deletion. When you select the Yes button, the service is removed.

If the service you want to change displays the Manage link, when you click it, your Microsoft Account page appears, showing you the permissions you have granted to that service. You can disable some of the services if you like by clearing the adjacent check box. (For example, if you want to stop sharing with LinkedIn, clear the the Share To LinkedIn check box.) Then, click the Save button to save your changes. If you want to remove the service completely, scroll down to the bottom of the list and click Remove This Connection Completely.

Managing your Office 2013 account

In the Backstage view, on the Account tab, you can set up your Office 2013 account the way you want it. First, you can change the Microsoft Account you're using to sign in to Office 2013—and switch accounts if you like—and review your account settings and change your account photo. You can also find information about which Office 2013 installation you're using.

Manage your account

1 With an Office 2013 app open on the screen, click the File tab to display the Backstage view.

2 Click the arrow to the right of your user name.

A list showing your profile information and giving you access to your account settings appears.

3 If you want to change your photo, click Change Photo and choose a new photo from your computer.

4 If you want to add information about yourself, click About Me.

5 If you click Account Settings, the Backstage view Account tab appears, showing your user information, connected services, and the Office background you've selected.

6 If you want to switch the account you're using, click Switch Account.

Setting program options

As you become familiar with the Office 2013 apps, there are sure to be things you'd like to tweak to suit your own personal tastes. Perhaps you want to change the way Word shows ScreenTips or you want to customize the look of the Quick Access toolbar. You can review and change the program settings in each of your Office 2013 apps by clicking the File tab to display the Backstage view and then clicking Options.

In most cases, the options already set in Office 2013 will be fine. The tabs you see in the Options dialog box vary slightly from app to app. On the General tab, ensure that all the items are selected in the User Interface Options so that you get the maximum amount of onscreen help at any one time. These options control whether you can see the previews of choices before you click them and the style of ScreenTips that appear when you hover the pointer over a tool or screen element.

The Display tab contains selections about the items that appear on the screen while you work. These might include formatting marks and page display options, such as whether white space appears between pages in Print Layout view. On the Display tab you can also choose printing options, such as whether you want to print drawings, background colors and images, document properties, hidden text, and more. On the Proofing tab, you can choose the way you want Office 2013 to correct spelling and grammatical errors.

On the Save tab, you select the defaults for the files you create. You can also choose the way you want Office 2013 to handle AutoRecover options and where you want to save files by default. If you are using the subscription version of Office 2013, your files will automatically to your SkyDrive account. If you want to change this, you need to modify the setting on the Save tab of the Options dialog box.

On the Language tab, you can choose the languages that you want to use with Office 2013, and the Advanced tab contains options for a variety of tasks related to the specific app. You might see editing options; cut, copy, and paste choices; image size and quality choices; options for charts; and document display, printing, and saving choices.

Using the Customize Ribbon tab, you can add, hide, or reconfigure the tabs on the Office 2013 ribbon. Note that when you change the ribbon, it is altered only for the app you're using when you make the changes. You can also reset and even export or import your ribbon changes. The Quick Access Toolbar tab makes it easy for you to add tools to the Quick Access toolbar in the upper-left corner of your app window. The Add-Ins tab shows you all the add-ins that have already been added to your Office 2013 application. You can also manage additional add-ins here, as well. The Trust Center tab gives you information about your privacy and security as you use Office 2013. You can make additional choices to set Trusted Publishers, Trusted Locations, and more.

Getting help

Help in Office 2013 is only a click away, no matter which app you are using or what you might be doing with it. You can find the Help tool, which resembles a question mark, in the upper-right corner of your application window. When you click it,

Office displays a Help window you can use to search for specific assitance, click a popular help category, or browse through articles and training options related to the main features and functions in your app.

Get help

1 In your current Office 2013 app, in the upper-right corner of the screen, click Help.

2 Click to enter a word or phrase for which you want to search.

3 Click Search.

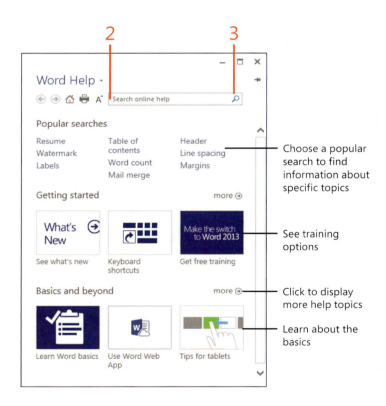

Choose a popular search to find information about specific topics

See training options

Click to display more help topics

Learn about the basics

4 Scroll through the list that appears if necessary.

5 Click the title of the article you'd like to view.

6 Read through the article.

7 Click Print if you want to print the article to refer to later.

8 Close Help by clicking the close icon.

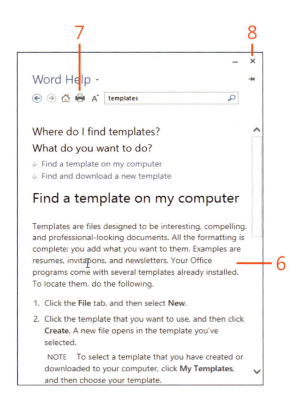

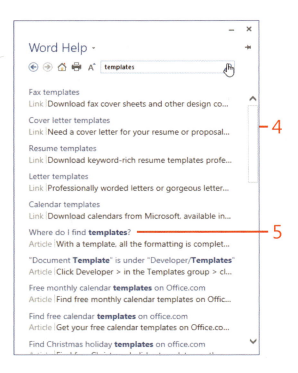

TRY THIS! You can choose whether you want to search for help on line or access the Office Help files installed on your computer. Click the arrow to the right of the Help title at the top of the Help dialog box. By default, the help displayed is from *Office.com*. If you want to change that, click Help From Your Computer; the Office program searches the help information on your computer and displays results according to the search text you entered.

Moving among open apps

With Windows 8, you can easily work with a number of apps open at any one time. You can cycle through them by dragging them in from the left side of the screen, using the thumbnails panel to click the app you want to use, or by pressing the Alt+Tab key combination to display a pop-up window of open apps that you can use to navigate to the program you need. The great thing about the way Windows manages memory is that only the active program—the one you're viewing on your screen at any given time—is actually using power; the rest of the apps are in suspended mode until you make one them the active program; the apps wake up so quickly that you'll never know they weren't fully at the ready, waiting for you to use them.

Move among open apps

1   Open the Office apps you want to work with by clicking the app tiles on the Windows 8 Start screen.

2   Swipe inward from the left side of the screen by using your finger or the mouse.

    The next open app appears.

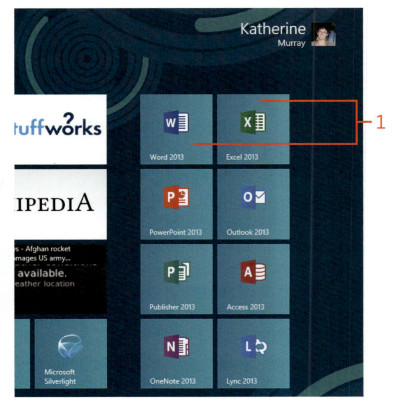

3 Alternately, point the mouse or your finger to the upper-left corner of the screen and then move it down the left edge.

The thumbnails panel appears.

4 Click the Office app that you want to view.

5 Or, press Alt+Tab to display a pop-up window of open apps.

6 Click the app that you want to view.

✓ **TIP** Windows 8 groups all open Windows 8 desktop apps together, which means that you won't be able to cycle through Microsoft Excel, Word, and PowerPoint as open apps if you're pulling them in from the left side of the Windows 8 Start screen. Instead, when an Office 2013 window appears in the rotation, use Alt+Tab to display the additional open apps on the Windows 8 desktop. You'll then be able to choose the open file with which you want to work.

Docking apps

Windows 8 makes it easy for you to dock apps open on the screen so that you can perform two tasks at once. For example, you might be working with a shared document in Word 2013 while you're instant messaging one of your co-authors in the Messaging app, which is docked along the right side of your screen. That way you can easily review the document and ask your co-author questions while you work. Docking apps positions one app in place while still allowing you to cycle through other open apps by dragging them in from the left edge of your screen.

Dock apps on the screen

1 Display the first app that you want to appear on your screen.

2 Swipe apps in from the left until you find the Office app that you want to dock on the screen.

3 Swipe the screen toward the top of the window.

The app is docked along the side of the screen. You can scroll through apps as normal in the other app area.

4 When you're ready to remove the docked app, click the divider and drag it to the right.

> **TIP** When you are swiping open apps in from the left, Windows 8 doesn't recognize each individual Office app as a separate app and only shows one representative app from the desktop at a time. This means that you might have Word, Excel, and PowerPoint open all at once, but when you swipe the apps in from the left, only the most recently used Office app will be included in the rotation as the desktop app example. If you want to dock two Office apps side by side on the desktop, you're better off right-clicking the Windows taskbar and choosing Show Windows Side-by-Side.

> **CAUTION** If you are having trouble getting apps to dock on your monitor, check your screen resolution. Microsoft announced that you need a widescreen monitor to use docking successfully, and although some tablet screens still qualify, you need to have your screen resolution set to 1366x768 before your docking will "stick."

Adding Office apps to the Windows 8 taskbar

If you find yourself working with the Windows 8 desktop more than the Windows 8 Start screen, you might want to add your Office 2013 apps to the taskbar so that you can launch them easily from the desktop.

Add apps to the Windows 8 taskbar

1 Open the Windows 8 Start screen.

2 Scroll to the far right to display the Office app tiles.

3 Swipe down on or right-click the app that you want to add to the taskbar.

4 Click Pin To Taskbar.

The app will now be available on the taskbar when you display the Windows 8 desktop.

Using app jump lists

A jump list makes it easy for you to open a file you've recently used or move quickly to a file that is still open in Office 2013. When you hover the pointer or tap and hold the Office 2013 icon in your Windows 8 taskbar, a thumbnail or a list of open or recently used files appears. You can move directly to the file you want by clicking it.

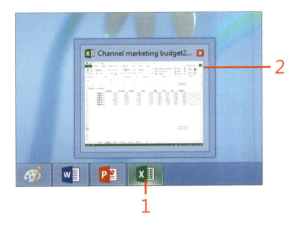

Use jump lists

1 Point to or tap and hold an icon on the taskbar.

The current file appears as a thumbnail above the app icon.

2 To display the file, click it.

3 Right-click an app icon in the taskbar.

A listing of recently used files appears.

4 Click the file you want to open.

5 When you're ready to close the app, click Close Window.

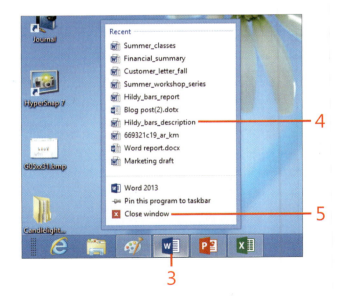

Opening new files

Many of the basic tasks you'll perform in your Office programs will be similar from app to app. You'll need to know how to open a new file in Word, Excel, PowerPoint, and Microsoft Publisher, for example. You can easily open a new file on the Start screen for the different apps, and you can also click the File tab and then choose New to start the process.

Open a new file

1 Launch the Office app you want to use.

2 On the app Start screen, click Blank Document to open a new, blank file.

3 Alternatively, click and enter a type of template for which to search.

4 Scroll through the results list.

5 Click the template that you want to use as the basis for the new file.

> **✓ TIP** What is a template? A template is a ready-made file that can include one or several pages and include images, placeholder text, and special layouts. When you start a new file based on a template, the format and layout are already done for you, and you can simply add your own text and images to complete the file.

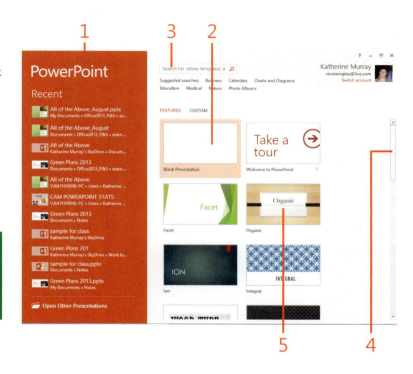

Opening existing files

Office 2013 makes it easy to find the files you worked on previously so you can continue your creative work.

Open an existing file

1   Launch an Office app.

    The Start screen for that app appears.

2   In the Recent list, click the file that you want.

3   If you don't see the desired file in the list, click Open Other Documents.

4   In Places, click the location at which the file is stored.

5   In the list on the right, click the folder in which the file is stored.

6   Alternatively, click Browse.

    The Open dialog box appears so that you can navigate to the folder that contains your file.

7   Click the file you want to open.

8   Click Open.

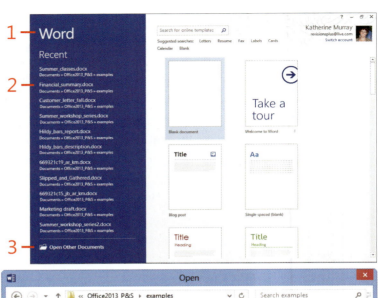

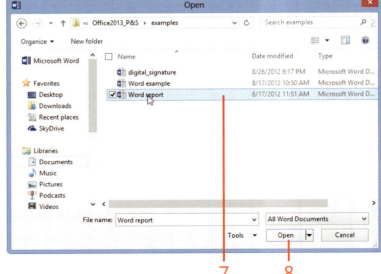

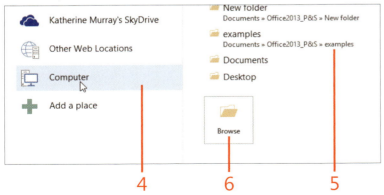

Saving files to the cloud

Office 2013 is set by default to save your files to the cloud, which is great if you're an avid SkyDrive or SharePoint user, but it might leave you a bit cold if you prefer to keep all your files as close as possible. Luckily the setting is easy to change, and you can choose to save your files—by default or otherwise—wherever you choose. Saving to the cloud is easier than you might think, however, and it does give you the extra perk

of being able to share your files easily and work on them no matter what device you are using or where you might happen to be.

Save to the cloud

1 Finish working on your Office file and click the File tab to display the Backstage view.

2 Click Save As.

3 In Places, choose the SkyDrive location.

4 Click the folder in which you want to save the file.

5 Alternatively, click Browse and navigate in the Save As dialog box to the SkyDrive folder you need.

6 Click the Save button to save the file.

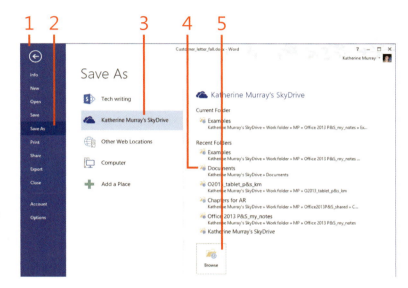

Add a place to save

1 Click File to open the Backstage view and then click Save As.

2 Click Add A Place.

Office 2013 displays two cloud locations that you can choose for the new place.

3 Click Office 365 SharePoint if you are an Office 2013 subscriber and use SharePoint Online to store, organize, and share your files.

4 Click SkyDrive if you prefer to use your SkyDrive account.

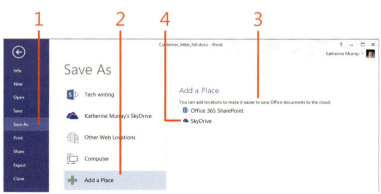

Saving files on your computer or device

If you would prefer to not save your files to the cloud, you can easily choose to keep your files closer at hand by saving them directly to your computer or other device.

Save files on your computer or device

1 Complete the file you want to save and then click File to display the Backstage view.

2 Click Save As.

3 In Places, click Computer.

4 Choose the folder in which you want to save the file.

5 Type a name for the file.

6 Click Save.

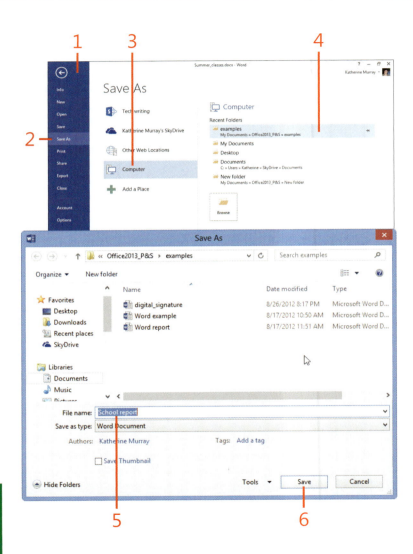

TIP Tagging your files makes them easier to find in searches. To add tags, click the File tab, and then in the Backstage view, click the Info tab. In the Properties on the right side of the screen, click in the Tags area and type the words you want to use as tags, separating them with commas.

Closing files

When you're finished with a file, closing it is a simple matter. And, if you forget to save it first, don't worry: Office 2013 will remind you so that you can save your changes before closing the file.

Close a file

1 With the file you want to close active on the screen, click the File tab to display the Backstage view.

2 Click Close.

1 —

Info

New

Open

Save

Save As

Print

Share

Export

2 — Close

Account

Options

> **TRY THIS!**   There are two more simple ways to close a file. The first is to click the close box (the "x") in the upper-right corner of the app window. The second way is to use the Windows 8 method and swipe down from the top of the screen, dragging the app all the way to the bottom. The app window becomes smaller and then finally disappears, which lets you know the file is closed.

Exporting files

If you want to use the data from your Office 2013 apps in other non-Office applications, you'll be pleased to know that you can export your data in a variety of formats. To do so, in the Backstage view, click the Export tab. From here, you can create a PDF/XPS file with the exported data or change the file type and export the information in a file format that is compatible with your other application. Excel 2013 also offers an export option with which you can share the data in a web browser so that others will be able to view the data you export.

Export a file

1 In Backstage view, click the Export tab.

2 Click the format that you want to use for the exported file. (The Export choices you see will vary from app to app.)

3 Click the Create PDF/XPS button to complete an export that saves the current file as a PDF or XPS file.

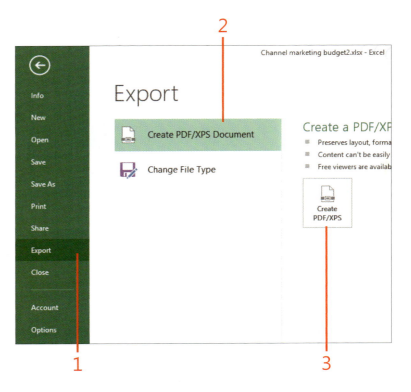

4 If you want to export the file in a format other than PDF or XPS, click Change File Type.

5 Choose the file type from the right panel.

6 Click Save As.

The Save As dialog box opens.

7 Navigate to the folder in which you want to save the file.

8 Type a new name if you want to.

9 Click Save.

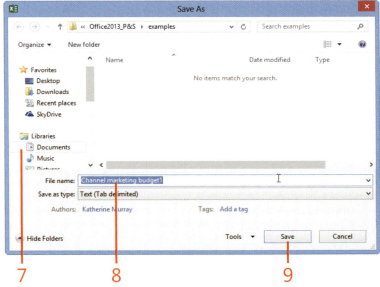

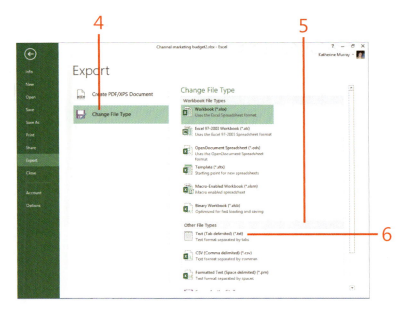

Previewing and printing files

Office 2013 makes it simple for you to see how your files are shaping up and print them in a single window in the Backstage view. When you click the File tab and choose Print, your file displays on the right side of the screen and printing options appear in the center. You can preview your file by clicking the arrows at the bottom of the preview pane and easily make choices about printing, including the number of copies you want to print, the printer you want to use, and specific settings such as the paper type, orientation, and page range that you want to include.

Preview and print files

1 In the Backstage view, click the Print tab.

2 Choose the printer that you want to use.

3 Click to select the pages you want to print.

4 Select whether to print on only one side of the page or both.

5 Select the paper size.

6 Choose portrait or landscape orientation for your printed file.

7 Click to preview other pages.

8 Scroll through the previewed document.

9 Enter the number of copies that you want to print.

10 Click Print.

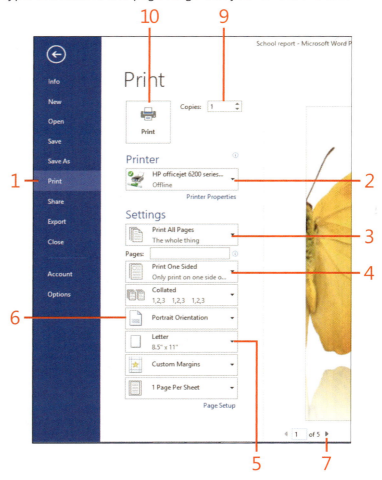

> **TIP**   If you choose two-sided printing, Word and Publisher will display the previewed file as it would appear if images appear on both sides of the page. This helps you see whether text or pictures will be visible from the other side of the page so that you can make adjustments before you print. Pretty neat, eh?

Changing view controls

Being able to change the view magnification means that you can get up close and personal with numbers you need to double-check or zoom out for a big-picture view when you need to eyeball the design of an entire page. With most of the apps, you can control the view of your app easily by using the view controls in the lower-right corner of the app window.

Work with view controls

1 Drag the Zoom control to the right.

   The display enlarges.

2 Click the Zoom level.

   The Zoom dialog box appears.

3 Click a new zoom level.

4 Alternatively, click Custom and enter a percentage for the size of the display.

5 Click OK to close the dialog box.

6 Click the view tools to the left of the Zoom control to see a different view.

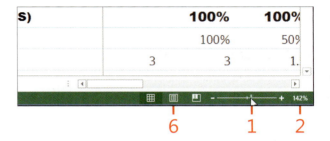

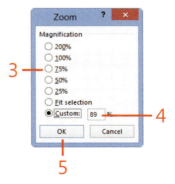

TRY THIS! Zoom your Office 2013 file to 75 percent, down to 35 percent, and then back up to a zoom level that feels comfortable for you. Click the view tools to the left of the Zoom control to see your file in different views.

TIP Word, Excel, PowerPoint, Publisher, and Outlook each display slightly different view controls, all employing the same basic idea. In each view, you'll be able to zoom the view and control the level of magnification.

Protecting files

Knowing that your files are secure in Office 2013 gives you peace of mind, and Office 2013 includes a number of features you can use to ensure that the content you create is protected in the way that's best for you. You might mark a file as final so that no one can make further changes; you could assign a password to the file; or you might add a digital signature or restrict editing to ensure that your content is safeguarded.

Mark a file as final

1 In the Office 2013 app, click the File tab to display the Backstage view.

2 Click the Info tab.

3 Choose Protect Document.

   A list of protection options appears.

4 Click Mark As Final.

   A message box informs you that the file will be marked as final.

5 Click OK to complete the operation or Cancel to abandon it.

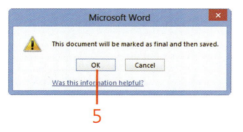

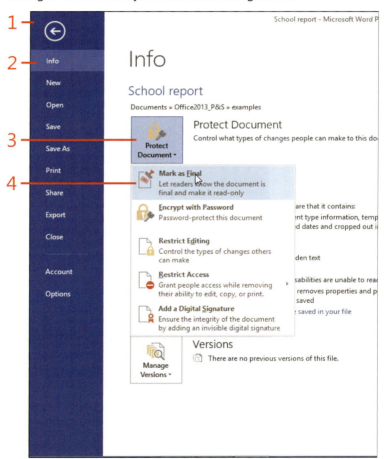

Save a file with a password

1 In your Office 2013 app, click the File tab to display the Backstage view and then click Info.

2 Choose Protect Document.

3 Click Encrypt With Password.

The Encrypt Document dialog box opens.

4 Click in the Password box and type a password for the file.

5 Click OK to save the password.

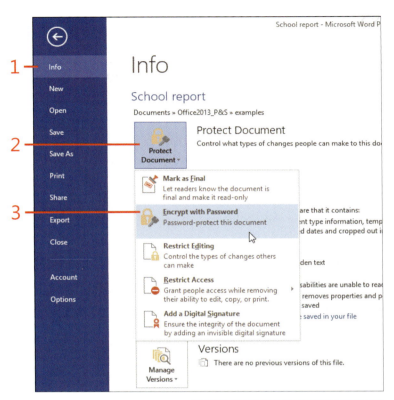

> ✓ **TIP** What makes a good password? The best passwords are ones that mix uppercase and lowercase letters, numbers, and punctuation.

> ⚠ **CAUTION** Ensure that you save the password you assign to the file because there is no way to recover it later if you lose or forget it. That could mean you are no longer able to open a file you need. So, keep a backup copy of the file in a safe place and write your password down.

Sharing files

Once upon a time, when you wanted to share a file, it entailed putting it on a disk and handing it to another person. Today, thankfully, sharing a file can be literally as easy as saving it. With Office 2013, you can invite others to share your file and then you can choose the way you want to share it easily, with no fuss and no bother.

Invite others to share your file

1 In your Office 2013 app, click the File tab to display the Backstage view.

2 Click the Share tab.

3 Choose Invite People.

4 Click Save To Cloud.

The Save As dialog box opens, in which you can choose the location in the cloud where you want to save the file.

5 Click the place where you want to save the file.

6 Click the folder in which you want the file to be stored.

When the Save As dialog box opens, click Save. Office saves your file to the cloud and displays the Share tab that contains additional options with which you can share the file with others.

> **TIP** If you want to ensure that those who are viewing or editing your file log on before they can access the file you've shared, select the Require User To Sign-In Before Accessing Document check box.

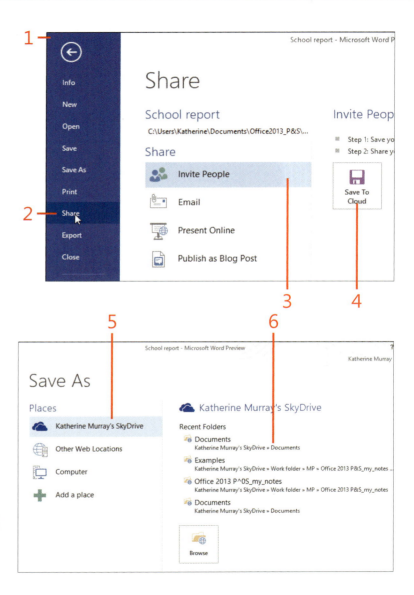

7 Enter the email addresses of the people with whom you want to share the file.

8 Choose the permission level you want to assign these folks.

You can choose between Can Edit and Can View.

9 Type a message to go along with your invitation.

10 Click Share.

The Office 2013 app displays a message that the file is being sent and then displays the recipient's information at the bottom of the screen so that you can see easily who has access to the shared file.

 TIP You can click the Address Book icon to the right of the email address line to choose recipients from your contacts list.

Sending files via email

You can easily send files by email if you prefer. The process begins in the Share tab of the Backstage view.

Emailing files

1 In your Office 2013 app, click the File tab to display the Backstage view and then click the Share tab.

2 Click Email.

Email options appear in the right panel.

3 Click the way in which you want to save the file.

If you send the file as an attachment, the Office file is attached to the email message. If you send a link (which becomes available only if you've previously saved the file to the cloud), you can copy the link to the file and insert it in the body of the email message you send. Send As PDF and Send As XPS save the file in PDF or XPS format and attach the file to the email message. Finally, Send As Internet Fax uses a fax service to send the message.

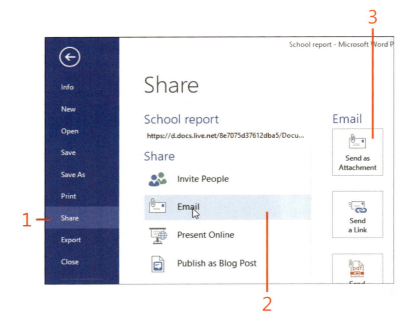

✓ **TIP** A fax service is a third-party vendor that will likely charge you a fee for faxing the file. After you choose Send As Internet Fax, a message box appears informing you that Office will open a browser page where you can locate a provider to use to send the fax.

✓ **TIP** Everyone needs an editor, and Office 2013 helps you to ensure that your files are ready to share by enlisting the Document Inspector's help. In the Backstage view, you can click the Info tab and choose Check For Issues. Your Office application displays a list of choices designed to help you ensure that your file is ready to share with others and doesn't include any sensitive information you'd rather not share.

The Inspect Document tool looks for comments, personal information, and more and lets you know if anything worrisome is found. You can then make changes and run the Document Inspector again to verify that the file is ready to share.

Creating and saving a Document in Word 2013

5

If you write letters, prepare reports, create booklets, send invoices, draft proposals, print mailings, or publish research, you can use Microsoft Word 2013 to complete your projects efficiently and professionally. The new Word 2013 Start screen offers the links and tools you need as you begin to use the program; you might choose to start a new blank document, create a document based on a template, or choose a document on which you've already been working.

Once you open the document, you'll notice right away that the Word 2013 window has been redesigned to give you the maximum amount of room to work on your document. Gone are the heavy window borders and the ribbon full of tools. Now, you see screen, and lots of it.

In this section, you'll learn how to find your way around Word 2013; navigate the Word window, and explore the tools you'll use to begin your document, add text and pictures; do some simple editing; and add some special elements such as tables, text boxes, and videos.

Getting started with Word 2013

The first thing you'll notice after you click the Word 2013 app tile on your Windows 8 Start screen is the Word Start screen experience. This new screen is designed to help you find the file with which you want to work, whether it's a beautiful template that you can use as the basis for a report you need to write, a document you've already worked on previously, or a new blank file.

Open the Word 2013 Start screen

1 On the Windows 8 Start screen, scroll to the right to display the Office 2013 app tiles.

2 Click the Word 2013 tile.

The Word 2013 Start screen appears.

1

2

TIP   The Start screen is convenient if you want to move directly to a specific document or you often search for templates when you begin to work with Word. But, if you find that the Start screen is getting in your way, you can configure Word to display a blank document window when you click the Word 2013 tile on the Windows 8 Start screen and bypass the Word Start screen altogether. To turn off the display of the Word Start screen, click the File tab, choose Options, and then clear the Show The Start Screen When This Application Starts check box. Click OK to save your changes.

Choose a template category

Search for a template

Your Microsoft Account information

Recent documents you've viewed in Word

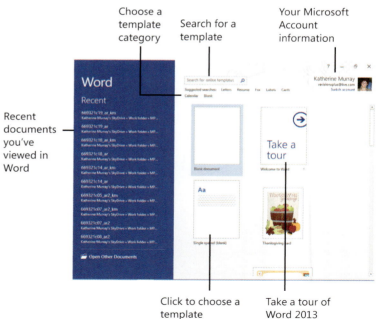

Click to choose a template

Take a tour of Word 2013

Tour the Word window

1 On the ribbon, click the Home tab.

2 Choose Pages.

The Navigation pane changes to show a thumbnail of your current document.

3 Right-click the status bar.

The Customize Status Bar list appears, showing all the items you can add to the status bar. These items give you information about the status of settings and content in your document.

4 Click an item that you want to add to the status bar.

A check mark appears adjacent to the item in the list and the element displays on the status bar.

5 To remove an item from the status bar, click it.

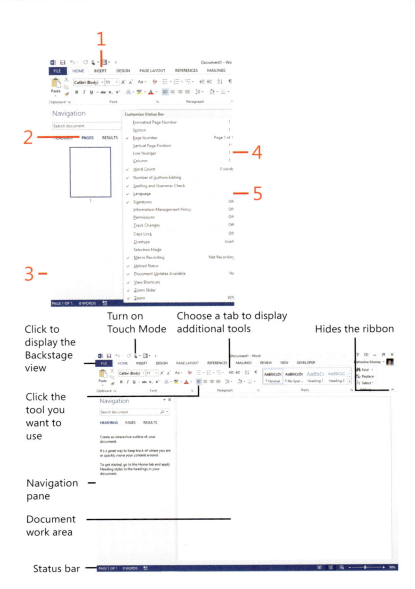

Turn on Touch Mode

Choose a tab to display additional tools

Hides the ribbon

Click to display the Backstage view

Click the tool you want to use

Navigation pane

Document work area

Status bar

Creating documents

Thanks to the new Word 2013 Start screen, you can start a new document in one of several different ways—all of them simple. You can choose to open a blank document, start typing, and then embellish the content by using your own design ideas and skills, or you can use a template to jump-start your design. Additionally, the Start screen makes it easy for you to open an existing document you've worked on previously.

Start with a blank document

1 On the Windows 8 Start screen, click the Word 2013 tile to display the Word Start screen.

2 Click Blank document.

A blank document appears on the screen.

3 Begin typing the content for your document.

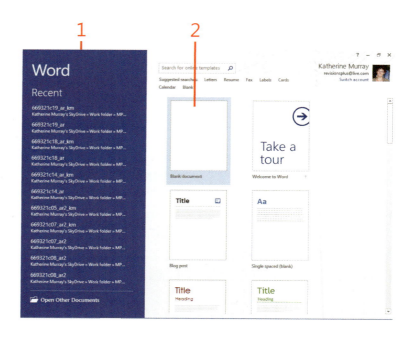

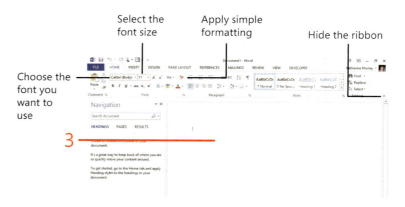

Choose the font you want to use

Select the font size

Apply simple formatting

Hide the ribbon

TIP If you want to start a new, blank document when you're already working with Word, simply click the File tab and choose New. The Word Start screen will appear and you can select Blank Document to get started.

TRY THIS! On the Word Start screen, click Blank Document to display the Word window. Experiment by typing (or tapping) a few characters on the screen to experience how quickly Word responds.

Start with a template

1 Display the Word 2013 Start screen.

2 Enter a word or phrase describing the template you'd like to find.

3 Click Start Searching.

4 Alternatively, click a template category.

5 Scroll down to display more templates.

6 Click the template that you want to use.

✓ **TIP** If you choose to search for a template or select a template category, Word displays the Filter By list along the right side of the Start screen. You can use the Filter By list to narrow the search results that display in the center of the screen. For example, you can narrow the results you receive for Fax templates by choosing a design set you like (such as the Oriel Design Set) or by selecting another characteristic, such as Professional.

Opening existing documents

Of course, not all of the documents you'll work with in Word will be brand new; you also need to be able to open documents that you've already created. Luckily that's a simple task with the Start screen and the Backstage view.

Open an existing document

1 On the Word 2013 Start screen, in the Recent list, review the available documents.

2 Click the document that you want to view.

3 If you don't see the document that you want, click Open Other Documents.

The Open screen appears.

4 Click the location where the file is stored.

5 Choose the file that you want to open.

> **TIP** To open a document when you're already working in Word (which means the Word Start screen isn't displayed), click the File tab and choose Open. You can then choose the location for the file and select the document in the Recent Documents list.

> **TIP** Depending on the location you choose in the center column of the Open window, the choices on the right side of your window might be folders rather than files. Click the folder containing the file you want to open. The Open dialog box will open so that you can choose the file you want. Click the file and choose Open to open the document in the Word window.

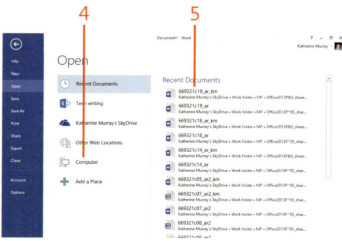

Adding text to your document

Chances are good that the first thing you'll want to do in a new document is enter text. You can do that several different ways in Word. First, and most obvious, you can type the content you want to save in the document. You can also copy and paste content from another file—even from another program—into your Word document. You can also incorporate the text from other documents into your active document. That means you won't need to retype finished work after all. Nice!

Enter text

1 Click in the document work area and then type your content.

 If you tap on the screen, the onscreen keyboard automatically appears.

2 To copy and paste content from another document, highlight the content in the document from which you're copying, and then in the Home tab, in the Clipboard group, choose Copy.

3 Switch to the document in which you want the content, click where you want the text to appear, and then choose Paste.

> ✓ **TIP** You can also drag content from one window to another when you have more than one open document in Word.

> ✓ **TIP** You can easily add text from another document at the cursor position in your current document. Just click at the point where you want to insert the text, choose the Insert tab, and then click the Object tool. Choose Text From File, and then in the Insert File dialog box, choose the folder in which the file is stored, and then select the file and click Insert. The contents of the file are added to your document.

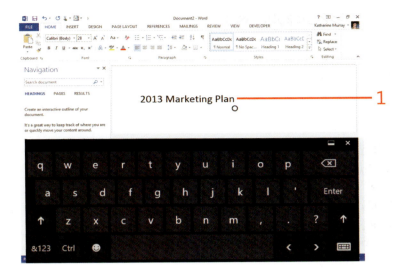

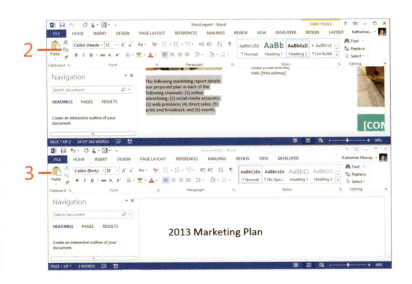

Changing the view

As you work with your document, you'll probably want to view it in different ways. If you're focusing on creating a good outline, for example, you might want to work in Outline view. When you are in a writing mood and just want to concentrate on the text, you might prefer to work in Draft view. And, when you're reviewing a document—either one you created or one shared with you by someone else—you can use Word's new Read Mode to review the content without screen elements to distract you.

Change the view

1 Open the document that you want to view.

2 Click the View tab.

By default, your document appears in Print Layout view.

3 Use the Zoom controls to adjust the display so that you see the number of pages you want on the screen at one time.

4 In the Views group, click Draft.

Draft view shows your document without pictures so that you can focus on the text.

5 In the Views group, choose Outline.

In Outline view, the various hierarchal levels of your text are indented to show the overall organization.

6 Change the level of text displayed.

7 Click to select all content in the section.

8 Click Close Outline View and return to the previous view.

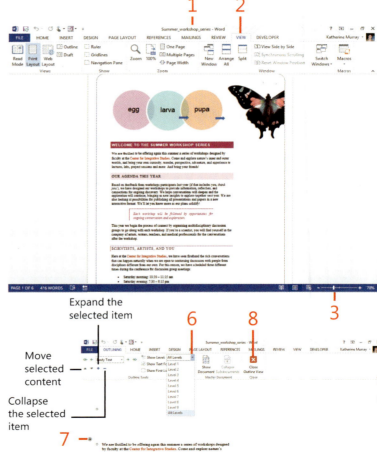

Use Read Mode

1 Display the document that you want to review.

2 Click the View tab.

3 In the View group, choose Read Mode.

4 In Read Mode, click the right arrow to display the next page.

5 Click View to display viewing and editing options.

6 Click Layout.

The different layout choices for Read Mode appear.

7 Choose Paper Layout.

The display of Read Mode changes so that you use the horizontal scroll bar—rather than the arrows on either side of the columnar page—to move through the document. If you prefer Column Layout, return to that layout by choosing View, Layout, and then selecting Column Layout.

5

4

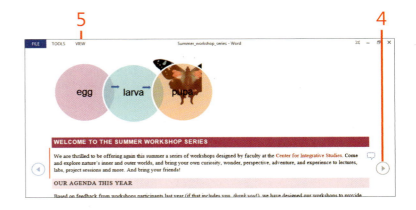

Search for content in your document or online using Bing

Click to return to Print Layout to edit document

Add Navigation Pane to ReadMode

Open a column on the right for comment display

Change column width to narrow or wide

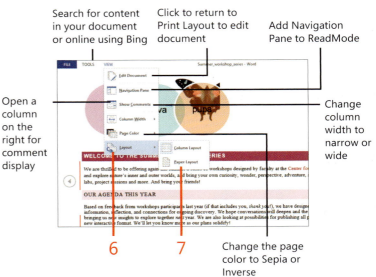

3 1 2

6 7

Change the page color to Sepia or Inverse

Inserting pictures

Today's documents just aren't complete without a little color, a bit of art, or some good old-fashioned visual interest. In Word 2013, you can easily insert and edit photos, choose clip art or photos from online sources, draw shapes, add custom charts, and even take pictures of your screen to include in your document. The process is simple, and you can personalize it so that you can easily get to the pictures you want to use most.

Insert a picture

1 Open a document in the Word window.

2 Click the Insert tab.

3 Choose Pictures.

   The Insert Picture dialog box opens.

4 Navigate to the folder in which the picture you want to add is stored.

5 Select the check box of the picture you want to use.

   If you want to add more than one picture, you can select multiple check boxes.

6 Click Insert.

   The picture (or pictures) you added appear on the page.

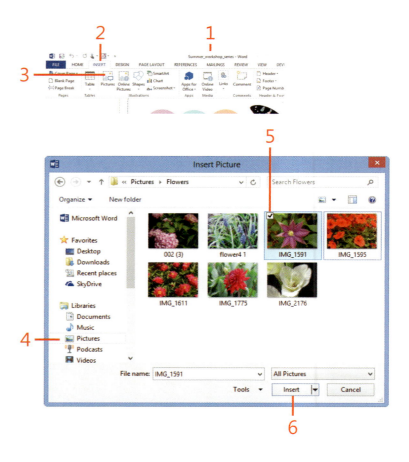

> ✓ **TIP** You can search for pictures online or choose pictures that you've saved in your own photo-sharing accounts by selecting Online Pictures in the Illustrations group. Choose whether you want to search for clip art, search Bing, choose a photo from a photo-sharing site you've connected to Office 2013, or access pictures you've stored in the cloud. Navigate to the folder or site where your picture is stored, select the picture and then click Insert to add it to your page.

Ways to Add Illustrations in Word 2013

Tab	Tool	Use to
View	Pictures	Insert photos, drawings, and other picture files from your local storage device or cloud storage
View	Online Pictures	Find images on Office.com, the web, or on your connected picture sites and cloud storage
View	Shapes	Draw a variety of shapes on your document page and add a new drawing canvas
View	SmartArt	Create a diagram with the color, text, and style you want
View	Chart	Add a chart based on numeric and label values
View	Screenshot	Insert a screenshot of a current screen image

TRY THIS! Add a picture to your document by searching for one you like on Office.com or one of your favorite photo sharing sites. Click Insert to add it to your page. If you add pictures from other sites, be sure that you are using only public domain images; pictures posted by others—online or otherwise—are protected by copyright law.

TIP When you are creating a manual for others to use, capturing and including screenshots in the document you're preparing is a valuable feature that allows readers to visually follow along with your tutorial. To add a screenshot to your document, click the View tab and then choose Screenshot. Select the image you want to add from the displayed pictures. If you want to capture only a portion of the screen, choose Screen Clipping and drag a rectangle around the portion of the screen image that you want to illustrate in your document.

Editing pictures

After you add a picture to the page, you can use the editing tools offered by Word to change its brightness and contrast, sharpen up the focus, alter the coloring, or even apply artistic effects if you want a special look.

Edit a picture

1 Click the picture that you want to change.

The Picture Tools Format tab appears.

2 Click Artistic Effects to view a gallery of special enhancements for your pictures.

3 Select the effect that you want to apply to your picture.

Sharpen or soften the image

Change brightness or contrast

Reset picture to original settings

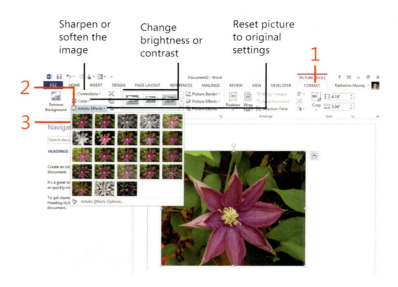

✓ **TIP**   You can also use the Select tool (on the Home tab, in the Editing group) to choose the options you want to use for selecting text. You can select all content in the document, select specific objects, select all text with similar formatting to that at the current location, or display the Selection pane. The Selection pane displays all objects on the current page so that you can reorder the items and hide or redisplay specific objects.

Flow text around a picture

1 Select the picture around which you want to flow text.

2 To the right of the image, click the Layout Options button.

The Layout Options menu appears.

3 Choose the way in which you want the text to flow around the image.

4 Select whether you want the image to move with the text or remain in one position on the page so that text reflows around it.

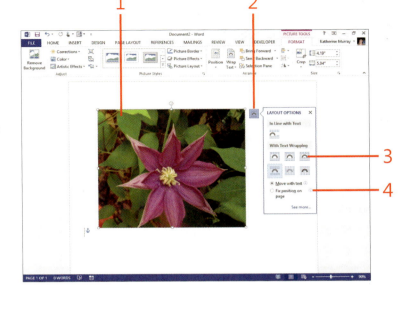

> ✓ **TIP** If you aren't certain what the different text wrapping choices do, hover the mouse pointer over the selection; Word displays the name of the option to give you more information. Again, unfortunately, this does not apply when using your finger on touch-screen devices.

Making simple text edits

You might be a great writer straight out of the blocks, but most of us need a good editor (or maybe more than one). After you add content to Word 2013, you are likely to want to tweak a word here or revise a phrase there. You'll also want to add formatting to specific phrases; for example, you might want to italicize a book title, boldface a product name, or underline a link you want others to be able to find easily.

Edit text

1 Display the document with the text that you want to edit.

2 Click to position the cursor at the end of the section of text you want to delete and use the backspace key to remove the unwanted text.

3 Type the corrected text.

4 Additionally, you can tap and drag or click and drag to select text that you want to change. Type the corrected text and the new text replaces the text you selected.

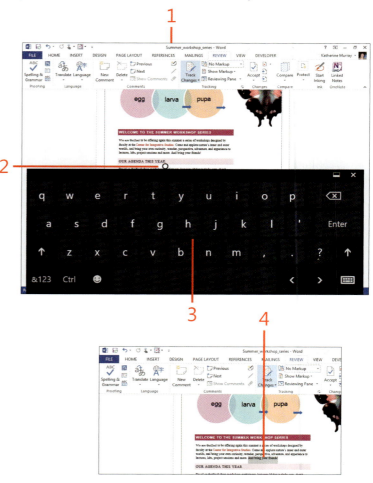

Ways to Select Text in Word

Use this action	To do this
Double-click	Select the current word
Triple-click	Select the current paragraph
Ctrl+click	Select the current sentence
Shift+click	Select all text from the previous cursor position to the point at which you click
Ctrl+A	Select all content in the current document

Find and replace text

1 Display the document that you want to use and click the View tab.

2 In the Show group, click to select the Navigation Pane check box.

3 To find all occurrences of a word or phrase in a document, type the text in the search box.

4 Click Results to see where in the document the word is used.

5 Click a result to move to that location in the document.

6 To search and replace text, click the More arrow.

7 Choose Replace. **The Find And Replace dialog box opens.**

8 Enter the word or phrase for which you're looking.

9 Type the replacement text that you want.

10 Click Replace All to replace all occurrences in the document.

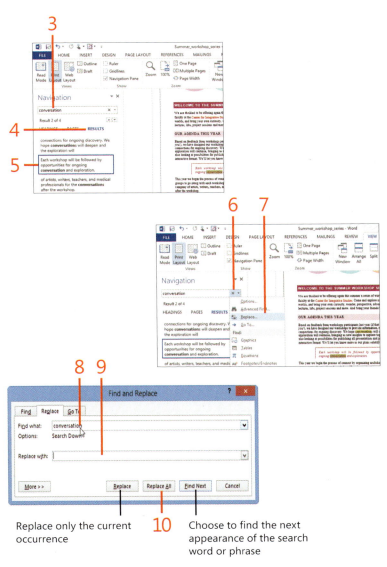

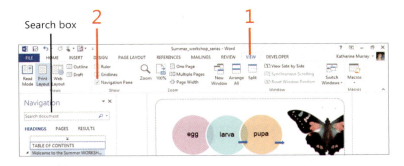

Search box

✓ **TIP** Because Office 2013 includes a live preview feature, you can see how an effect will look on your picture before you select it. Simply hover the mouse pointer over the setting you're considering applying. If it looks the way you want, click it to apply the setting to the image in your document. Unfortunately, there's no way to take advantage of this feature if you're using your finger on a touchscreen device.

Replace only the current occurrence

Choose to find the next appearance of the search word or phrase

Correcting misspellings

Most of us need an extra pair of eyes when we review our documents—it's easy to miss typos we've skimmed over again and again. Word has a spelling checker that keeps an eye on the words you type as you type them. You can run the spelling checker when you're finished writing or pay attention to the spelling checker icon in the status bar to see when Word thinks you have one of more misspelled words.

Correct Misspelled Words

1 Right-click a word with a red-squiggly underline. (This is how Word lets you know it thinks a word is misspelled.)

2 Click the suggested correction you want to use.

3 If the word is spelled correctly, select Ignore All.

All occurrences of the word will be ignored by the spell checker.

4 If you want to add the word to Word's dictionary, choose Add To Dictionary.

Spelling and Grammar Check tool

> ✓ **TIP** In the status bar, the small icon to the right of the number of words is the Spelling And Grammar Check tool. The tool alerts you when Word has found any proofing errors in your document that need correcting.

> ⊙ **TRY THIS!** Click the Spelling And Grammar Check tool. Word checks your document and lets you know if any spelling or grammatical problems are found.

Customizing spelling checks

You can control what Word checks for during a spelling check by changing the Proofing options. To do this, on the File tab, choose Options and then click Proofing to display the Word Options dialog box.

In the When Correcting Spelling In Microsoft Office Programs area, you can choose global spelling settings that will apply to all Office 2013 programs. In the When Correcting Spelling And Grammar In Word area, you can choose settings that apply only to Word. You can select whether you want to check for spelling and grammar errors as you type, check words that are often confused (such as "their" and "there"), and whether you want to show readability statistics.

You can also add a custom dictionary to Word so that words and phrases used commonly in your industry will be recognized by the spelling checker.

Formatting text

Word includes a number of tools with which you can enhance the formatting of your document. It presents the tools you need when you select content on your page. You can then choose the tools you want from the formatting minibar, which appears just above the text you've selected or by clicking the tool you want to use on the Home tab.

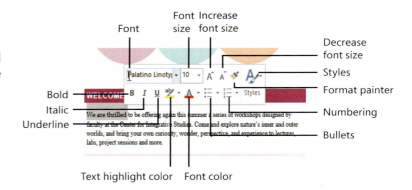

Format selected text

1 Select the text that you want to format.

2 Click the tool in the formatting toolbar that represents the change you want to make.

Add a bulleted or numbered list

1 Click to position the cursor in the document where you want to begin the bulleted or numbered list.

2 Click the Home tab.

3 Click the Paragraph group, select Bullets (or Numbered List).

   A bullet (or number 1) appears at the cursor position.

4 Type the text for the first bullet or numbered item and then press Enter.

   A new bullet or the number "2" appears, ready for you to enter the second item.

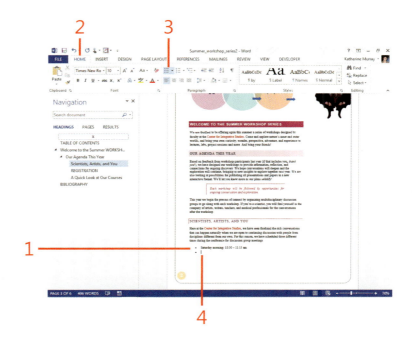

Tools in the Formatting Toolbar

Use this tool	To do this
Font	Change the font of selected text
Font size	Adjust the size of selected text
Increase font size	Enlarge the size of selected text by one point size
Decrease font size	Reduce the size of selected text by one point size
Format painter	Copy the formatting applied to selected text
Styles	Display a gallery of styles that you can apply to selected text
Bold	Make selected text bold
Italic	Italicize selected text
Underline	Underline selected text
Text highlight color	Add a highlight to selected text
Font color	Change the color of selected text
Bullets	Add bullets to selected text
Numbering	Add numbering to selected text

TIP You can easily turn text into a bulleted list or a numbered list after you type it, as well. Just select the text you want to use and then choose either Bullets or Numbered List. Word formats the list as you selected, assigning one bullet or numeral to each paragraph. The text is also formatted so that the list text aligns to an indent and the bullets or numbers hang out to the left of the list items.

TIP If you want to choose the character used for the bullet or change the bullet style or color, select the arrow to the right of the Bullets tool. A gallery of bullet choices opens. If you want to create a new bullet, choose Define New Bullet, and then in the dialog box that appears, select your choices. Click OK to save your settings.

Inserting tables

In addition to the text and pictures you add to your Word document, you might want to use some special elements to help showcase your content. One easy way to share information with readers is through the use of tables. With tables, you can line up data items so readers can see how the items compare side-by-side. The table tools offered by Word give you a lot of flexibility in how you create tables in your document. You can draw a table on the page, choose a Quick Table design, or insert a table with the number of rows and columns you want.

Create and modify tables

1 Click to position the cursor at the point in the document where you want to add the table.

2 Click the Insert tab.

3 In the Tables group, click Table.

4 On the grid that appears, drag to select the number of rows and columns that you want to add to the table you create.

Word displays a preview of the table at the cursor position, giving you a chance to see how the table will look before you click to confirm your choice.

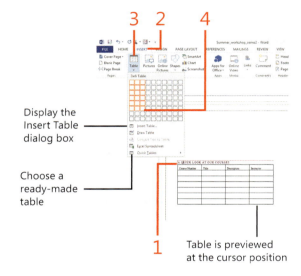

Display the Insert Table dialog box

Choose a ready-made table

Table is previewed at the cursor position

TIP   You can use a shortcut key combination Ctrl+H to display the Find And Replace dialog box if you know you want to search and replace a word or phrase right off the bat. Open the dialog box, enter the search text as well as the text you want to replace it with, and then click Replace All.

5 Click in a table cell and type the information you want to add. Press Tab to move to the adjacent cell.

6 To add a row to the table, position the pointer along the left edge of the table and click the + that appears in a small bubble along the table border.

A blank row is added to your table.

7 To add a column to the table, point to the top edge of the table along one of the column borders and click the + that appears.

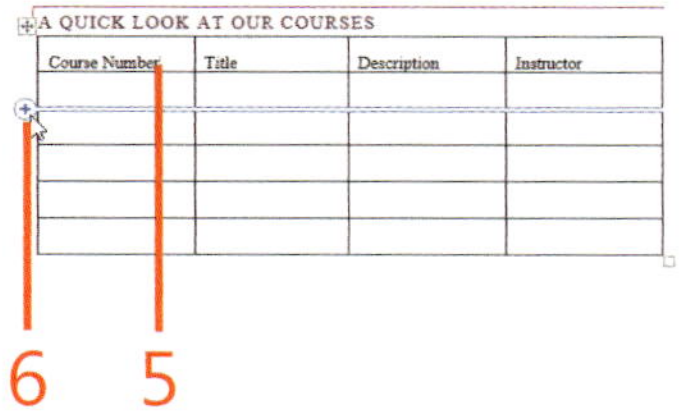

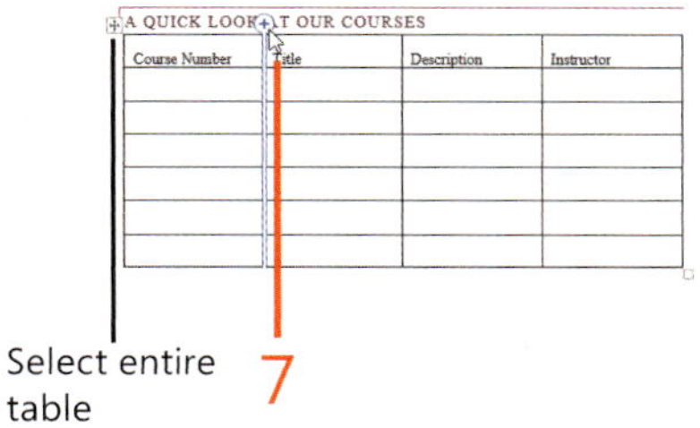

TIP After you add content to your table, you can format the information by using the various tools on the Home tab. You can also select your text and choose the formatting options you want to use from the formatting toolbar.

TIP Tables can contain more than text. You can add pictures to tables if that fits what you need in your document. You can also use shading and borders to give your table a professional look.

Adding text boxes

Adding text boxes is another flexible and easy way to add unique content to your pages. You can choose to add a pre-designed text box from the Text Box gallery, draw your own text box on the page, or choose another text box design from Office.com.

Add a text box

1 Click to position the cursor at the point in the document where you want to add the text box.

2 Click the Insert tab.

3 In the Text group, click Text Box.

4 Choose the text box that you want to add.

5 Click to draw a text box on the page.

If you select this option, move the pointer to the page and drag a rectangle on the page. Word adds a text box at that location on the page.

✓ **TIP** If you choose a text box from the Text Box gallery, Word displays the text box on the page with placeholder text. To remove the text, simply click it and begin typing the information you want to use in its place. You can now change the format of the text or apply other formatting changes from the Drawing Tools Format tab that becomes available when you select the text box.

Adding apps for Office

Apps for Office extends the functionality of Word 2013 by making it possible for you to add apps that bring tools, information, and more right into your line-by-line document work. For example, you might want to add your favorite dictionary as an app in Word. Or perhaps you regularly fax contracts to others—in this case, adding an app with which you can fax from Word is a real time-saving feature.

If you want to add Apps for Office, click the Insert tab and choose Apps for Office. In the list that appears, click See All. A window appears, showing you the apps that are currently available for Word 2013. Click the app that you want to add. A webpage opens displaying additional information about the app. Click Add. Click the close box to close the webpage.

Back in the Insert App dialog box, click Office Store and then click Refresh. Now, you can choose the app that you want to add and choose Insert.

The app appears in a panel along the right side of the Word window. You can close the app by clicking the close box. In the future, you'll be able to launch the app on the Insert tab by choosing Apps for Office and selecting the app from the displayed list.

Adding and playing online video

In Word 2013, you can incorporate online video clips in your documents. That's a great thing if you want to share a clip that illustrates the point you're making in the written text, or if you want to offer readers another way to understand the importance of a product or service.

Add and play online video

1 Click the Insert tab.

2 In the Media group, choose Online Video.

The Insert Video dialog box opens.

3 Click in the Bing Video Search and type a word or phrase that reflects the type of video you want to add.

4 Alternatively, if you have the embed code from one of your own videos (for example, a video you uploaded to YouTube that you want to include in your Word document), click in the From A Video Embed Code box and paste the embed code.

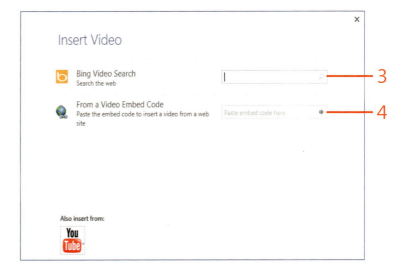

5 Click the thumbnail of the video you'd like to add.

6 Click Insert.

The video is added to your document at the cursor position.

7 You can play the video clip at any point by clicking Play on the added clip.

8 The video clip opens and begins to play.

You can use the standard player controls to adjust playback.

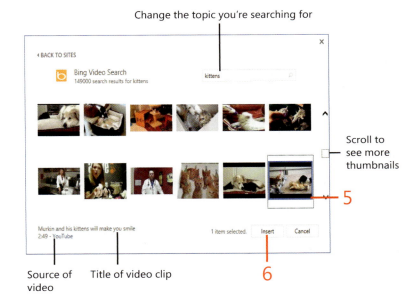

Change the topic you're searching for

Scroll to see more thumbnails

Source of video

Title of video clip

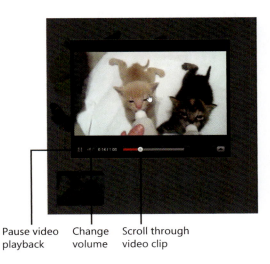

Pause video playback

Change volume

Scroll through video clip

Formatting your content in Word 2013

6

Here's a simple fact of modern publishing life: if you want someone to actually *read* the document you prepared in Microsoft Word, you're probably going to have to put a little artistic effort into it. Nobody wants to read paragraph after paragraph (after paragraph!) of dry, boring text. Think about the last thing you read with interest. Was it a webpage, with colorful pictures, big headlines, and lots of white space around the page? Was it a magazine layout, inviting you in with eye-catching color and interesting fonts?

If you want your reader to become interested in the information you're presenting, you need to be able to share it in an inviting, engaging way. That's what the design features are all about in Word 2013.

This section introduces you to the various ways that you can make your words look good by using themes and styles to spruce up your message in an organized, logical way. You'll also learn how to format and control spacing for your paragraphs; use tools such as tabs, indents, and margins to arrange your content on the page; and make design choices (for instance, page color and borders) that impact the entire page and hopefully impress your readers, as well.

In this section:

- Understanding design tools in Word 2013
- Choosing a theme
- Choosing and saving a style set
- Adjusting the colors of your document
- Selecting fonts
- Saving a new theme
- Applying styles
- Modifying styles
- Creating a new style
- Managing styles
- Using the Style inspector
- Formatting and spacing paragraphs
- Working with tabs, indents, and margins

Understanding design tools in Word 2013

When you're creating a document in Word, you can get as much—or as little—design help as you'd like. If you want someone professional to do everything for you, you can choose to create your new document by using a template. You learn how to start a new document based on a template in Section 5, "Creating and saving a document in Word 2013," but in addition to the templates you'll find in the Word Start screen, you can search online and choose from thousands of templates in all sorts of styles and types.

Once you've started a new document, however, there are many additional design tools that you can use to give your document the look you want, whether that look is professional, whimsical, creative, or structured.

Themes

Word 2013 themes are coordinated design tools that pull together a variety of formatting settings in one orchestrated group that you can apply to your document. By default, each new blank document you create is assigned the Office theme. That means that a set of formatting configurations is already controlling the look of the following items in your document:

- The font, size, style, and color of headings

- The font, size, style, and color of text (including body text and special text items such as captions and tables)

- The overall color scheme used in your document

- The spacing applied to the paragraphs in your document

- Any dimensional effects applied to objects, such as shapes, borders, and boxes

> ✓ **TIP** The font settings that the theme orchestrates are part of the style sets available within the theme. You can change font settings as you like; you're not limited to using only what the theme offers you. To do so, choose a different style set or in the Document Formatting group, select Fonts.

Office theme is the current theme

Color reflects the theme choice

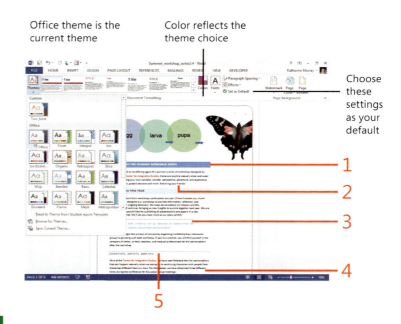

Choose these settings as your default

1
2
3
4
5

Style sets

Style sets are collections of settings that control the look of the text on your page. When you choose a theme in Word 2013, you can choose from different style sets that appear in the Document Formatting group on the Design tab. You can click the More button on the Style Set gallery to view all available style sets for the selected theme. You can also create your own style sets, uniquely configured to your project and preferences. After you save a style set, it becomes available in the gallery, where you can click it to apply it easily.

Styles

When it comes to working with words, sentences, and paragraphs on your page, you will want to use Word styles to keep your content formatted and organized. You'll find styles on the Home tab, in the Styles group, where you can access them easily. The fonts, styles, and colors used in the styles that appear by default are connected to the theme selected for your document. When you change the theme, you change the styles that are available. You'll find styles in Word that cover a wide range of formatting needs, including:

- Heading levels 1 (largest) through 9 (smallest)
- Title and subtitle
- Emphasis in various degrees (including subtle and intense)
- Quote and intense quote
- Book title
- List paragraph
- Caption
- Subtle reference and intense reference

Set style in use

Built-in style sets

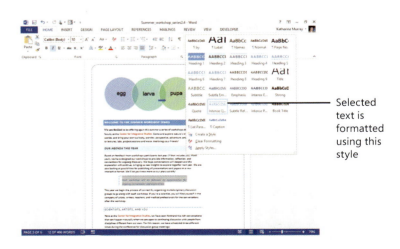

Selected text is formatted using this style

Why use styles?

If you're perfectly happy adding bold to a word here, under-lining a phrase there, or increasing the font size of some text to make it look like a heading, why do you need to mess with styles and style sets and themes? At first, it might seem like busywork that doesn't really benefit you.

But, the beauty of working with orchestrated styles is that when you use a style to format a particular element on your page—for example, suppose that you use Heading 3 for the section heads in your report—you can easily change the look later by simply choosing a different theme or style set. Because the Heading 3 setting is tied to a particular theme and style set, when you decide you want a new look, you can simply click your choice; everything connected to that theme or style set changes accordingly. So, your heading might go from having a blue background to a green one; the fonts might change; the effects of the picture borders on the page might change. That's a whole bunch of reformatting, all tied to one simple choice.

If you go through and increase the font size of each head-ing in your document individually rather than using a style to format them, if you want to change the heads later, you would have to go back through the document and change each one individually, all over again. How much better would it be to format them all with styles and then make all the changes with a simple click? That's why using styles is a good idea. They give you more time to do fun stuff and ensure that all the items you wanted to change actually get changed (rather than accidentally leaving that one renegade heading in the wrong font in the final document).

Choosing a theme

When you first fire up Word 2013, you'll notice that on the Design tab, in the Themes gallery, you have a set of 10 themes available. You aren't limited to these themes, however; you can also create your own themes, find additional themes on Office.

com, or even go back to the original theme used on the template you started with. (Assuming, of course, you started with a template.)

Select a theme for your document

1 Open the document with which you want to work.

2 Click the Design tab.

3 Choose Themes.

   The themes palette appears. The selected theme is shaded blue.

4 Click the theme that you want to apply to the document. Depending on the theme you select, you might see the font change slightly as well as the colors and effects used in the document.

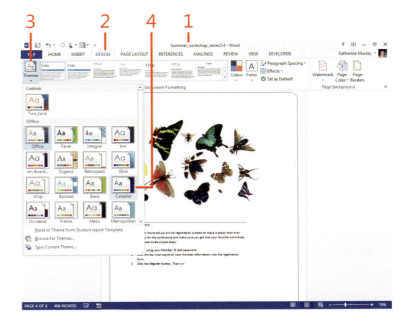

Choosing and saving a style set

Because style sets go along with themes, whenever you choose a new theme, you get new styles sets to go along with it. The various style sets give you options about the way your headings look, the types of graphic elements used (borders, boxes, and lines, for example), and the way color is assigned to elements and text on the page.

Choose and save a style set

1   On the Design tab, in the Document Formatting group, review the style sets.

2   Click More to see additional style sets.

3   Click the style set you want to apply.

4   If you would like, modify the set by changing other settings in the Document Formatting group.

5   Click Save As A New Style Set.

6   In the dialog box that opens, enter a file name for the new style set.

7   Click to change the title of the style set.

8   Choose Save to save the new style set with your current settings.

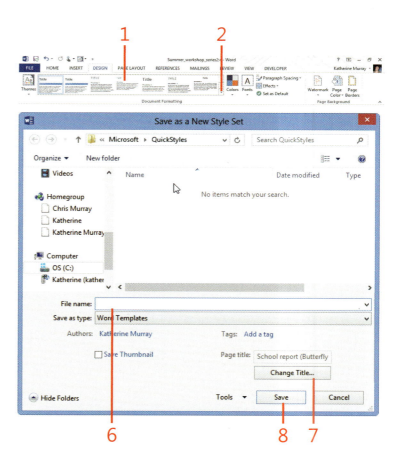

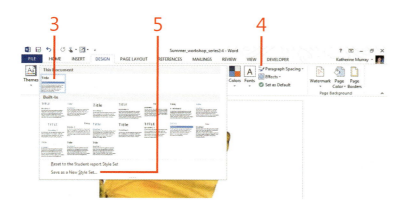

Adjusting the colors of your document

Although the color scheme for your document is set automatically when you choose a theme and a variant, you can select a different coordinated color scheme if you like. Word includes a number of palettes with complementary colors already assembled for you.

Adjust the document color

1 On the File tab, in the Document Formatting group, click the Colors arrow.

A palette of color schemes appears.

2 Scroll through the list to find the color scheme you like.

3 Click the color scheme you want to apply.

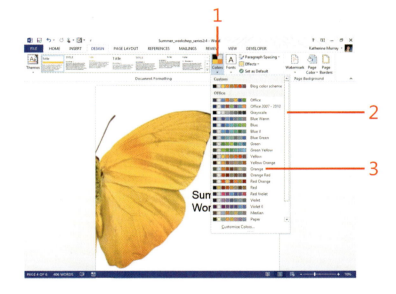

> **TIP** You can also create your own custom color scheme. At the bottom of the Colors list, click Customize Colors and choose the different colors you want to assign to various elements in your document. When you click Save, the custom color palette is added to the top of your Colors list so that you can apply it easily.

> **TRY THIS!** Open a document with which you want to experiment and display the Design tab. Click Colors and experiment with the different color schemes to find a look you like.

Selecting fonts

The font family applied to the design of your document is also controlled by the theme, but you can change the font selections available to you by using the Font tool in the Document Formatting group.

Select a font

1 On the Design tab, in the Document Formatting group, click the Fonts arrow.

2 Scroll through the list to see the font families available for the selected theme. Each font grouping shows the Heading font and the body font.

3 Choose the font you want to use for your document.

4 If you want to create your own font combination, click Customize Fonts.

5 In the Create New Theme Fonts dialog box, click the Heading font arrow and choose the font you want from the displayed list.

6 Click the Body Font arrow and select the font from your the drop-down list that appears.

7 In the Sample window, review the changes.

8 Enter a name for the new font combination.

9 Click Save.

The new font group is added to the Custom area at the top of the Fonts list.

✓ **TIP** Once you get all your settings just the way you want them, you can click Set As Default in the Document Formatting group to make them the defaults for new documents you create in the future. This is an easy way to create a design standard for your business or department.

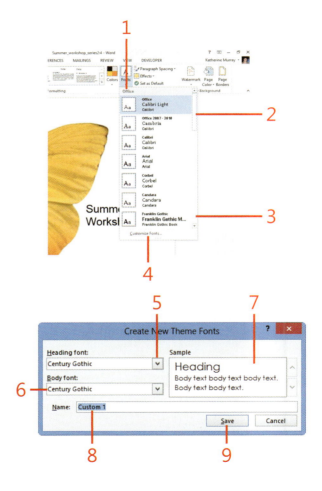

Saving a new theme

After you create the look you want with color, fonts, and effects, you can save your settings as a new theme that you can apply to other documents you create. The new custom theme will then be available at the top of the Themes gallery so that you can find and apply it easily.

Save a theme

1 After you've made all the changes in Document Formatting you want to make, click Themes.

2 Click Save Current Theme.

The Save Current Theme dialog box opens.

3 Type a name for the theme.

4 Click Save.

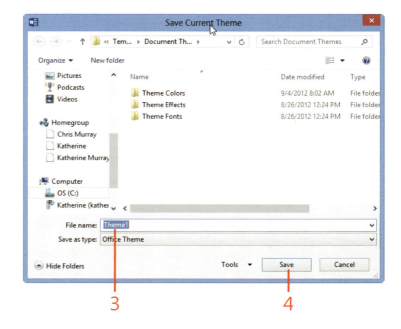

> ✔ **TIP** When you save your theme, Word displays the folder in which all the theme settings are stored. Be sure to save your theme in the selected folder so that Word will be able to access and display your new theme in the Themes gallery on the Design tab.

Applying styles

The styles you assign to the text and paragraphs in your document are available on the Home tab, in the Styles gallery, but there are more where those came from. Your business or organization might have its own style sheet with particular styles used for correspondence with customers (you'll learn how to attach a style sheet later in this section). You might want to create or tweak your own styles so that you can get just the look you want. Then, you can even save those styles so that you can use them consistently in your other documents, as well.

Apply a style to text

1   Click in, tap, or select the text to which you want to apply the style.

2   Click the Home tab.

3   In the Styles gallery, click the style that you want to apply.

4   If you want to see additional styles, on the far right side of the Themes gallery, click the More arrow.

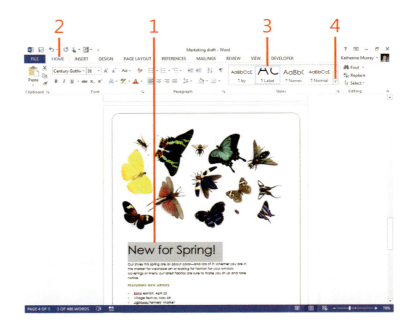

Work with the style pane

1 On the Home tab, in the Styles group, click the Styles button in the lower-right corner to display the Style pane. You can use the Style pane to view, organize, modify, and assign styles to the text in your document.

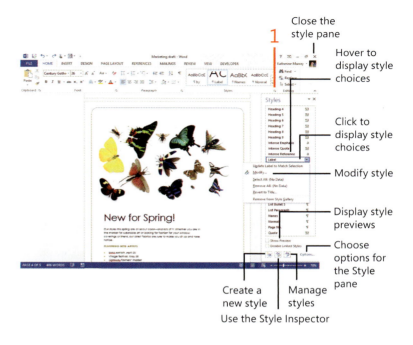

Close the style pane

Hover to display style choices

Click to display style choices

Modify style

Display style previews

Choose options for the Style pane

Create a new style

Manage styles

Use the Style Inspector

TRY THIS! If you want to reduce the number of styles shown in the Style pane, in the lower-right corner of the pane, choose Options. In the Style Pane Options dialog box that opens, click the Select Styles To Show arrow and choose In Use. This limits the display of styles to only those you have applied in the current document. If you have a long list of available styles, this will help to pare that down to display the ones you're really looking for.

Modifying styles

You can easily change the various settings included in a style so that you get just the look you want. To do so, in the Styles pane, click Modify to display the Modify Style dialog box, in which you can set the font, size, and formatting for the style.

Modify a style

1 Display the Styles pane and click the arrow that appears to the right of the style that you want to change.

A list of style options appears.

2 Click Modify to open the Modify Style dialog box.

3 Change the formatting settings that you want to include with this style.

For example, you might change the font or size of the text, alter the way the text is aligned on the page, alter the text color, or adjust the line spacing.

4 Review your changes in the preview window.

5 Click Format to display additional choices you can use to change settings related to the style's border, language, numbering, text effects, paragraph settings, and more.

6 If you want Word to change all occurrences of the style currently being used in your document, select the Automatically Update check box.

7 Click OK to save your changes.

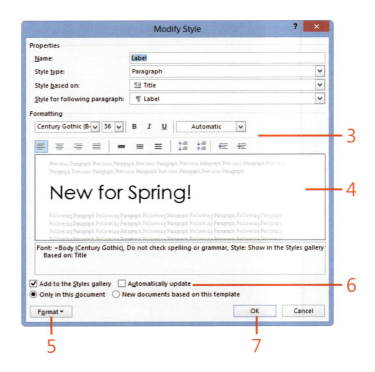

Creating a new style

If you want something a little different from the default styles or even those that you modify yourself, you can create a style from scratch. Word makes it easy for you to base your new style on an existing one or to start with a blank slate.

Create a new style

1 In your document, apply the formatting that you want to include in the new style to a paragraph of text and then select that formatted text.

2 In the Style pane, click New Style to open the Create New Style From Formatting dialog box.

3 Enter a name for the style.

4 Choose the type of style you want to create.

When you click the arrow, a list appears, showing five types of styles: Paragraph, Character, Linked (paragraph and character), Table, and List).

5 Choose the style on which you want this style to be based.

6 Add any additional desired formatting.

7 Preview the new style.

8 Click OK to save the style.

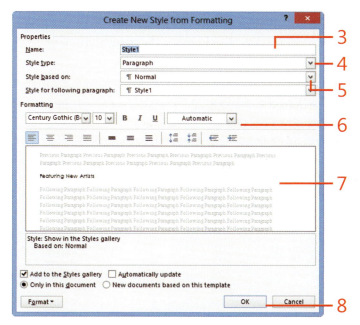

> ✓ **TIP** By default, the Only In This Document option is selected in the Create New Style From Formatting dialog box, which means that the new style you created will be available only for the file in which you're working. If you want the style to be available to other new documents that use the current template, click the New Documents Based On This Template option.

Managing styles

As you add styles to your document, you can organize how they appear in the Styles pane. By choosing which styles you want to appear and arranging them in the order you want them, you can streamline the amount of time you spend looking for the styles you want and get back to working on the document at hand.

Organize your styles

1 In the Style pane, click Manage Styles to open Manage Styles dialog box.

2 Click Sort Order and choose to display styles Alphabetically (which is the default setting), As Recommended, or by Font, Based On, or Type.

3 Click to choose styles you want to appear in the recommended list of styles.

On this tab, you can also rearrange the styles and determine their priority in the Style pane.

4 Click to restrict the use of some styles available in this document.

5 Set the default formatting values for new styles you create in this document or in all new documents.

6 Import or export styles for use in this or other documents.

7 Click OK to save your changes.

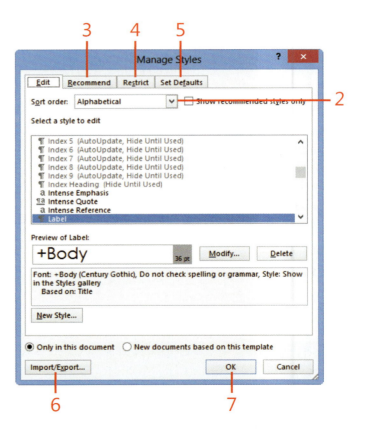

Using the Style inspector

The Style Inspector in Word helps you check the styles in your document to ensure that your formatting is consistent throughout your document. You can also modify styles and make other style selections using the Style Inspector.

Use the Style inspector

1 Select the text you want to check, and then in the Style pane, click Style Inspector.

The Style Inspector pane appears, showing you the current settings related to the paragraph style and the character style of the selected text.

2 Click the Clear/Reset buttons on the right to remove or reset the styles for the text.

3 To make more changes, hover the mouse over the style and click the arrow.

4 Click to modify the style.

5 Highlight all occurrences of the style in the document.

6 Remove the style where it is used in the document.

7 Reveal the formatting settings assigned to the style.

The Reveal Formatting pane appears along the right side of your document window.

8 You can review all the formatting settings and change them by clicking the setting links (Font, Language, Paragraph Style, and more).

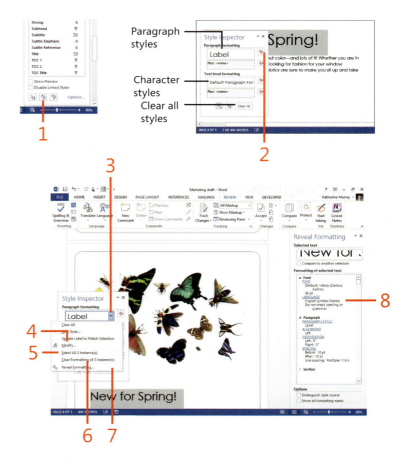

Formatting and spacing paragraphs

It can be tempting to focus a lot of your design energy on fancy things like the title and heading of your document, the pictures you include, and the charts and diagrams you place. But, paying careful attention to the way your paragraphs are formatted goes a long way toward making the document easier to read, which means your readers will be more likely to stick with you until the final page. When you apply formats to your paragraphs, you can choose the way the text is aligned, change the spacing before and after paragraphs, adjust the line spacing, and create special indents.

Choose paragraph alignment

1 Click to place the cursor in the paragraph that you want to change.

2 On the File tab, in the Paragraph group, click the alignment setting you want.

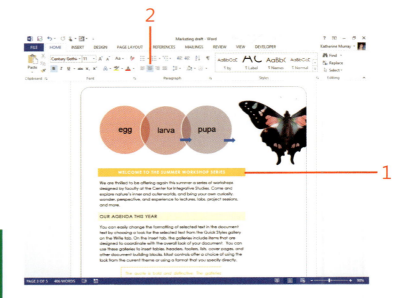

> **✓ TIP** Bullet lists and numbered lists are two formats that are available on the Home tab, in the Paragraph group. You can easily add bullets or numbers to a list by clicking the tool you want in the Paragraph group.

> **✓ TIP** Why would you use the Justify alignment in the Paragraph group? Justify inserts spaces between words to cause both the right and left margins of your text to align. This style is sometimes jarring to read. If you are creating a multi-column format, however, using Justify alignment can help your readers see clearly where one column ends and another begins. This can add continuity to your page and help lead readers' eyes from one column to the next.

> **✓ TIP** If you're trying to center text and find that it's not centering correctly, the ruler can help you see what's going on. To display the ruler, click the View tab, and then in the Show group, select the Ruler check box. Notice the margin indicators on the horizontal ruler, and check the amount of space available for centering your text. If necessary, you can drag the margin indicator on the right toward the edge of the page to widen the text area of your document and allow for true centering.

Control paragraph spacing

1 Position the cursor in the paragraph that you want to change.

2 In the Paragraph group, click the Paragraph Settings button in the lower-right corner.

3 Click to change the amount of space displayed before the paragraph.

You can enter a new value in the text box or click the up-arrow or down-arrow to change the setting.

4 Change the amount of space displayed after the paragraph.

5 If you want to keep paragraphs of the same style close together with no additional space between them, select this check box.

6 Click to choose the line spacing for paragraph text.

You can select Single, 1.5 lines, Double, At Least, Exactly, or Multiple.

7 Choose the number of lines you want to be used for the spacing.

For example, if you set the line spacing to Double and then increase the "At" setting to 2.5, additional space will be inserted between the lines of the selected paragraph.

8 Preview the changes you have made.

9 If you want to keep these settings as default values, click Set As Default.

10 Click OK to save your changes.

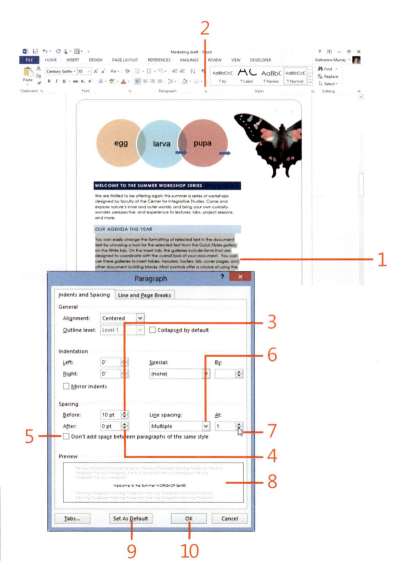

> **SEE ALSO** If you create just the spacing you like for your document text, you can easily save those settings and use them again by creating a new style to store your settings. See "Creating a new style" earlier in this section for the steps on how to do that.

Working with tabs, indents, and margins

It might sound funny, but the unused space on your page is as important to your document as the words on the page. That's because the unused space gives readers' eyes a rest and sets off the rest of the page so the entire layout is as readable as possible. You can use tabs, indents, and page margins to control the amount of space on your page, and to align the text as it appears in the space.

Display the ruler

1 Display the document with which you want to work.

2 Click the View tab.

3 In the Show group, select the Ruler check box.

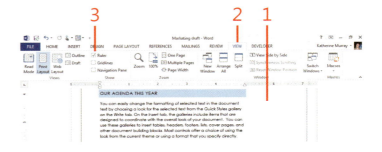

 TIP If you want to hide the ruler again later, repeat the steps, but this time clear the check mark.

 TIP The ruler appears in Print Layout, Web Layout, Draft, and Full Screen views, but it isn't visible in Read or Outline view.

Add tabs

1 Click to display the tab type that you want to add to your document.

2 Click on the ruler to add the tab.

3 Alternatively, in the lower-right corner of the Paragraph group, click Paragraph Settings to display the Paragraph dialog box, and then in the lower-left corner, click Tabs to display tab choices.

4 Type a position for the new tab.

5 Choose the tab type that you want to create.

6 Click the leader type to add, if any.

7 Click Set.

8 Click OK.

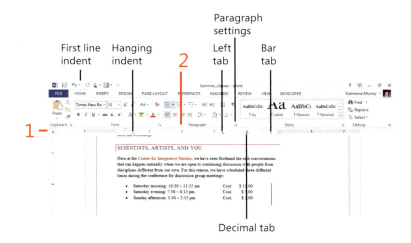

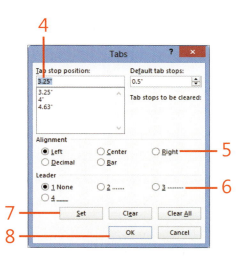

> **TIP** Word documents include left tabs set at .5 inch increments across the width of your page, so each time you press the Tab key, the cursor moves a half inch to the right. You can change the amount of space you want to allow for default tab stops by displaying the Tabs dialog box, and then in the upper-right corner, in the Default Tab Stops setting, increasing or decreasing the value. Choose OK to save your changes.

Tab types in Word 2013

Symbol	Description	
L	Left tab	Aligns text along the left at this tab
⊥	Center tab	Centers text on the tab
⌐	Right tab	Aligns the right edge of text at this tab
⊥	Decimal tab	Aligns values at their decimal points
I	Bar tab	Inserts a bar character at the tab location
▽	First-line indent	Sets the position for the first line indent of paragraphs
△	Hanging indent	Sets the position for wrap-around text in a list item

Indenting your content

You can call attention to specific passages in your document by changing the way the text is indented. You can increase and decrease the way your text is indented by using tools in the Paragraph group of the Home tab.

Indent your content

1 Click in the paragraph that you want to change, or, if you want to indent the entire document, press Ctrl+A.

2 Click the Home tab.

3 In the Paragraph group, click Increase Indent

The selected text is moved farther away from the left edge of the page.

4 Alternatively, click Decrease Indent to move the selection closer to the left edge of the page.

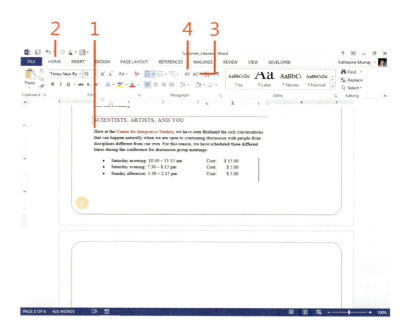

> ✓ **TIP** If you want to set the indents in your document precisely, use the Indention settings in the Paragraph dialog box. You can type a value in the Left and Right text boxes and choose the amount of space you want to assign to first line indents or hanging indents.

> ✓ **TIP** If you are working on a document in which you want to vary the indents, in the Paragraph dialog box, turn on the Mirror Indents setting. Mirror indents means that the page indents will mirror each other, allowing you, for example, to create a larger margin on the inside of the page (where the document will be bound) than the outside.

Adding a border

Adding a border is an easy way to set off a section of your document so that others can find and read it easily. Using the Page Borders tool, you can choose the color, line thickness, and border style that you want to apply to selected text.

Add a border to a page

1 Click the Design tab.

2 In the Page Background group, click Page Borders.

   The Borders And Shading dialog box opens.

3 Click the type of border that you want to add.

4 Select the line style you like.

5 Choose to apply a color to the border.

6 Select the width of the border line.

7 Choose to add Border Art, if you like.

   This adds a border of small graphical images, like cupcakes, apples, or palm trees.

8 View your border in the preview area.

9 Choose the portion of the document to which you want to apply the border. Your choices are Whole Document, This Section, This Section - First Page Only, This Section - All Except First Page.

10 Click OK to save your settings and display your border.

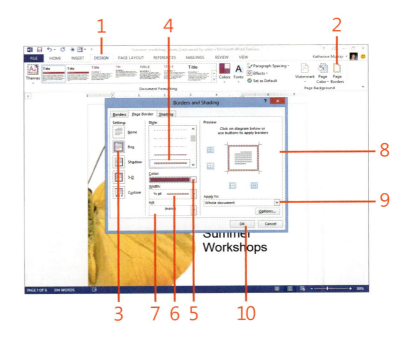

TRY THIS! There's another option in the Page Background group with which you can add a watermark to the background of your page to add a subtle message; for example, to let others know your document is protected or private. Word provides a gallery of watermarks that include the messages Confidential and Do Not Copy. You can also create custom watermarks or download additional watermarks from Office.com. To add the watermark to your page, on the Design tab, in the Page Background group, click Watermark and click the watermark that you want to add. If you later decide you want to delete the watermark, display the Watermark gallery again and choose Remove watermark.

Collaborating with Word 2013

7

Once upon a time, if you wanted someone to review what you'd written, you had to print it out, take it down the hall, and hand it to the other person. Those were the old days when we got more exercise in the office (every little bit helps). The downside, however, is that it took forever to get people to sign off on what you were doing.

Today, thankfully, reviews can happen almost instantly, thanks to tools that make it possible for us to share files in real time. What's more, you can comment on and edit files that others are working on at the same time.

Microsoft Word 2013 makes this kind of seamless collaboration possible by saving files to the cloud, where Word can keep versions organized, allow access from users who have the appropriate permissions, and enable you to get to your content using any device or computer you like. Tracking makes it easy for you to see what others have done in your document, and you can use the new threaded commenting feature to read through the side conversations that are happening around your content ideas. This section shows you how to make the most of the collaboration features offered by Word 2013 and spotlights how simple it is to get input and incorporate your colleague's ideas in your finished piece. Maybe you'll save enough time preparing your document that you can get outside at lunchtime and take a *real* walk!

In this section:

- A bird's-eye-view of the collaboration features in Word
- Co-authoring in the cloud
- Working collaboratively in a document
- Opening and editing PDF files
- Tracking document changes
- Turning on Simple Markup
- Choosing the markup you want to see
- Adding and responding to comments
- Accepting or rejecting changes
- Presenting your document online
- Setting up a blog
- Publishing content to your blog
- Comparing and combining documents
- Restricting document editing

A bird's-eye-view of the collaboration features in Word

No matter what your job or hobby might ask of you, the chances are good that at some point you'll need to share the files you create with others. Perhaps you're writing a report for the local historical society. When you're done, you'll want to send it to somebody on staff to ensure that everything you've written is correct. You might be preparing a paper for school, but at some point you'll need to turn it in. If you're drafting a marketing plan for next year, the director of your department is likely waiting to see it. And, maybe she was hoping for it yesterday.

Word 2013 makes it easy to share your files. You'll find the sharing features you need on the Share tab of the Backstage view.

With the sharing features offered by Word 2013, you can:

- Save your file to the cloud and invite others to share it

- Choose to create one of two links that you can share with others—those given one link can only view the file; those using the other link can edit the file

- Post your file to your favorite social media account

- Send the file by email to others

- Present the document online so that others can go through it with you—even if they don't have Word 2013

- Create and post content directly to your blog

Additionally, the collaboration features built in to Word 2013 have been enhanced so that you can work together easily. After you save your file to the cloud, you and your co-authors can all work in the file at the same time; Word keeps track of the changes you're making and synchronizes them all when you close the file. What's more, the commenting and tracking features have been dramatically improved so that you can read through others' comments and see what changes have been made without having to wade through a document crowded with comment balloons and text markup.

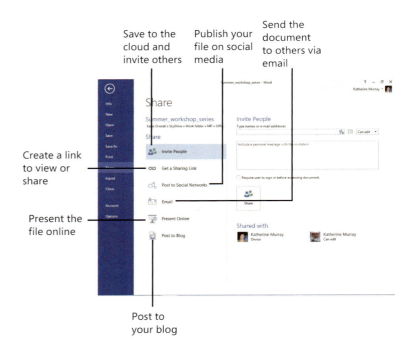

Save to the cloud and invite others

Publish your file on social media

Send the document to others via email

Create a link to view or share

Present the file online

Post to your blog

Co-authoring in the cloud

Saving to the cloud means that you can access your Word document by using any computer, device, or smartphone that has web access or the Microsoft SkyDrive app installed. This makes it easier than ever for you to do a little editing while you're waiting in line somewhere, or review a coworker's report and make suggestions before he turns in the final draft.

The sharing features in Word makes it easy for multiple authors to work on the document at the same time. Word shows you who else is working in your document by displaying an indicator at the bottom of the document window. You can hover the mouse pointer over the indicator to see a list of authors currently editing and then click the name of a person you want to contact in real time.

Open a shared document

1 Click the File tab to display the Backstage view.

2 Click Open.

3 Choose the online location where your shared file is stored.

4 If necessary, click Browse to look through folders and files in your cloud space.

5 Click the folder containing the file that you want to use, select the file, and then click Open.

The document opens on your screen.

6 Hover the mouse pointer over the indicator in the status bar to see who else is working on the document.

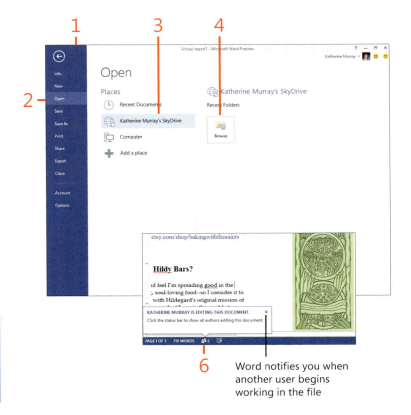

Word notifies you when another user begins working in the file

> 🔍 **SEE ALSO** Before you work collaboratively on a document, you need to go to the Backstage view, select the Share tab, and then use the Invite People selection to save the file to the cloud and give others the permission they need to access the file. You can see how to do that in Section 4, "Accomplishing basic tasks In Office 2013."

Working collaboratively in a document

Word keeps track of all the changes being made in the file and displays a bracket adjacent to areas to which any other people working in the file have applied changed. When you save the document, Word lets everyone else know that an update of the file is available, and when they save their versions of the file, Word synchronizes all the changes and highlights added text so that each person can see what their co-authors have changed.

Work collaboratively in a document

1 Open a shared document and make the desired changes.

2 When a co-author makes changes in the document, a bracket shows where the changes have been made along with the name of the individual who made the change.

3 When the other author saves changes, Word notifies you that updates are available. Click Updates Available. Word displays a message box informing you that when you save the document, Word will update it with any changes made by others. You can see those changes by looking for a green overlay in the text.

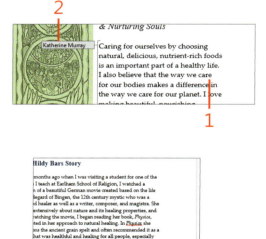

Contact your co-author while you work

1 While you're working in the shared document, hover the mouse pointer over the authoring indicator in the status bar.

The list of current authors appears.

2 Click the author whom you want to contact.

The contact information for that author appears.

3 Click the messaging icon to send an instant message to the co-author you selected.

4 Click the email link or the email icon to send an email message.

5 Click the phone icon to call your co-author.

6 Click the video icon to start a video call.

7 Click the Schedule A Meeting link to set up a new meeting and invite your co-author.

8 If you choose to launch instant messaging, you can dock the messaging window in Windows 8 so that you can work on the document and continue your conversation thread.

9 Click to type a new message; press Enter to send it.

10 To close the docked window when you're done, drag the window divider off the right side of the screen.

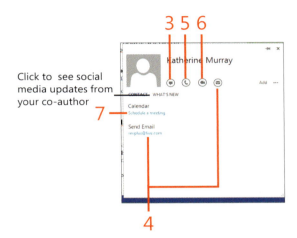

Click to see social media updates from your co-author

Opening and editing PDF files

Portable document format (PDF) files have become increasingly popular in the past few years. Previously, a major limitation of PDF files was that you were unable to open and edit them unless you had a special (and expensive) program with which to do that. Now, however, in Word 2013, you can open and edit PDF files in much the same way you can work with any Word document.

Open a PDF file

1 Click the File tab to display the Backstage view.

2 Click Open.

3 Choose the location of the PDF.

4 Click the folder you want.

The Open dialog box appears, displaying the contents of the folder you selected.

5 Alternatively, click Browse to display the Open dialog box and browse to the folder you need.

6 Select the PDF file that you want to open.

7 Click Open.

The document appears in the Word window in Print Layout view, looking just like a traditional Word document. You can now edit the file as you would any document; all of the editing tools in Word are available as you edit the PDF.

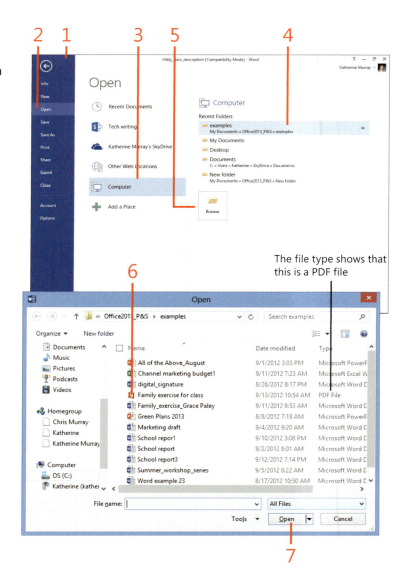

The file type shows that this is a PDF file

Save the PDF file

1 When you're ready to save your changes, click the File tab to display the Backstage view.

2 Click Save As.

3 Choose where you want to save the file.

4 Select the folder in which you want to save it.

5 Alternatively, click Browse to navigate to the folder.

6 Select where you want to save the file.

7 By default, Word saves the edited PDF file as a Word Document. If you want to resave the file in PDF format, click the Save As Type arrow.

8 Click PDF.

9 Click Save to save the file.

Tracking document changes

When multiple people are working on your document, it's helpful to be able to see at a glance the changes that others have made. When you turn on Track Changes, Word displays all additional changes made after that point so that you can scan them easily. You can also use Lock Tracking so that tracking stays on. This ensures that no one is making changes in your document that you're not seeing.

Turn on track changes

1 Open the Word document that you want to review.

2 Click the Review tab.

3 Click the Track Changes arrow.

   A list of options appears.

4 Click Track Changes.

Lock tracking

1 Click the Review tab.

2 Click the Track Changes arrow.

   A list of choices appears.

3 Choose Lock Tracking.

   The Lock Tracking dialog box opens.

4 Type a password in the Enter Password box.

5 Retype the password.

6 Click OK.

   The Track Changes option in the list that appears when users click Track Changes is now disabled so that the feature cannot be turned off.

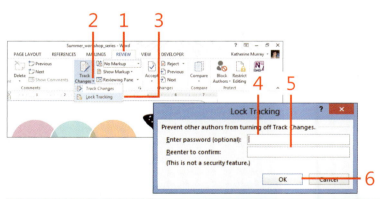

> **TIP** When you select Track Changes again, you'll see that Lock Changes appears with a check mark to the left of the option name. When you click Lock Changes, you are prompted to enter the password assigned to the tracking setting in the current document.

Show and hide the Reviewing pane

If you prefer to work with changes and comments in the Reviewing pane, you can display and hide it easily. On the Review tab, in the Tracking group, simply click Reviewing Pane to display the revisions in a panel alongside your document window.

By default the Revisions pane appears as a vertical column, but you can also display it horizontally, along the bottom of your document, if you prefer. To do so, click the Reviewing Pane arrow and choose Reviewing Pane Horizontal.

Turning on Simple Markup

In Word 2013, the entire process of reviewing and evaluating the changes made in a shared document with Track Changes has been simplified. Thanks to a new feature called Simple Markup, you are alerted to changes with a small mark in the page margin. When you click the mark, the changes become visible and you can easily see who made the changes in your document and what changes were made.

Turn on and use Simple Markup

1 With Track Changes turned on, make the desired changes.

2 Click the Review tab.

3 In the Tracking Group, click the Display For Review arrow.

A list of tracking displays appears.

4 Click Simple Markup.

The page simplifies; changes are noted by a vertical bar along the left margin, and comments collapse into small balloons.

5 To display all changes, click one of the vertical bars. You can return to Simple Markup by clicking the vertical bar a second time.

6 Display the comment you want to see by clicking the comment.

The comment opens in a window on the document page.

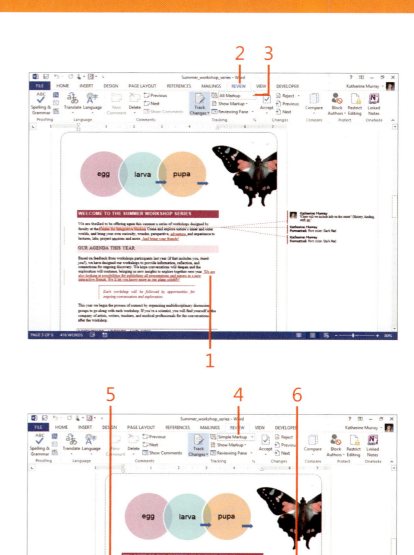

Choose the markup you want to see

Depending on how many people have reviewed your document and the types of changes they've made, the page you see might be full of comment balloons and multiple colors of edited text. Using the Simple Markup feature in Word 2013, you can choose what types of changes you want to see and what changes you want to remain hidden.

1 Click the Review tab.

2 Click the Show Markup arrow.

A list of different markup elements appears.

3 Clear the check mark that appears to the left of any item that you want to hide from the display.

4 To change the way balloons are used to show changes in the document, click Balloons.

5 To display changes made by specific reviewers, click Specific People and choose the individuals whose changes you want to review from the list that is displayed.

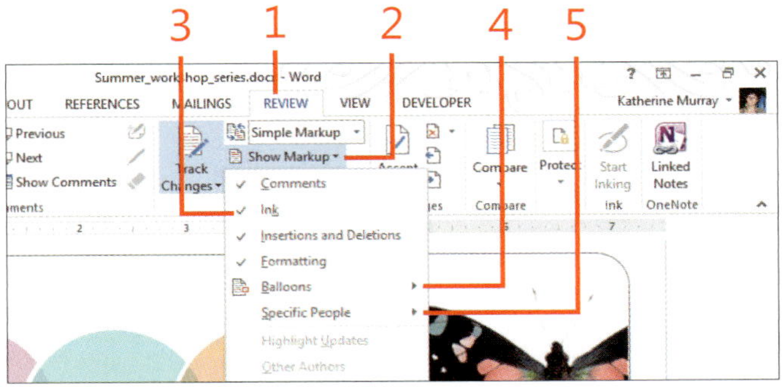

> **TIP** If you're working with a document that has undergone a lot of changes, you might want to display the original document to see how much has changed. To view the original document—without losing any of your changes—on the Review tab, in the Tracking group, click the Display For Review arrow and choose Original. All markup is hidden and you are able to read through the content as it was originally.

Adding and responding to comments

Another collaboration perk in Word 2013 involves the way comments are handled. In previous versions of Word, a new comment balloon appeared each time someone added a comment to the document. That was fine when you had just a few comments, but if you have a entire team weighing in on a draft of an important report, you might spend all afternoon trying to sort through the hundreds of comment balloons in a mere 20-page document.

Word 2013 adds a simple but elegant fix to the comment-balloon problem. Now, comments are threaded like conversations so that you can read through and respond to a comment in a particular place in the document. Gone are the myriad responses all related to one original comment; instead they are threaded into one comment balloon and you can easily read through the discussion and make the document changes you want to make. Ah, nice! It's the simple things that make all the difference.

Add a comment

1 In your document, highlight the text about which you want to comment.

2 Click the Review tab.

3 Click New Comment.

4 A comment balloon opens on the right side of the window.

5 Type your comment in the space provided.

6 Close the comment by clicking anywhere outside the comment balloon.

> **TIP** To add comments more quickly, you can highlight the text, right-click it, and then in the options menu that opens, choose New Comment.

> **TIP** You can make the size of the comment balloon bigger if you like by positioning the pointer on one edge of the balloon. When the pointer shape changes to a double-arrow, drag the border in the direction you want to resize the comment balloon.

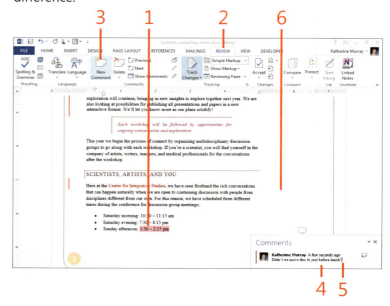

Respond to a comment

1 Display the comment by clicking the comment balloon that appears beside the text.

2 Click the Reply button to add a new place in the comment for your response.

3 Type your reply.

Word 2013 adds your picture and name to the left of the comment.

Delete a comment

1 Display the comment you want to delete by clicking the comment balloon.

2 Click the Review tab.

3 Click the Delete arrow.

4 Choose Delete to remove the last comment added in the thread.

5 Click Delete All Comments In Document if you want to remove all comments added.

> ✓ **TIP** You can easily move from one comment to the next in your document by clicking the Previous and Next tools in the Comments group. You can also open the Comments panel along the right side of your document if you want to read through all comments at once (or prefer this display to viewing comments in balloons).

> ✓ **TIP** If you want to delete a comment response you've added in a comment box, you can simply highlight the text you want to delete and then press the Delete key.

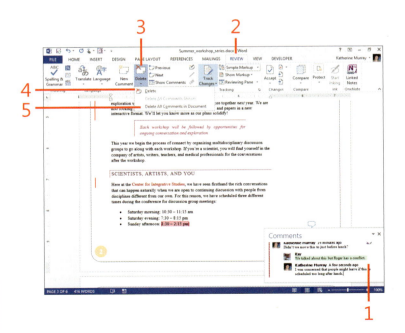

Accepting or rejecting changes

The whole idea of tracking changes is that you can easily see what changes others have made in your document so that you can choose whether you want to accept or reject the changes when you prepare the final version of the file. On the review tab, in the Changes group, you'll find the tools you need to display changes and decide whether you want to accept or reject the edits made.

Navigate to changes

1 Open a document that has changes made with Track Changes and then click the Review tab.

2 Click Next to find the next change in the document.

3 Click Previous to move to the preceding change.

Accept changes

1 Go to the change that you want to accept and click Accept.

2 Alternatively, click the Accept arrow to view more options.

3 You can move through changes one by one, accepting each as you go, by choosing Accept And Move To Next.

4 Click to accept all changes.

5 Click to accept all changes and turn tracking off.

Reject changes

1 Display the change that you want to resolve.

2 Click Reject.

A list of options appears.

3 To cancel the change at the cursor position and display the next change, click Reject And Move To Next.

4 To remove the edits at the cursor position, click Reject This Change.

5 To cancel all edits in the document, click Reject All Changes.

6 To remove all changes and turn tracking off, click Reject All Changes And Stop Tracking.

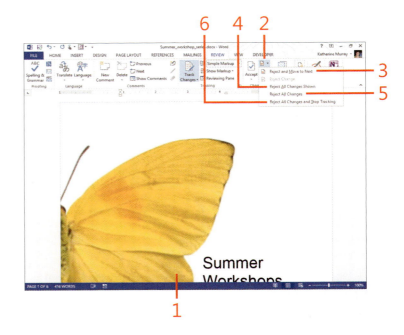

✓ **TIP** If you reject a change and then immediately realize that shouldn't have, you can use the trusty Ctrl+Z key combination to undo your last action.

Presenting your document online

In Word 2013, you can now present your document live online to colleagues, even if they don't have Office 2013 installed. The Present Online feature gives you the choice of using Microsoft Lync 2013 or the free Office Presentation Service to connect to others. This way, you can walk them through a review of your document. You can also share meeting notes you've prepared in Microsoft OneNote 2013, and participants will be able to download a copy of your document, if they choose.

Get ready to present

1 Open the document that you want to use in your presentation and click the File tab to display Backstage view.

2 Click Share.

3 Click Present Online.

4 Choose whether you want to use Lync or Office Presentation Service to present your document online.

5 Click Present Online. If prompted, enter your Microsoft Account user name and password and click Sign In.

The Present Online dialog box opens.

6 In the Present Online dialog box, click Copy Link.

7 Alternately, choose Send In Email. You can send the link by email message or instant message to those whom you want to view the presentation.

8 When you're ready, click Start Presentation.

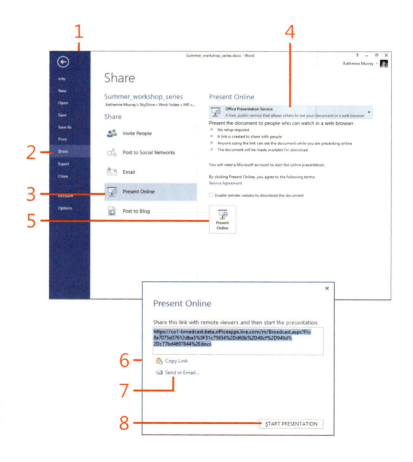

TIP Participants will be able to download a copy of the document you're presenting by clicking the File tab in their browser window and choosing Download in the Save As tab.

Present your document

1 To send additional invitations at the start of the presentation, on the File tab, click Send Invitations. Send the link to those whom you want to participate in the meeting.

2 Click Edit if you'd like to change something in the document while you're presenting.

This pauses the presentation so that you can make the change without others seeing what you're doing.

3 When you're finished making changes, click Resume Online Presentation.

4 Share notes with participants by choosing Share Meeting Notes.

5 Find content in your document by clicking Find.

The Navigation pane opens on the left side of the presentation window so that you can enter the phrase you want to find. The Navigation pane isn't visible to those watching the presentation.

6 Scroll through the document, sharing the information you want to share.

7 When you're finished, click End Online Presentation.

TIP It's not necessary for the other people who are viewing your presentation to have Office 2013 installed on their computers to view your Word 2013 document; because you send a link and the presentation is hosted either by Lync or by using the Office Presentation Service, they will be able to view the presentation in their browsers. Additionally, a Comment tab appears in the upper left of their browser windows. When participants click Comments, a Comments pane opens on the right side of the window so that they can read through comments added to the document.

Sharing and taking notes while you present

This is one of the circumstance in which the interconnected-ness of the Office 2013 apps really shines. While you present your Word document to others online, you can share the OneNote notebook that goes along with the document (or you can create one on the fly if you haven't created one previously). This makes it possible for you to capture good ideas from the feedback you receive or add notes for follow-up later.

Others will be able to see and add to the notes, as well. To use this feature, click Share Meeting Notes while you're presenting your document online. In the options menu that opens, choose Share Notes With Meeting, and then in the Choose Notes To Share With Meeting dialog box, display the page or section where you want to add notes. Click OK. Now, choose Share Meeting Notes again, but this time select Open Shared Meeting Notes. The Shared Meeting Notes tab appears at the top of the screen for those who are viewing your presented document so that they can see and add to the notes in your shared notebook.

Setting up a blog

Whether you're an experienced blogger or just getting started, you don't need to use a tool like WordPress or Blogger to post your blog updates. You can set up your blogging account so that you can use Word to post directly to the blog service of your choice.

Set up your blog

1 Click File to display the Backstage view and then select New.

2 Click Blog Post. When the Blog Post dialog box appears, click Create.

3 The first time you select this option, the Register A Blog Account dialog box opens. Click Register Now.

4 In the New Blog Account dialog box, click the Blog arrow and choose your blog service from the list.

5 If you don't see your blog service in the list, click My Provider Isn't Listed.

6 If you haven't yet signed up for a blog, click I Don't Have a Blog Yet.

7 Click Next.

8 If prompted, enter the blog post URL for the blog service you selected.

9 Click in the User Name field and type your user name.

10 Type your password and select the Remember Password check box to avoid having to enter the password every time.

11 Click Picture Options.

12 Choose the location at which to store your pictures.

13 Click OK.

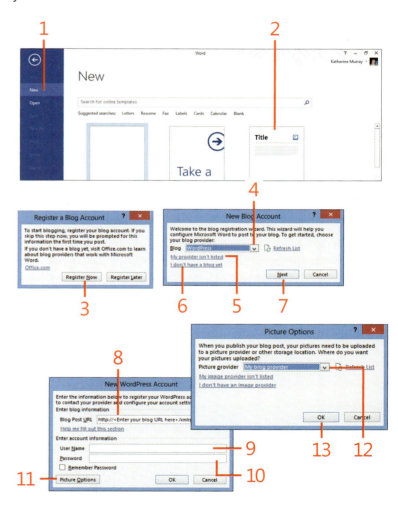

Publishing content to your blog

Now that your blog is set up to work with Word, you can write blog posts and publish them directly to your blog without ever leaving Word.

Post to a blog

1 Click File to display the Backstage view and then select New.

2 Click Blog Post.

A blank blog post document opens on your screen.

3 Click and type the title for your blog post.

4 Add the content for the post.

5 Click Publish.

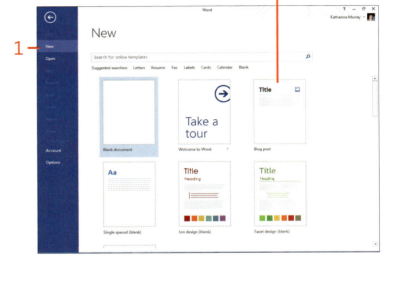

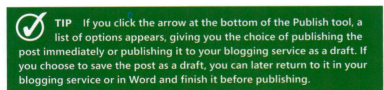

TIP If you click the arrow at the bottom of the Publish tool, a list of options appears, giving you the choice of publishing the post immediately or publishing it to your blogging service as a draft. If you choose to save the post as a draft, you can later return to it in your blogging service or in Word and finish it before publishing.

Add images to your blog post

1 With your blog post open on the screen, click to position the cursor at the point where you want to add the image.

2 Click the Insert tab.

3 To choose a picture from your computer or connected cloud accounts, choose Pictures.

The Open dialog box appears, in which you can navigate to the folder where the picture you want to use is stored.

4 To search for a picture from an online source, click Online Pictures.

The Insert Picture dialog box opens.

5 Click to enter a word describing the picture you'd like to find on Office.com.

6 Alternatively, use Bing to find an image to go along with your blog post.

7 Click a picture thumbnail to see photos you've stored on a photo-sharing site that is connected to Office 2013.

8 Click Browse to retrieve a picture from cloud storage.

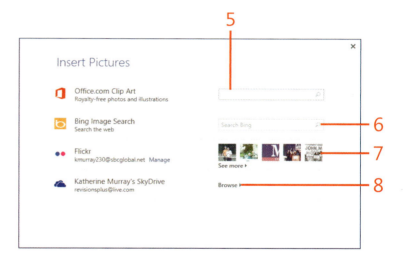

> ⚠️ **CAUTION** Before you can upload images to your blog, in Picture Options, you need to have selected the location to which your pictures will be uploaded when you post. For popular blog services such as Blogger and WordPress, you can choose to post the images to your blog account space. You can also choose None, which prevents you from posting pictures, or My Own Server, which enables you to enter the URL to which you can upload the pictures you want to use.

Comparing and combining documents

When others are working on your document, you aren't always sure what kinds of changes are being made. Even if you have turned Track Changes on, you might want to see at a glance what some of the big changes are between two versions of the same file. Word offers the Compare tool to easily identify the changes when you evaluate two documents. In addition, the Combine tool brings together the changes in two or more documents to create a merged draft that you can use to finalize your content.

Compare two document versions

1 Open the first document that you want to use.

2 Click the Review tab.

3 Click Compare.

  A list of choices appears.

4 Choose Compare.

  The Compare Documents dialog box opens.

5 Click the Original Document arrow to display a list of recent files.

6 Alternatively, click the Folder icon to browse for the file you want to use.

7 Click the Revised Document arrow and choose the file with which you want to compare the original.

  Word adds your user name in the Label Changes With box.

8 Click OK.

  A new document opens, using Simple Markup to point out the places in the document where changes have been made.

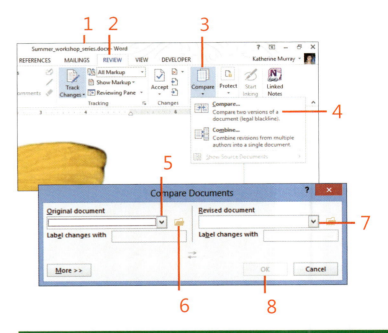

> ✓ **TIP** You can click More to have Word compare additional elements such as comments, formatting, tablets, and headers and footers.

> ✓ **TIP** By default, Word shows the changes found when comparing documents in a new file. If you prefer, you can change the setting so that Word displays the changes in either the original or the revised document. In the Compare Documents dialog box, click More and then click your choice in the Show Changes In settings in the lower-right corner.

Combine documents

1 Click the Review tab.

2 In the Compare group, click the Compare tool.

The list of options appears.

3 Click Combine.

The Combine Document dialog box opens.

4 Click the Original Document arrow and choose the first document you want to combine.

5 Alternatively, you can click the Folder icon to navigate to the file you want to use.

6 Click the Revised Document arrow and choose the second file you want to combine.

7 Click OK.

The combined file is displayed in a new document window, with Simple Markup turned on. You can review the changes in the document by clicking the bar indicator along the margin of the page.

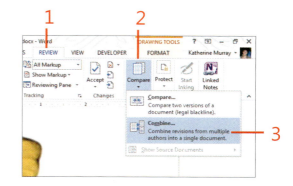

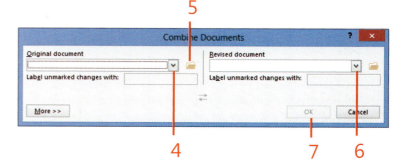

Restricting document editing

You can limit the types of changes other users are allowed to make in your document by limiting the formatting choices or determining the type of editing you allow in a document you share. On the the Review tab, in the Protect group, use the Restrict Editing tool to choose the restrictions that you want to add to your documents.

Restrict editing

1 Open the document for which you want to restrict editing.

2 Click the Review tab.

3 Click the Protect arrow.

4 Choose Restrict Editing.

The Restrict Editing task pane appears along the right side of your document window.

5 To limit the formatting others can do in your document, select the Formatting Restrictions check box.

6 To control the type of edits other users can make, select the Editing Restrictions check box.

7 Choose the type of editing you want to allow from the list.

8 Click Yes, Start Enforcing Protection.

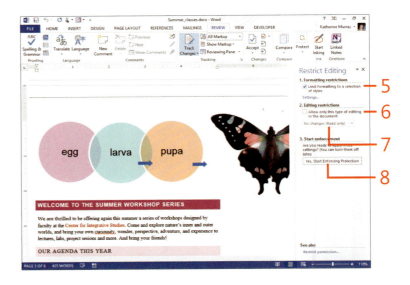

Choose the styles allowed in restricted formatting

1 In the Restrict Editing task pane, select the Formatting Restrictions check box.

2 Click Settings.

The Formatting Restrictions dialog box opens.

3 To remove styles you don't want to be allowed, clear the check box.

4 Choose Formatting options for AutoFormat, Theme, and Quick Style Set selections.

5 Click OK to save your changes.

6 In the Restrict Editing task pane, click Yes, Start Enforcing Protection.

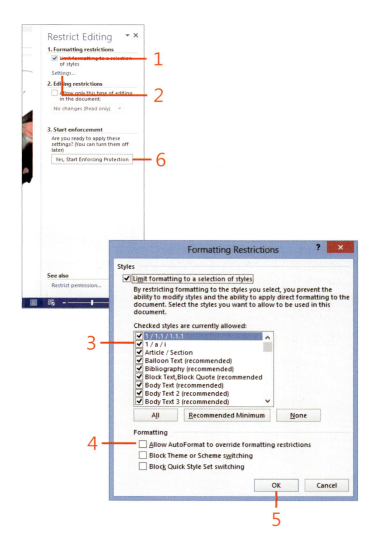

Creating long documents in Word 2013

8

If your work involves creating documents that are longer than a few pages, Microsoft Word 2013 offers a number of features that can make your life easier. Oh, you will still do all the same basic tasks—entering, editing, and formatting text; adding and enhancing pictures; applying themes and styles to give the document a professional look—but larger documents mean that your readers might need some help finding their way around. You might want to add page numbers, headers and footers, and maybe even a table of contents. You might want to shake up the layout a bit by using columns, sidebars, or pull quotes to make special passages of text stand out. This section shows you how to add all those elements to your long document.

In addition to creating volumes of text to share with others, you might also have some projects in mind that you'd like to do in Word. For example, Word can help you put together a mailing to all the members of your book club or create a custom form letter so that the non-profit where you volunteer can send fundraising letters to everyone on its email list.

Inserting page numbers

There might be nothing more important in a long document than a page number. If you've ever accidentally dropped a long document that you had printed and had to sort the pages out by hand, you probably agree wholeheartedly with that assessment. Word 2013 gives you a variety of ways to add page numbers. You can choose from among a wide collection of predesigned page number styles or create your own to fit the needs of your particular document.

Add page numbers

1 Open the document with which you want to work.

2 Click the Insert tab.

3 Click Page Number.

A list of options appears.

4 If you want to display the page number in the header, click Top Of Page.

A gallery of styles opens. Alternatively, you can choose Bottom of Page, Page Margins, or Current Position.

5 Click the style that you want.

The page number is inserted on your page.

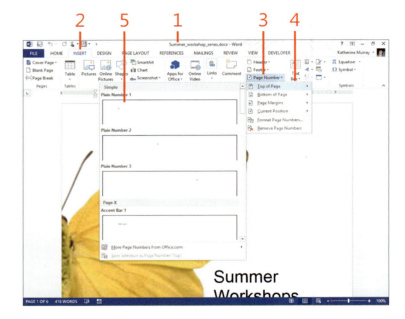

TIP If you want to include other information in the header or footer along with the page number, you can also add a page number after you insert the header or footer on your page. See the section "Adding Headers and Footers" later in this section to find out how to add a predesigned header or footer to your page.

Format page numbers

1 Select the page number you added.

The formatting minibar appears above your selection.

2 Choose the Font that you want to apply to the page number.

3 Select the size at which you want the page number to be displayed.

4 Change the color of the page number if you like.

5 Click Styles to display a palette of style choices that you can apply to the page number.

Remove page numbers

1 Click in the header or footer area where the page number is displayed.

2 On the Header & Footer Tools Design tab, click Page Number.

3 Choose Remove Page Numbers.

Word deletes the page numbers without any further action required by you.

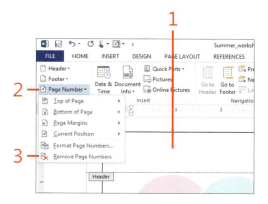

TIP The formatting changes you make to the selected page number are applied to all page numbers in the current section.

Adding headers and footers

Maybe instead of just adding a single page number to the top and bottom of your page, you want to include a bit more information. Headers and footers in a long document help readers orient themselves as they read. Headers appear at the top of the page and footers appear at the bottom of the page. Word reserves space at the top and bottom of your document so that you can easily add headers and footers.

Word also provides a gallery of header and footer styles so that you can choose predesigned, professional-looking headers and footers for your document. Or, if you prefer, you can create your own from scratch. What's more, you can add page numbers, document information, and even images such as logos. You can also vary the way the headers and footers appear so that they look different on odd and even pages or so that your first page looks different from the rest of your document. Because headers and footers are similar (in every way except, obviously, where they appear on your page), the following tasks apply to both headers and footers.

Choose a header or footer from the gallery

1 Open the document in which you want to add the header or footer.

2 Click the Insert tab.

3 Click Header or Footer.

   A gallery of header or footer styles opens.

4 Scroll through the gallery to find the style you like.

5 Click the header or footer that you want to add to the document. Word inserts the item you selected and displays the Header & Footer Tools Design tab.

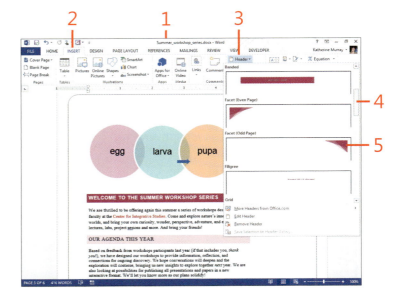

Create a header or footer from scratch

1 Double-click in the area at the top or bottom of the page. Word displays the Header & Footer Tools Design tab.

2 Type the information you want to include in the header or footer.

3 Click Page Number to add a page number.

4 Click Date & Time to insert the date and time.

5 Click Document Info to add document information, such as the author name, file name, file path, or document title.

6 Click Pictures to insert a picture in the header or footer.

7 Click Quick Parts to add AutoText, a document property, a data field, or another building block to the header or footer.

8 Click Close Header and Footer to close the header and footer area.

Working with headers and footers

Once you add headers and footers to your document, there' a little bit of mastery involved in moving among them and getting them to do what you want them to do. This is especially true if you plan to change the way headers or footers appear depending on whether they're on a right or left page; you'll need to change a few header and footer options to pull that off.

Move among headers and footers in your document

1 Double-click the header or footer area to display the Header & Footer Tools Design tab.

2 In the Navigation area, click Next.

   The header or footer of the next page is displayed.

3 Click Previous.

4 If the cursor is positioned in the header of your document, move to the footer on the same page by clicking Go To Footer.

5 If the cursor is in the footer, click Go To Header.

> ✓ **TIP** Even if you begin a new section and unlink the header in one section from the headers or footers that follow it, you will still be able to use Next and Previous to display headers or footers on other pages in your document.

Change the header and footer display

1 Click in the header or footer that you want to change to display the Header & Footer Tools Design tab.

2 If you want to create a different first page display (for example, headers and footers typically don't appear on the first page of a document), select the Different First Page check box.

3 To vary the layout and change the alignment or content of headers and footers so that they appear differently on even and odd pages, select the Different Odd & Even Pages check box.

4 If you want to hide the document text while you're working with headers and footers, clear the Show Document Text check box.

5 To change the amount of space between the top of the page and the header, type a new value or click the arrows to increase or decrease the amount shown.

6 To adjust the space between the bottom of the page and the footer, change the Footer Position From Bottom value.

7 Insert a tab to help align elements in the header or footer.

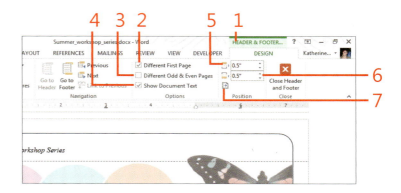

> **→ TRY THIS!** If you've created more than one section in your document, the headers and footers are linked between the sections by default. If you want to change the header or footer content or format of a subsequent section, you need to unlink the header or footer. To do this, click in the header or footer of the section you want to change to display the Header & Footer Tools Design tab. Click the highlighted Link To Previous tool in the Navigation group to unlink this header or footer from the ones that preceded it. Now, you can format or modify the header or footer as you'd like, and it will remain different from those displayed on preceding pages.

Creating sections

Sometimes in long documents you might want to vary the page layout or change the headers to reflect new headings in major sections of the text. When you want to change the layout or create new headers or footers for another part of your document, you can insert a section break to instruct Word to stop carrying the formatting forward at that point. You might add section breaks before the beginning of each new chapter in a book manuscript, for example, or add breaks in a report in which you need to change from portrait orientation to landscape orientation.

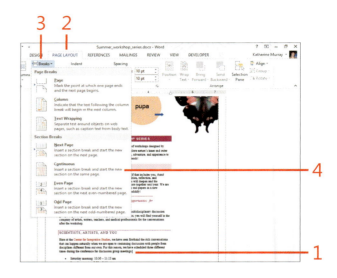

Insert a section break

1 Click at the point in the document where you want to begin a new section.

2 Click the Page Layout tab.

3 Choose the Breaks arrow.

A list appears, offering two types of breaks: page breaks and section breaks.

4 Click the type of section break you want to insert at the cursor position.

Types of section breaks in Word

Symbol	Break Type	Description
	Next Page	Adds a section break and begins the next section on a new page
	Continuous	Inserts a section break at the cursor position and continues with new text after the break
	Even Page	Adds a section break and begins the text for the next section on the next even-numbered page
	Odd Page	Inserts a section break and begins text on the next odd-numbered page

View section breaks

1 After you have added section breaks to the document, click somewhere on the page where you want to view a break.

2 Click the Home tab.

3 In the Paragraph group, click the Show/Hide tool.

The section break appears in your document.

Remove a section break

1 On the Home tab, click Show/Hide to display the section breaks in your document.

2 Click at the right end of the section break to select it.

3 Press the Backspace key twice to delete the section break.

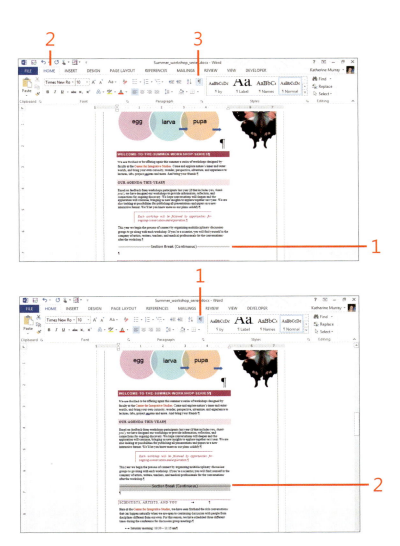

 TIP You can also click at the beginning of the section break and press Shift+Right Arrow key to highlight the break.

⊕ TRY THIS! You can apply the formatting of a section, which might include column settings and headers and footers, to a new section. In the Paragraph group, click Show/Hide to display all the formatting and character marks in your document. Next, select the section break character at the end of the section that contains the formatting you want to use. Copy the section break to the end of the text you want to format with the same settings and paste it in place. Section breaks store the section formatting for the text preceding the break. If all section breaks in a document are removed, the last paragraph mark in the document will contain the formatting settings for the text preceding it.

Choosing columns

Word makes it easy for you to vary the layout of your pages by flowing your text in multiple columns on the page. You can create a variety of column layouts, including multiple columns of equal widths, columns of unequal widths, and differing column styles—perhaps two columns on the top and three on the bottom—even on the same page.

You can use the Columns tool in Word to set the columns for the current section. To do so, on the Page Layout tab, in the Page Setup group, choose to apply the column format to the entire document or from the current point forward in the document.

Create columns

1 Open the document in which you want to create columns.

2 Click the Page Layout tab.

3 Click Columns.

A list of column options appears.

4 Click the number of columns that you want to create.

5 Alternatively, choose whether you want to create a two-column layout with the narrower column on the right or the left.

The columns are added to your document and the text reflows automatically.

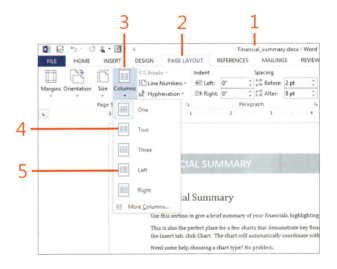

> **TIP** To display the rulers in your document, click the View tab, and then in the Show group, choose Ruler. In the ruler you'll be able to see the column divisions as well as the text indents and tabs set for the individual columns.

> **TIP** If you need to add more than three columns, on the Page Layout tab, choose Columns and click More Columns. In the Columns dialog box that opens, increase the Number Of Columns setting to reflect the amount that you want to include on your page.

Change column width and spacing

1 Click the Page Layout tab.

2 Choose Columns.

3 At the bottom of the options list, click More Columns.

The Columns dialog box opens.

4 If you want to set different widths for your columns, clear the Equal Column Width check box.

5 Increase the width value to make a column wider; decrease the value to make the column narrower.

6 When columns are equal widths, by default Word separates them with a quarter-inch "gutter." When the columns are not set to equal widths, you can change the spacing for each column individually. Click to increase or decrease the spacing value, whether columns are equal or different widths.

7 Check the preview to see if this is the way you want your columns to look.

8 Click OK to save your changes.

> ✓ **TIP** If you want to include a line between the columns in your document, in the Columns dialog box, select the Line Between check box. Lines appear between all columns you've created. If you want to remove the lines later, simply clear the Line Between check box.

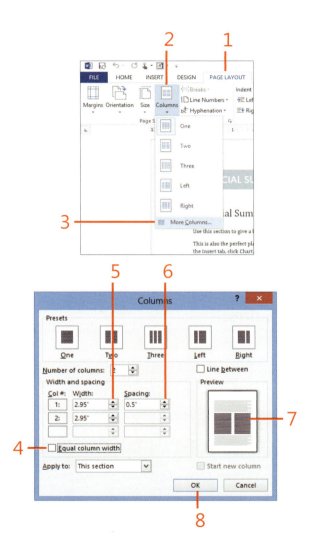

Adding footnotes and endnotes

Footnotes and endnotes give your readers more information about the content in your document. You can use footnotes or endnotes to list the resources you used in your research for a report or to provide extra information about your topic. Word provides the tools to insert footnotes and endnotes and format them according to your preferences. You'll find the tools you need on the References tab, in the Footnotes group.

Insert a footnote

1 Position the cursor at the point in the document where you want to add the footnote and click the References tab.

2 Click Insert Footnote. A superscript number is inserted at the cursor position, and a small superscript indicator appears below a divider line at the bottom of your document.

3 Type the footnote text. The footnote text appears in a smaller font. It will be printed and displayed at the bottom of the page on which the footnote reference number appears.

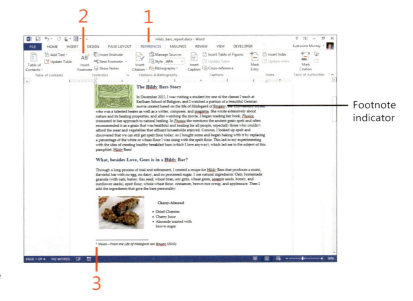

Footnote indicator

Add an endnote

1 Click the References tab.

2 In the Footnotes group, click Insert Endnote. A small indicator is added at the cursor position and the cursor is moved to an endnote entry at the end of your document.

3 Type the endnote text.

> **TIP** You can tell the difference between footnotes and endnotes: footnotes appear at the bottom of the page on which they are inserted; endnotes appear at the end of the document. Footnotes often provide information about specific resources used in main text, whereas endnotes often provide notes about the larger topic or bibliographical resources that readers can consult for more information.

Format footnotes and endnotes

1 Click the References tab.

2 In the lower-right corner of the Footnotes group, click the Footnote & Endnote dialog launcher.

The Footnote And Endnote dialog box opens.

3 Choose whether you want to set the format for Footnotes or Endnotes.

4 If you choose the Footnotes option, select either Bottom Of Page or Below Text from the list.

5 Set the endnote location by clicking Endnotes and choosing either End Of Document or End Of Section.

6 Click the Columns down-arrow and choose whether you want Word to display footnotes according to the section layout or in a specific column pattern.

7 Choose the Number Format down-arrow and select the numbering you want to use for footnotes or endnotes.

8 You can choose a custom symbol to serve as the indicator for footnotes or endnotes.

9 Indicate which number you want Word to use as the starting point for your footnotes or endnotes.

10 Choose whether you want to number continuously or start the numbering with each new section or page.

11 Click to choose whether you want to apply these changes to the whole document or to the current section only.

12 Click Apply to save your settings.

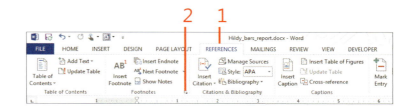

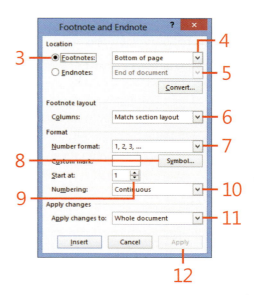

> **TIP** You can to convert footnotes to endnotes, and vice versa, by clicking the Convert button in the Footnote And Endnote dialog box. In the Convert Notes box, choose what you want to convert and click OK.

Working with footnotes and endnotes

Once you've added the footnotes and endnotes to your document, you need a way to review them. You can navigate among your notes or use the Show Notes tool to display them in a dialog box in which you can click the one you want to see next.

Navigate footnotes and endnotes

1 Click the References tab.

2 In the Footnotes group, click Next Footnote.

   A list of navigation options for footnotes and endnotes appears.

3 Click your choice; Word displays the next or previous note, depending on what you selected.

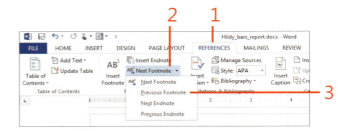

Show your notes

1 After entering your footnotes and endnotes, click the References tab.

2 Click Show Notes.

   The Show Notes dialog box opens.

3 Choose whether you want to view the footnote area or the endnote area.

4 Click OK.

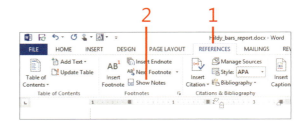

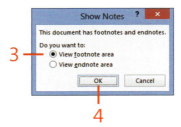

Creating sidebars and pull quotes

Sidebars and pull quotes are common layout methods for making certain passages of text stand out from the flow of your normal text. Typically, sidebars are text sections that are related to the current text but not central enough to be included in the regular text. Pull quotes are usually shorter than sidebars, displaying a memorable quote or significant phrase or sentence from the primary text.

Click the Insert tab and then select the Text Box tool to access a gallery of pull quotes and sidebars provided by Word 2013. You can choose from a variety of predesigned text boxes (you can get more on Office.com) or you can draw your own text box and format it the way you like it.

Add a sidebar or pull quote

1 Open the document to which you want to add the text box element.

2 Click the Insert tab.

3 In the Text group, click Text Box.

A gallery of sidebars and pull quotes opens.

4 Scroll through the list to view all available styles.

5 Click the style you like.

Word adds that sidebar or pull quote to your document.

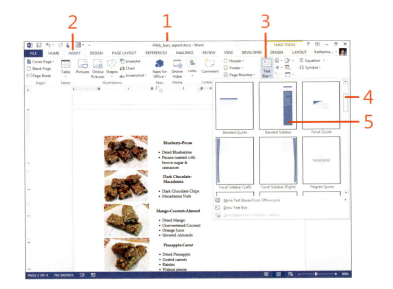

> ✓ **TIP** To draw your own text box and format it the way you like, click the Insert tab and choose Text Box. The gallery opens. At the bottom of the gallery, click Draw Text Box. The cursor changes to a crosshair. Drag on the page to create the text box in the size and shape you want and then type the text you want to include. Format the box by using the tools in the formatting minibar.

Inserting a table of contents

What's the first thing you look at when you are handed a document that's more than 30 pages long? The table of contents, right? The table of contents shows you all the major sections in the document and provides page numbers to guide you directly to the content you're most interested in reading.

You might be surprised how easy it is for you to add a table of contents to your Word document. It all begins on the References tab, with the Table Of Contents tool on the Table Of Contents tab (no surprise there).

Add a table of contents

1 Click to position the cursor at the point in the document where you want to add the table of contents.

2 Click the References tab.

3 In the Table Of Contents group, click the Table Of Contents arrow.

A gallery of table styles opens.

4 Click the table style that you want to add.

Word inserts the table of contents at the cursor position and includes all headings formatted with heading styles in your document, along with the page numbers on which they're found.

Remove the table of contents

1 Click the References tab and choose Table Of Contents.

2 Click Remove Table Of Contents.

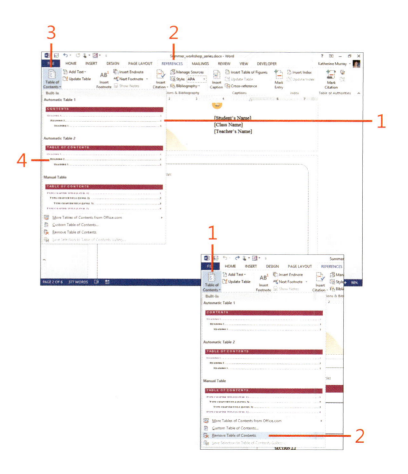

> ✓ **TIP** If you want to bypass using tools in the ribbon, you can delete the table of contents in your document by highlighting it and pressing the Delete key.

Create a custom table of contents

1 Click to position the cursor where you want to add the table of contents.

2 Click the References tab.

3 Click Table Of Contents.

4 Choose Custom Table Of Contents.

The Table Of Contents dialog box opens.

5 Click the Formats arrow to choose a new style for the table.

6 Review the change in the Print Preview and Web Preview boxes.

7 Click to change the tab leader character.

8 Click the Options button and then increase or decrease the number of heading levels displayed in the table of contents.

9 Click OK to save your changes and create the table of contents.

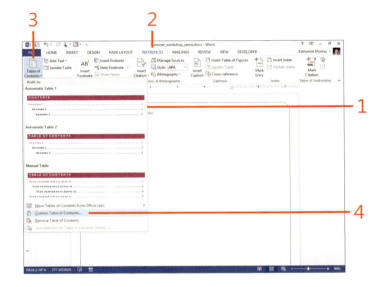

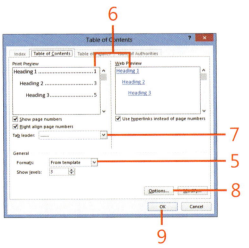

Preparing a mail merge

You might have heard that mail merge in Word isn't for the faint-hearted, but the steps are actually simple if you follow the basic process.

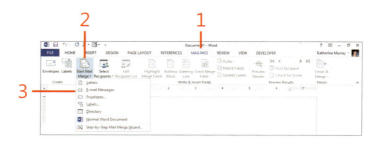

Start a mail merge

1 Click the Mailings tab.

2 Click Start Mail Merge.

A list of mail merge options appears.

3 Click the type of merge project that you want to create.

You can choose to create a merge letter, email message, envelopes, labels, or a directory.

Enter your recipient list

1 On the Mailings tab, click Select Recipients.

2 Click Type A New List.

The New Address List appears.

3 Type the data you want to use in the merge in the fields provided. Press the Tab key to move to the next field.

4 To start a new record, click New Entry.

5 To change the data columns shown in the dialog box, click Customize Columns, and then in the Customize Address List dialog box that opens, choose the columns that you want to include.

6 If you want to remove an entry you don't need, click Delete Entry.

7 When you're finished typing new data, click OK.

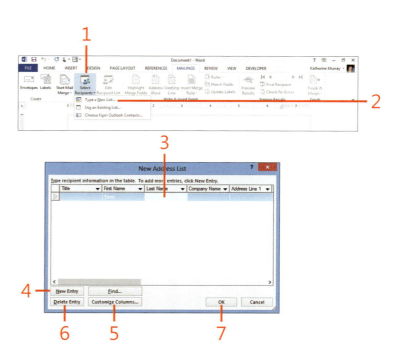

Use an existing recipient list

1 On the Mailings tab, in the Start Mail Merge group, click Select Recipients.

2 Click Use An Existing List.

The Select Data Source dialog box opens.

3 Choose the data list you want to include in the mail merge.

4 Click Open.

Edit the recipient list

1 On the Mailings tab, click Edit Recipients List to open the Mail Merge Recipients dialog box.

2 Clear the check boxes of any entry you want to leave out of the merge.

3 Click to sort the list.

4 Filter the data list based on criteria you enter.

5 Click OK to save any changes.

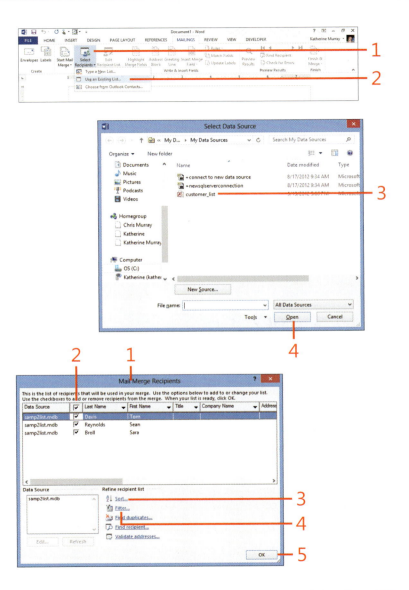

Creating the mail merge document

After you add the data source to your mail merge project, you're ready to create the document itself. This can be as simple as a traditional letter or as complex as a catalog. The process involves entering the content, adding the merge fields, previewing the merge, and then actually merging the data into the type of document you selected.

Create the merge document and insert fields

1 Create the merge document that you want to send.

2 If you want to add the address of a customer, click Address Block.

3 To open a letter or email message, click Greeting Line.

4 Click at the point where you want to add data from your data list and choose Insert Merge Field.

A list of fields appears. These fields are taken from your data list.

5 Click the field that you want to insert at the cursor position.

Preview the merge

1 Click Preview Results.

2 Click Next Record to preview the next entry.

3 Click Previous Record to preview the prior entry.

4 Click to move to the last record.

5 Click to move to the first record.

6 Click to check for errors in the merge document.

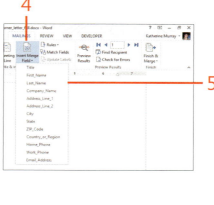

Complete the merge

1 Click Finish & Merge.

   A list of options appears.

2 Click to display each merged letter or message on its own page in a merge document.

   The Merge to New Document dialog box opens, in which you can choose whether to merge all records, the current record, or the records in a range you indicate. Click OK and the merge is completed and displayed in a new document.

3 Click to print the merged documents.

   This opens the Merge To Printer dialog box, in which you can choose whether to print all records, the current record, or a range of records that you specify. Click OK to print the documents.

4 Click to send email messages.

   The Merge To E-mail dialog box opens, in which you can specify the To line, Subject line, and mail format that you want to use. You can also select which records to send. Click OK to complete the merge.

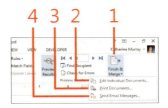

TIP Save the document you created for the merge to use again in the future with other similar communications. You can always tweak the document if necessary, but with the fields already in place, you won't have to start again from scratch.

What are Quick Parts?

Quick Parts are content items in Word that help you add content to your document... well, quickly. They aren't specifically intended to work with Word headers and footers, but you can insert them as part of headers and footers if the information fits what you want to include.

The Quick Parts tool, which is located on the Header & Footer Tools Design tab, in the Insert group, includes several content items. AutoText is text that you use often in documents and want to save so that you can insert it easily as needed. For example, you might save your organization's mission statement to AutoText or add your mission statement as AutoText so that you can add it easily wherever you need it. You can use the Document Property selection to choose from a variety of properties, including author, category, keywords, publish date, subject, and title. With the Field tool, you can insert a data field in the header so that it displays variable information, such as UserName, NumPages, Subject, Template, or FileName.

To add a Quick Part to your header or footer, click to position the cursor where you want the item to appear and then click Quick Parts. Choose the type of Quick Part you want to insert and then select the item from the displayed list. It appears in your document header or footer as you indicated.

Creating and saving worksheets in Excel 2013

9

Microsoft Excel 2013 is the application you'll use if you need to work with numbers and formulas on a regular basis. Whether you track expenses for your department, produce sales projections for a weekly meeting, monitor a basic inventory, or collaborate on elaborate financial reports, you'll find the tools you need for creating, managing, protecting, sharing, and analyzing your data in Excel.

Some of the new features in Excel 2013 are similar to those you'll find in the other Microsoft Office apps. Excel is now built to work basically anywhere, on any device. What's more, the new Excel Start experience makes it easy for those new to Excel to jump right into creating the worksheet they need. This section focuses on some of the basic tasks you're likely to want to accomplish with Excel.

In this section:

- Getting started with Excel
- Starting a new workbook from the Start screen
- Entering and importing worksheet data
- Editing your data
- Adding a new worksheet
- Creating a new worksheet from a template
- Creating and modifying charts
- Adding and formatting chart elements
- Saving and protecting a workbook
- Sharing a workbook
- Tracking workbook changes
- Commenting on a workbook
- Exporting a workbook

Getting started with Excel

Excel 2013 includes a number of new features designed to simplify your work. You can begin with the Excel 2013 Start screen to launch a new workbook from a predesigned template or easily choose the existing or blank file you want to use. You will find a variety of aids designed to put tools within easy reach; recommendations for charts and PivotTables to help you choose the right way to showcase your data; and a number of features that make it simple for you to share your work and collaborate with others.

Your first task involves launching Excel and starting with a blank workbook. The following task shows the process with Windows 8. If you're using Windows 7, the chances are good that you know the drill: click the Start button, select All Programs, click Microsoft Office 2013, and then choose Excel 2013.

Launch Excel in Windows 8

1 Scroll or swipe to display the app tiles that are beyond the right edge of the screen.

2 Click the Excel 2013 tile.

The program opens on your Windows 8 desktop.

Explore the Excel window

The Excel window includes all the tools you need to create worksheets, add and edit data, format cells and ranges, manage the layout of the worksheet, add formulas, work on the file with others, and much more. Along the way, contextual tabs appear when you select an item in the worksheet—such as a range of cells or a picture that you've added—giving you more choices related specifically to that item.

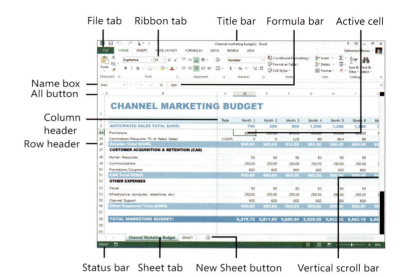

File tab   Ribbon tab   Title bar   Formula bar   Active cell

Name box
All button

Column header
Row header

Status bar   Sheet tab   New Sheet button   Vertical scroll bar

Starting a new workbook from the Start screen

After you launch Excel 2013, whether from the Windows 8 Start screen or the All Programs list in Windows 7, the Excel 2013 Start window opens. This screen is designed so that you can get started quickly, no matter if you're starting a new blank workbook, beginning with a template, or opening a file in which you've already worked.

Create a blank workbook

1 Start the Excel 2013 app.

The Start screen opens.

2 Click Blank Workbook.

TIP A blank workbook is just what it sounds like—a totally blank grid of columns and rows. If you have a unique worksheet in mind or you have something very simple that you want to add up, a blank worksheet might be just what you need. If your needs are a bit more elaborate, you might want to review some of the Excel templates, which provide ready-made worksheets with elements that you can use for your own data.

Start a worksheet from a template

1 Start Excel and display the Excel Start screen.

2 Scroll through the display to view the displayed templates.

3 Alternatively, click a template category to display specific templates in that type.

4 Click in the Search box and enter a word or phrase that describes the templates you'd like to find.

5 Click the Search tool to begin searching.

6 Click the template that you want to use to start the new workbook.

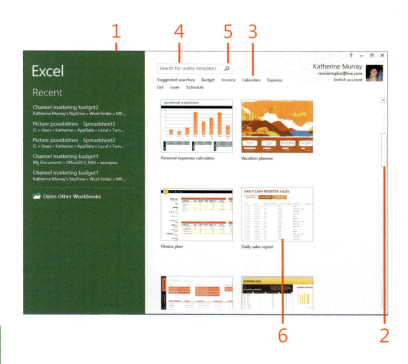

TIP If you choose one of the template categories in the Suggested Searches list, a Filter By pane will appear along the right side of the Start screen. You can use this list to choose the category of the template you'd like to find. You can choose multiple categories if you like (for example, you can click the Sales and Form categories to display forms related to sales). To clear the categories after you've selected them, position the pointer over or tap the category at the top of the list and click the X that appears to the right of the item.

TRY THIS! Start Excel 2013, and then in the Start screen, experiment searching for templates by using different words and phrases. Which styles do you like? Which ones will be helpful to you in the type of work you do?

Entering worksheet data

If you're creating a worksheet from scratch, you might be happy typing all of your data by hand. You can use the new Flash Fill feature in Excel 2013 to speed up the process and help you along the way.

Type new data

1 Click the cell into which you want to enter text.

2 Type the text that you want in the cell.

3 Press the Enter key.

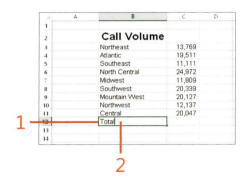

Enter data by using Flash Fill

1 In the cell to the right of the first item in the data list, type the string you want to extract from the first value in the list.

2 In the cell to the right of the second item in the data list, type the string you want to extract from the second value in the list.

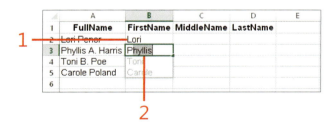

> **TIP** If the original Flash Fill suggestions miss some aspect of the data, such as a middle name, edit the first example of that sequence to correct the Flash Fill values.

> **TIP** In Excel 2013, the Formula bar doesn't expand to display all of the information in a cell. To scroll through its contents one line at a time, use the scroll buttons at the right edge of the Formula bar. To display the entire contents, click the Expand Formula Bar control to the right of the Formula bar. The Expand Formula Bar control changes to the Collapse Formula Bar control; clicking it returns the Formula Bar to its original one-line height.

Flash Fill is a little bit of Excel magic

Flash Fill is a new feature in Excel 2013, and although it can be used for simple tasks like entering data in a series or quickly filling up a data range, you can also use it to modify the format of data you've already added to your worksheet.

For example, suppose you've imported data that shows phone numbers as one long number (3175551212 instead of 317-555-1212). You can insert a new column beside the Telephone column on your worksheet and, in the first blank cell, type the phone number the way you want it to appear (317-555-1212).

Now press Enter to move to the next cell in the column. Type the first three numbers, followed by the dash, and suddenly Excel knows what you want to do. Flash Fill fills the whole row with telephone numbers formatted the way you want them. Simple, fast, and correct!

Importing worksheet data

One of the great things about Excel 2013 is that it plays nice with many other programs. You can easily import data you've saved in another program and use it in your Excel worksheet, whether the data is from a Microsoft Access database, a website, a text file, or other data sources.

Import worksheet data

1 Click the Data tab.

2 Click Get External Data.

A list of appears from which you can choose the type of data you want to import. Select From Access if you are importing data from an Access data table; choose From Web if you have a web query that you want to use in Excel; select From Text if you have text data that you want to organize in Excel; or choose From Other Sources if your data is from sources, including an SQL Server, XML data, a Microsoft Query, and more.

3 For this example, click From Text.

4 Navigate to the folder that contains the text file that you want to import.

5 Double-click the text file to select it.

The Text Import Wizard opens.

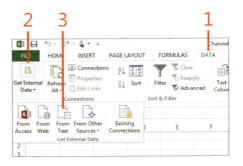

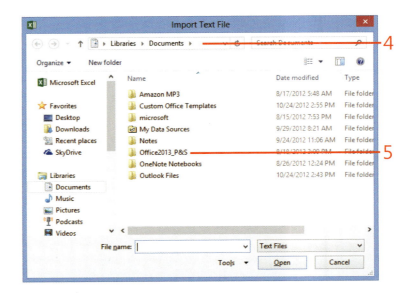

6 In the Original Data Type section, click the Delimited option.

7 Click Next.

8 In the Delimiters section, select the file's delimiter character.

9 Verify that the data appears correctly in the Data Preview pane.

10 Click Finish.

11 Click OK.

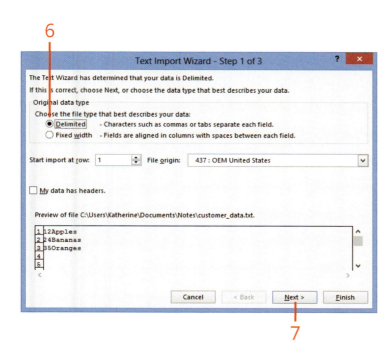

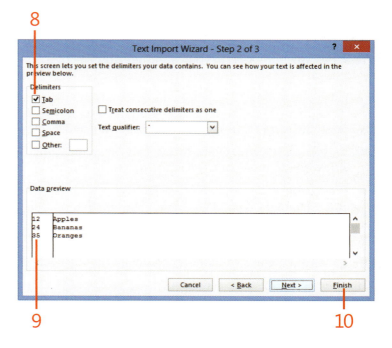

Editing your data

Once you have all of your values in the worksheet, you need to know how to page through the data and move and edit cell contents as needed. You can use the keys on your keyboard to move quickly through the worksheet or, if you're using a tablet device, you can swipe the screen to move to another area of the worksheet.

Navigate the worksheet by using the keyboard

To move between the cells in your worksheet, do any of the following steps:

- Press Ctrl+Home to move to cell A1.

- Press Ctrl+End to move to the last used worksheet cell.

- Press the Up Arrow, Down Arrow, Left Arrow, or Right Arrow key to move one cell in the named direction.

- Press PageUp to scroll up one screen.

- Press PageDown to scroll down one screen.

- Press Ctrl+PageUp to move to the previous worksheet.

- Press Ctrl+PageDown to move to the next worksheet.

- Pinch the screen to reduce the size of the worksheet so that you can navigate it easily

- Pinch outward to magnify an area of your worksheet

- Tap the worksheet tabs at the bottom of the worksheet to move among the various worksheets in the workbook

Edit your data

To edit your data, do either of the following:

- Click the cell and edit its contents on the Formula bar.

- Click the cell and edit its contents in the body of the cell.

Navigate the worksheet by touch

To roam around your worksheet on your touch device, do any of the following:

- Swipe up or down to move through rows on the worksheet

- Swipe left and right to move across columns on the worksheet

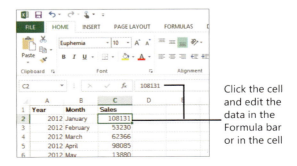

Click the cell and edit the data in the Formula bar or in the cell

Move data by using the mouse

1 Drag to select the cells that you want to move.

2 Hover the mouse pointer over the edge of the selected cell range.

3 When the mouse pointer changes to a four-way arrow, drag the range to its new location.

Move data by touch

1 Tap the cell in one corner of the range that you want to move.

Two handles appear on the cell.

2 Tap and drag one handle in the direction of the cells that you want to move and then release your touch..

3 Tap the selected area to display a minibar.

4 Tap Cut to copy the selection to the clipboard.

5 Tap the location where you want to paste the selected cells.

6 Tap Paste to insert the moved cells.

Copy and paste data

1 Drag to select the cells that you want to copy.

2 Click the Home tab.

3 Click the Copy button.

4 Click the cell at the upper-left corner of the target range.

5 Click Paste.

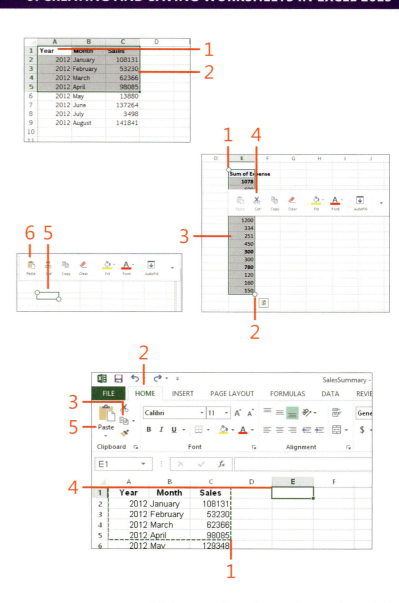

Adding a new worksheet to the workbook

Although the terminology at first can seem a little confusing, Excel 2013 uses the term *workbook* to refer to the Excel file, which might in fact comprise multiple *worksheets*. Each worksheet appears in its own tab. When you first open a new blank workbook in Excel, by default the program displays three blank worksheet tabs. You can add to those worksheets as needed by creating a new blank worksheet, and you can reorder the worksheets to appear just the way you want them to.

Add a blank worksheet

1 Open the workbook you want to use in Excel 2013.

2 Click the New Sheet button to the right of the rightmost worksheet tab.

✓ **TIP** You can rename a worksheet by right-clicking or double-tapping the tab at the bottom of the worksheet and choosing Rename. The tab name is highlighted so that you can type the new name.

Creating a new worksheet from a template

Excel give you access to hundreds of templates in different styles ranging, from budgets to invoices, to calendars and more. You can scroll through the available templates in the Start screen or you can display the Backstage view and look on the New tab. You can also search for templates by clicking in the Search Online Templates box and typing a word or phrase to locate a template that fits your needs.

Create a new worksheet from a template

1 Right-click and hold a sheet tab.

   A list menu appears.

2 Click Insert.

   The Insert dialog box opens.

3 Click Spreadsheet Solutions.

4 Click the template that you want to use.

5 Click OK.

> **TRY THIS!** Right-click or double-tap the worksheet tab and choose Insert to add a worksheet based on a template. Click the Spreadsheet Solutions tab and select a template that looks good to you. Click OK to open a new worksheet based on that template.

Creating charts

Charts have a big job in Excel because they are used to showcase the data you're presenting in an graphical, easy-to-understand manner. You can choose from a number of different chart types and then fine-tune the styles within those chart types to get just the effect you need for your data. One of the new features in Excel 2013 is the Recommended Charts tool, which suggests the types of charts that best fit the data you've highlighted on the worksheet.

Add a new chart

1 Click a cell in the data that you want to summarize.

2 Click the Insert tab.

3 Click the type of chart you want to create in the Charts group.

4 Click the desired chart subtype.

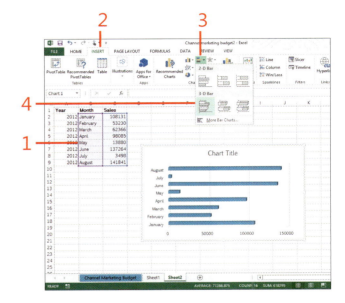

TRY THIS! Using a worksheet on which you've entered some data, select cells and click the Quick Analysis button below and to the right of your selection. Click Charts and choose a chart from the Recommended Charts that are displayed.

Use recommended charts

1 Select the data that you want to summarize in your chart.

2 Click the Quick Analysis action button.

3 Click Charts.

4 Click the type of chart that you want to create.

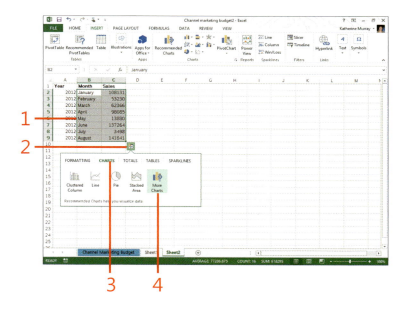

Modifying charts

The chart Excel 2013 adds by default—after you choose a chart type and a style you like—might be pretty close to the mark as far as you're concerned. But, it's good to know how to tweak charts so that they present what you're trying to convey in a clear, unambiguous manner. You can modify your chart by choosing a different chart style or changing the type after the fact.

Choose a different chart style

1 Click anywhere in the chart that you want to change.

2 Click the Style button.

3 Click the style that you want to apply.

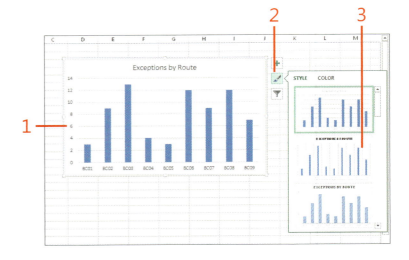

Change the chart type

1 Click anywhere in the chart that you want to change.

2 Click the Design tab.

3 Click Change Chart Type.

4 Click the type of chart you want.

5 Click the desired chart subtype.

6 Click OK.

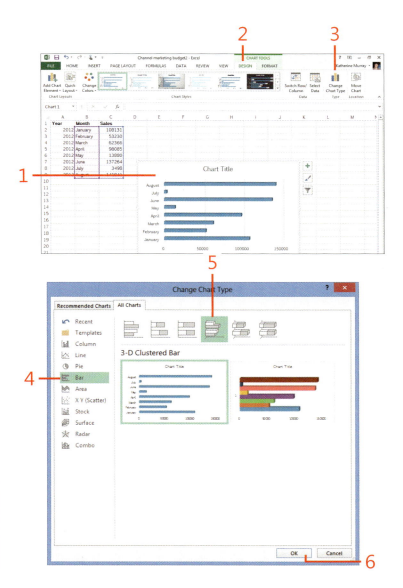

> ✓ **TIP** What might you want to format on your chart? You could change the style, color, or effect of the shapes used to create the chart; modify the text of your labels or titles; arrange the different elements in the chart area; or choose a specific height and width for the chart itself. The tools you need in the Chart Tools Format tab become available when you click the element that goes with those tools. For example, the WordArt Styles group won't be available for you to select until you click a text box on your chart. Similarly, you won't be able to set the size of the chart until you click the chart box so that object is selected.

Adding and formatting chart elements

In addition to the big color blocks (or pie slices or lines) and the title or labels added to your chart by default, there are other elements that you can add to help make your chart more clear for your readers. You might want to add gridlines, for example, or error bars. And, if you haven't added a chart title or legend,

you might want to do that to help readers see clearly what the different data items on your chart represent.

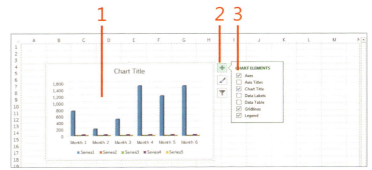

Add chart elements

1 Click anywhere in the chart to select it.

2 Click the Chart Elements button.

3 Select the check boxes adjacent to the elements that you want to add.

Format chart elements

1 Click anywhere in the chart to select it.

2 Click the Format tab.

3 Click the Chart Elements down arrow.

4 Select the chart element that you want to change.

5 Use the controls on the Chart Tools Format tab to format the chart element.

Filter chart data

1 Click the chart whose data you want to filter.

2 Click the Filter button.

3 Select the check boxes adjacent to the data series that you want to display.

4 Select the check boxes adjacent to the categories that you want to display.

5 Click Apply.

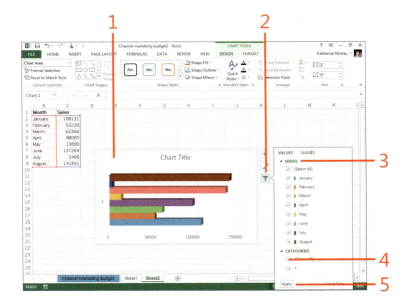

Saving and protecting a workbook

Once you've added text and values in your worksheet and you've included a chart or two, you need to ensure that your workbook is saved by clicking the Save button on the Quick Access toolbar (or by pressing Ctrl+S). You can also protect the workbook or individual worksheets in your workbook so that only those people whom you want to allow access to your Excel data will be able to do that.

Protect the current sheet

1 Click the Review tab.

2 Click Protect Sheet.

   The Protect Sheet dialog box opens.

3 Select the check boxes adjacent to the protection options you want to apply.

4 Click OK.

Add a password

1 Click the Review tab.

2 Click Protect Workbook.

3 Type a password for your workbook.

4 Click OK.

   A small Confirm Password dialog box appears.

5 Retype your password.

6 Click OK.

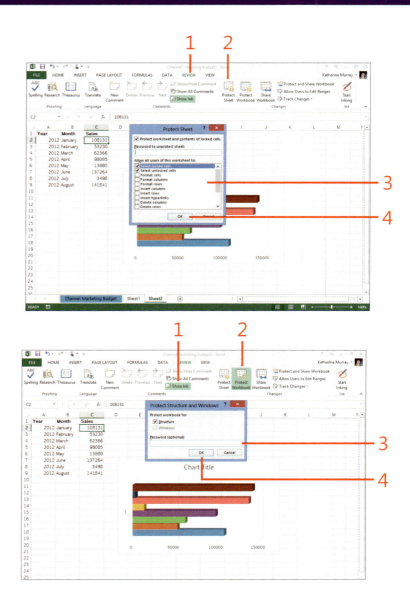

Mark the workbook as final

1 Click the File tab to display the Backstage view.

2 Click Info.

3 Click Protect Workbook.

4 Click Mark As Final.

5 Click OK twice to clear the message boxes.

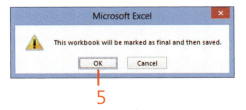

Sharing a workbook

If you're occupied with a workbook to which others also need to contribute, you can easily share your workbook in Excel 2013. On the Review tab, in the Changes group, you can choose to share your workbook by using either the Share Workbook or Protect And Share Workbook tools.

Moreover, you can use tools on the Share tab of the Backstage view to present your workbook online by using Microsoft Lync so that others can view and respond to your worksheet in real time. Be sure to sign in to Lync before choosing the Present Online option so that you don't have to stop and sign in before sharing your workbook.

Share your workbook with others

1 Click the Review tab.

2 Click Share Workbook.

The Share Workbook dialog box opens.

3 Select the Allow Changes By More Than One User check box.

4 Click OK to close the dialog box.

5 In the Quick Access toolbar, click Save to save the workbook.

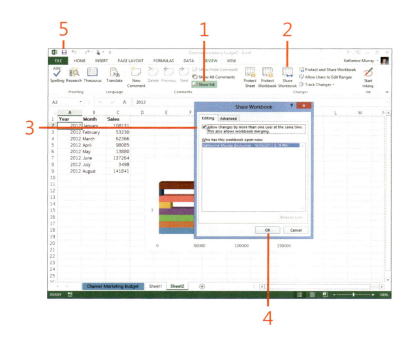

Present the workbook online

1 Click the File tab to display the Backstage view.

2 Click the Share tab.

3 Click Present Online.

4 Click Share.

The Share Workbook Window appears, listing any current meetings you've joined in Lync.

5 Click the meeting or conversation you want to join, if one appears in the list. If not, click Start A New Lync Meeting.

6 Click OK.

Lync makes the connection and displays the worksheet in the presenting window. You can use the tools along the top of the screen to switch the meeting control to another attendee or stop presenting.

7 When you're finished sharing the workbook online, click Stop Presenting.

You are returned to the Lync window, and you can continue your conversation as normal or close or minimize Lync.

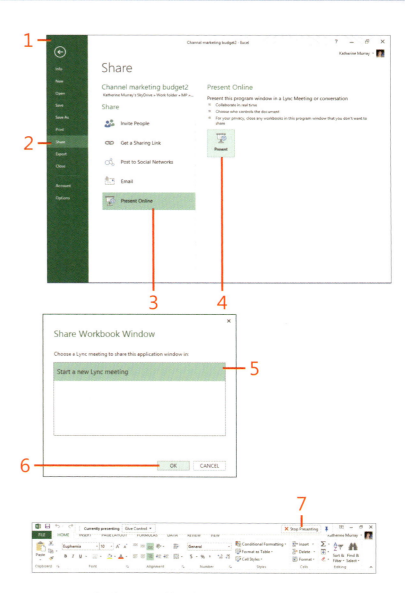

Tracking workbook changes

When you're collaborating on a workbook, it's important to be able to see what kinds of changes others who are working on it are making, too. You can use Excel 2013's Track Changes feature to easily identify additions and changes made by others who are sharing your workbook.

Turn on Track Changes

1 Click the Review tab.

2 Click Track Changes.

3 Click Highlight Changes.

The Highlight Changes dialog box opens.

4 Select the Track Changes While Editing check box.

5 Click OK twice to save and share the workbook.

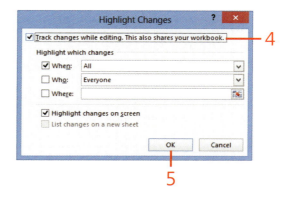

Review changes

1 Click the Review tab.

2 Click Track Changes.

3 Click Accept/Reject Changes to inform Excel that you want to work with the changes on the worksheet and then click OK to save your workbook.

The Select Changes To Accept Or Reject dialog box opens.

4 Click OK.

The Accept Or Reject dialog box opens, displaying the first of the changes made on the worksheet.

5 Do any of the following:

- Click Accept to accept the current change.
- Click Reject to reject the current change.
- Click Accept All to accept all the changes.
- Click Reject All to reject all the changes.
- Click Close to stop reviewing changes.

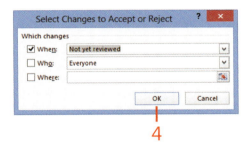

Commenting on a workbook

Being able to leave comments in a workbook is a saving grace when you're confused about a formula or a data series and you can't ask the person who might be able to help you in real time.

You can instead leave a comment in the workbook to which that person can respond.

Insert a comment

1 Click the cell to which you want to add a comment.

2 Click the Review tab.

3 Click New Comment.

4 Type the comment that you want to add.

5 Click anywhere outside the comment to discontinue adding text.

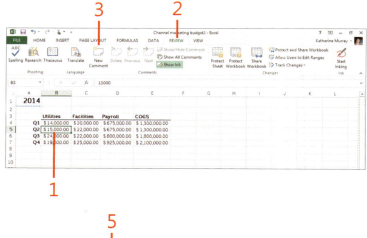

> **TIP** To view a comment on a non-touchscreen device, hover the mouse pointer over a cell that displays a red triangle in the upper-right corner.

Delete a comment

1 Select the cell that contains the comment.

2 Click the Review tab.

3 Click Delete.

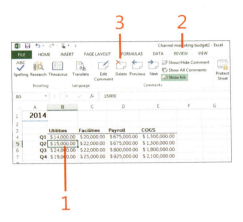

Exporting a workbook

Excel 2013 is such a popular program that you might use it for all kinds of things: the roster of your son's baseball team; the subscriptions to your gardening club newsletter; and of course work-related things like financial projections, payroll statements, and more. No matter what the content of your workbooks, you can export them—and individual worksheets, as well—in formats that make it easy to share the data or work with it in other programs.

Create a PDF of your worksheet

1 Click the File tab to display the Backstage view.

2 Click Export.

3 Click Create PDF/XPS Document.

4 Click Create PDF/XPS.

5 Navigate to the folder in which you want to save the workbook.

6 Type a name for the file.

7 Click the Save As Type down arrow and select PDF.

8 Select publishing options.

9 Click Publish.

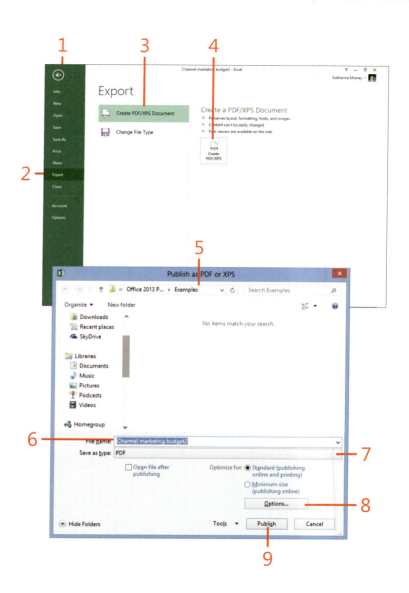

Export the workbook in other file types

1 Click the File tab to display the Backstage view.

2 Click Export.

3 Click Change File Type.

4 Select the desired file type.

5 Click Save As.

The Save As dialog box opens.

6 Navigate to the folder in which you want to save your workbook.

7 Type the file name you want.

8 Click Save.

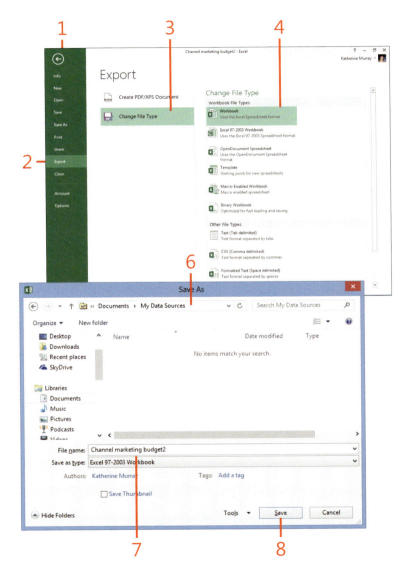

Formatting and enhancing an Excel 2013 worksheet

10

Once you create your Excel worksheet and enter some of your own data (and maybe add a chart or two), you might want to enhance the way it looks. Perhaps you want to change the format of the data in the cells—formatting numbers as dollar amounts, for example—or you might want to apply special effects to column headers and row labels.

Other ways you might want to modify the worksheets in your workbook can involve adding or removing columns and rows, inserting pictures (and applying them to the worksheet background if that's appropriate), and hiding and displaying worksheet information. Finally, you can manage multiple worksheets and preview and print your worksheets to achieve just the right effect in print that you want to produce.

In this section:

- Choosing a theme
- Formatting worksheet cells
- Adding images
- Adding a background image
- Adding and deleting columns and rows
- Hiding and displaying information
- Working with multiple worksheets
- Previewing and printing worksheets

Choosing a theme

A theme coordinates a set of colors, fonts, and special effects that are applied to objects in your worksheet. Excel 2013 includes a number of new themes that bring together designer color schemes, font families, and special effects. By default, the

Office theme is applied to any new blank workbooks that you create, but you can use the Themes tool on the Page Layout tab to choose another theme for your workbook.

Apply a theme

1 In an open Excel workbook, on the ribbon, click the Page Layout tab.

2 In the Themes group, click Themes.

3 Select the theme that you want to apply.

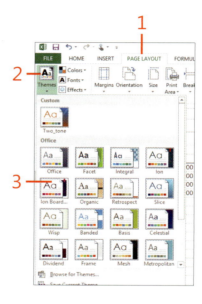

Modify and save a custom theme

1 Click the Page Layout tab.

2 In the Themes group, click Colors and select a new color scheme.

3 In the Themes group, click Fonts and select a new font scheme.

4 In the Themes group, click Effects and select a new effects scheme.

5 Click Themes.

6 Click Save Current Theme.

The Save Current Theme dialog box opens.

7 Navigate to the folder in which you want to save your custom theme.

8 Type a name for the new theme.

9 Click Save.

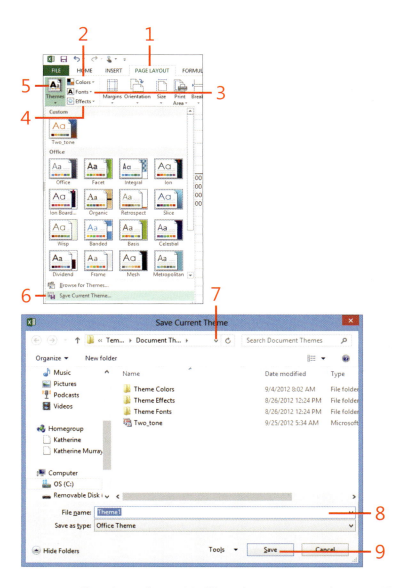

Formatting worksheet cells

Excel 2013 makes it easy to format the data you've added to your worksheet cells. If you've entered text in the cells—for example, as row labels or column headers—you can easily use the formatting tools that you'll find in the Font group on the Home tab to apply the formatting you want.

Format selected cells

1 Drag to select a cell range.

2 Click the Home tab.

3 Use the controls in the Font, Alignment, Number, and Style groups to format the cells.

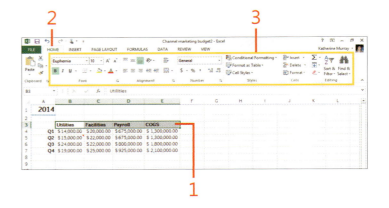

Format numbers

1 Click and drag to select a cell range.

2 Click the Home tab.

3 Use the controls in the Number group to do any of the following:

- Select a predefined number format.

- Assign the Currency style.

- Assign the Percent style.

- Assign the Comma style.

- Increase the decimal places displayed.

- Decrease the decimal places displayed.

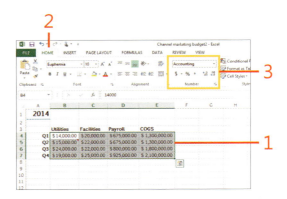

Adjust column width

1 Hover the mouse pointer over the right edge of a column header.

2 When the mouse pointer changes to a horizontal black bar with arrows on either side of it, pointing to the left and right, drag the column border to the desired width.

Adjust row height

1 Hover the mouse pointer over the bottom edge of a row header.

2 When the mouse pointer changes to a horizontal black bar with arrows above and below it, pointing up and down, drag the row border to the desired height.

> ✓ **TIP** If you missed a cell or two when selecting a cell range, you can still add an unconnected cell range to the selection without having to start over again. Simply hold down the Ctrl key, click another cell, and then drag to define the additional cells.

Adding images

Images can add a lot to your worksheets. Maybe you'll show a picture of a new product, include an image of your manager (or yourself!), or add an inspiring image to get people thinking about the new sales promotion. Whatever your motivations, you can add pictures easily in Excel 2013, whether they're from your computer or online sites like your SkyDrive account, photo-sharing sites, or Bing search.

Insert a picture file

1 Click the Insert tab.

2 Click Illustrations.

3 Click Picture.

The Insert Picture dialog box opens.

4 Navigate to the folder that contains the picture you want to insert.

5 Click the desired picture.

6 Click Insert.

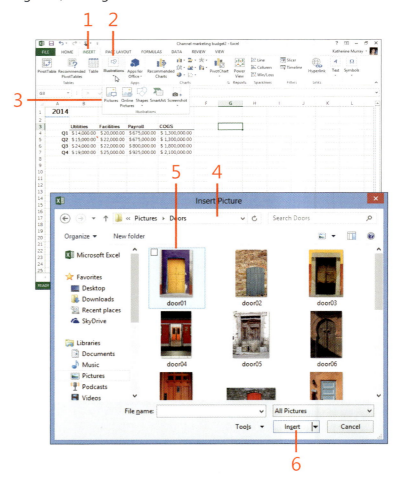

> ✓ **TIP** The new way you can search for and add images from online sites makes finding pictures on Office.com and Bing a snap. The Bing results show that the images displayed are licensed under a Creative Commons license, which is a good reminder that pictures you didn't take yourself don't belong to you. Check the copyright on any image you select from Bing before using it in your worksheet and verify that the image is licensed for public use.

Search for clip art

1 Click the Insert tab.

2 Click Illustrations.

3 Click Online Pictures.

4 In the Insert Pictures window, type a description of the clip art image that you want.

5 Click the Search button.

6 From the clip art choices that appear, click the one you would like to insert.

7 Click Insert.

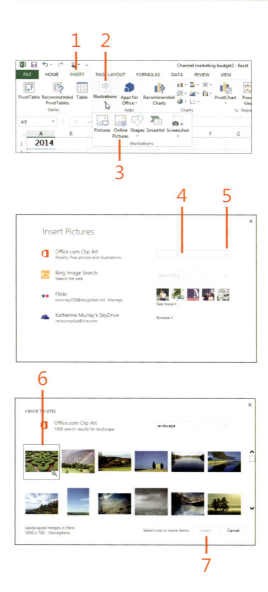

Adding and deleting columns and rows

As you continue to add to your worksheet, sooner or later you will need to insert columns and rows within the areas where you've already added values. You can easily insert a column—or more than one—and add rows, as well, and if you've inserted formulas on the worksheet, Excel 2013 will adjust the formulas automatically to accommodate the addition of the new cells.

Insert a column

1 Right-click and hold the column header immediately to the right of where you want the new column to appear.

2 In the options menu or minibar that appears, click Insert.

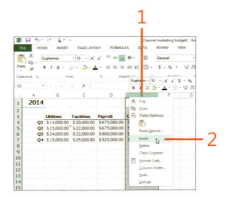

Insert a row

1 Right-click and hold the row header directly below where you want the new row to appear.

2 In the options menu or minibar that appears, click Insert.

Remove a column or row

1 Click the header of the column or row that you want to delete.

2 Right-click and hold the selection, and then in the options menu that appears, click Delete.

Delete selected content

1 Drag to select the content that you want to delete.

2 Press the Delete key or tap the minibar arrow to display additional touch options and then tap Delete.

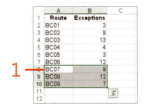

Adding a background image

If you want to add a special touch to your worksheet, you can insert a picture as a background image. You might do this when you want to showcase an image related to your worksheet, such as a company logo, a beautiful travel destination, or a picture of your corporate headquarters. If you add an image and then later think better of it, removing it is a simple thing.

Add a background image

1 Click the Page Layout tab.

2 Click Background.

3 In the Insert Pictures window, click Browse.

4 Navigate to the folder that contains the image you want to use as a background.

5 Click the image.

6 Click Open.

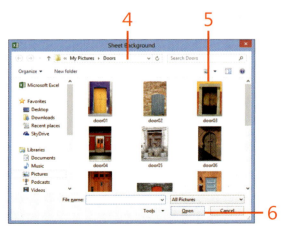

 TIP To remove a background image, simply click the Page Layout tab and then click Delete Background.

Hiding and displaying information

In some cases, you might share your worksheet with folks who don't need to see all the information it contains. Suppose, for example, that your worksheet includes the budget for your current project but you want to hide the information that shows how much you're paying individual contractors. You can choose to hide columns or rows that include sensitive information you don't want everyone to see. You can easily redisplay the rows or columns later when you want all data to be visible.

Hide columns or rows

1 Select the rows or columns that you want to hide.

2 Right-click and hold the selection, and then in the options menu or minibar that appears, click Hide.

Reveal hidden columns or rows

1 Select the rows or columns that surround the hidden rows or columns.

2 Right-click and hold any of the selected row or column headers, and then in the options menu or minibar that appears, click Unhide.

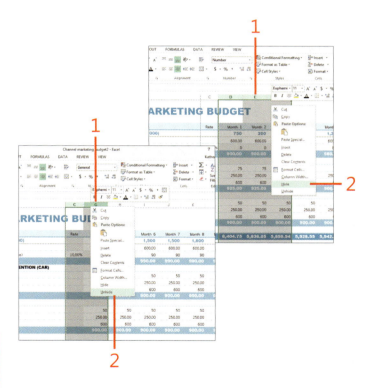

✓ **TIP** If you're wondering how you'll know whether columns or rows are hidden in a worksheet you inherited, look at the column headers or row labels. If you see columns named A, B, C, D and then the columns suddenly jump to H, I, J, K, you know that columns are hidden in the middle. Similarly, if the row numbering is out of sequence along the left edge of your worksheet, you know that some rows have been hidden from view.

Working with multiple worksheets

When you create a new workbook in Excel 2013, the program displays one blank worksheet by default. You can easily add to that worksheet by clicking the New Sheet button (+) located to the right of the worksheet tab. Soon, you might discover that

you have a whole set of worksheets in your workbook. You might also discover that you need to know how to rearrange and remove worksheets. You can also choose to enter data on all your worksheets at once if you choose.

Change the order of worksheets

1 Click the sheet tab representing the worksheet that you want to move.

2 Drag the sheet tab to a new position on the tab bar.

Remove a worksheet

1 Right-click and hold the sheet tab of the worksheet that you want to remove.

2 Click Delete.

3 If necessary, click Delete to confirm that you want to delete the worksheet.

Select multiple worksheets

1 Click the sheet tab of the first worksheet that you want to select.

2 Hold down the Ctrl key and click the sheet tabs of additional worksheets that you want to select.

Enter and format data on several worksheets at one time

1 Hold down the Ctrl key and click the sheet tabs of the worksheets that you want to edit.

2 Type the data that you want to appear in the same cell or cells on the selected worksheets.

3 Drag to select the cells.

4 Using the minibar, specify the formatting options you want.

5 Press the Enter key.

6 Click the sheet tab of any unselected worksheet.

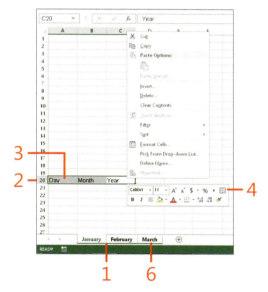

Previewing and printing worksheets

We do so much electronically today that you might not need to preview and print your worksheets as often as you used to. But, Excel 2013 makes it easy to prepare your page for printing and preview the worksheet pages to ensure that they look the way you want them to before you send them to the printer.

Set up your page for printing

1 Click the Page Layout tab.

2 In the Page Setup group, click the dialog launcher.

3 Use the controls in the Page Setup dialog box to prepare your worksheet for printing.

4 Click OK.

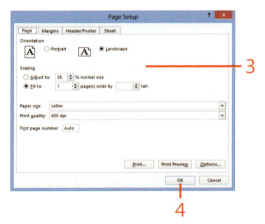

Preview your worksheet

1 Click the File tab to display the Backstage view.

2 Click Print.

3 Click the Zoom To Page button to magnify the page.

4 Click the Return button to close the Backstage view.

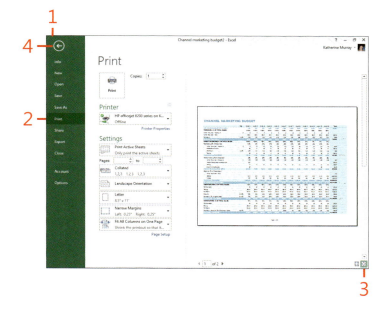

Printing your worksheets

Once your worksheets look the way you want them to, you can send them to the printer. First you'll need to choose the print area to ensure that all of the cells you want to print will be included. Then, in the Backstage view, click the Print tab and set the desired print options.

Choose the print area

1 Drag to select the cells that you want to print.

2 Click the Page Layout tab.

3 Click Print Area.

4 Click Set Print Area.

Print the worksheet

1 Click the File tab to display the Backstage view.

2 Click Print.

3 Click the printer that you want to use.

4 Set the other print options.

5 Click Print.

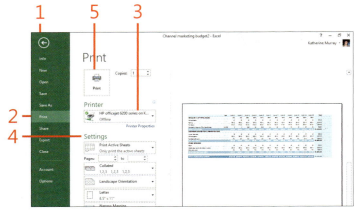

> **TIP** One of the features you'll find on the Print tab in the Backstage view makes it possible for you to send your worksheet to your OneNote notebook. Click the Printer arrow to display a list of available printers. At the bottom of the list, you'll see Send To OneNote 2013. When you select this option and click Print, the Select Location In OneNote dialog box opens. Here, you can choose the notebook in which you want to print the worksheet.

Analyzing your Excel 2013 data

11

One of the great things about Microsoft Excel 2013—and maybe you've already noticed this—is that you can use the program to do all sorts of things, not just manipulate numbers. You can enter your grade book in Excel and keep track of student assignments. You can manage your inventory using it. You can keep track of your checkbook, do sophisticated data analyses, or manage data, none of which necessarily has to have anything at all to do with numbers. This section shows you how you can use Excel to analyze and share the data you're gathering. You can use features such as *sparklines* and *conditional formatting* to show in an instant how the data trends look, or you can construct formulas by using Excel's functions to perform simple or complex calculations with your numeric data. Excel also makes it easy to report on and share your data via Power View Reports and PivotTables.

In this section:

- Using conditional formatting to showcase data trends
- Adding sparklines
- Understanding Excel formulas and functions
- Performing common calculations
- Subtotaling data values
- Entering formulas
- Troubleshooting formulas
- Working with functions
- Creating and modifying data tables
- Sorting data
- Filtering worksheet data
- Creating PivotTables
- Viewing data instantly with Quick Analysis

Using conditional formatting to showcase data trends

Conditional formatting makes it easy for you to see how your data is shaping up in different ways. You can display values as data bars of different colors, using a color scale to display differences in data. Additionally, you can display icons in the cells (such as an up arrow or down arrow), add greater-than or less-than symbols, highlight the top or bottom percent of values shown, or clear the formatting altogether. Conditional formatting is fun to apply and easy to use, and it can help those who are unfamiliar with your worksheet see easily what your data shows.

Highlight data results

1 Open an Excel workbook and drag to select the values that you want to format.

2 Click the Home tab.

3 Click Conditional Formatting.

4 Point to Highlight Cells Rules.

5 In the options menu that appears, click the type of rule that you want to apply.

6 If necessary, click to change the data range.

7 Click the down arrow next to the formatting list box to display your conditional formatting choices and select the format that you want to apply.

8 Click OK to apply the format to the cells.

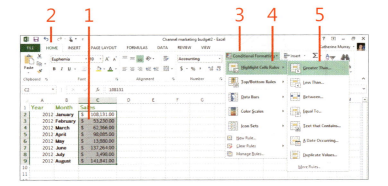

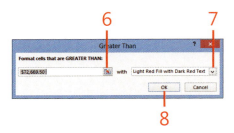

Display data bars

1 Drag to select the cells for which you want to display conditional formatting.

2 Click the Home tab.

3 Click Conditional Formatting.

4 Point to Data Bars.

5 Click the data bar style that you want to apply in the options list that appears.

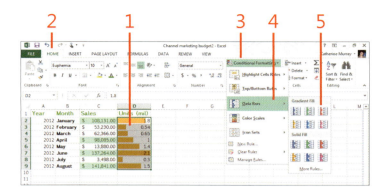

Add icon sets

1 Drag to select the values that you want to format.

2 Click the Home tab.

3 Click Conditional Formatting.

4 Point to Icon Sets.

5 In the options menu that appears, click the icon set style that you want to apply.

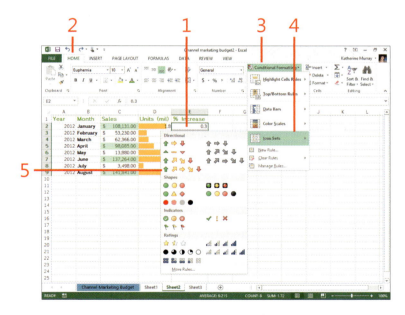

Adding sparklines

Sparklines are simple and fun conditional formatting tools that make it easy for you to show at a glance what the data trend is in the values on your worksheet. You can customize your sparklines so that they appear in different colors and styles.

Excel 2013 offers three types of sparklines: Line, Column, and Win/Loss. The Line option displays your data as a small line chart. The Column sparkline format shows your data as comparison values displayed as a small bar chart. The Win/Loss option displays values as a sequence of colored dashes that clearly indicate the high and low points in your data.

Create sparklines

1 Select the cells that you want to summarize.

2 Click the Insert tab.

3 In the Sparklines group, click the type of sparkline that you want to create.

The Create Sparklines dialog box opens. The data that you selected already appears in the Data Range box, and the cursor is positioned in the Location Range box.

4 Click the cell on the worksheet in which you want the sparkline to appear.

The cell address displays in the Location Range box.

5 Click OK to add the sparkline.

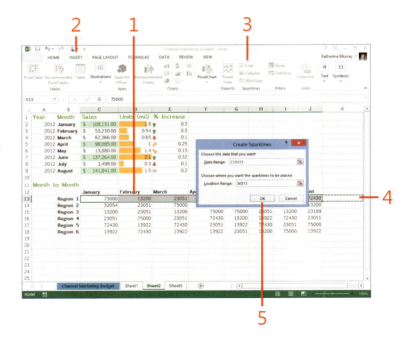

Edit sparklines

1   Click the cell that contains the sparkline you want to edit.

The Sparkline Tools Design tab appears, offering a number of tools that you can use to edit the sparklines.

2   In the Show group, select the desired check boxes to add data markers to your sparkline.

3   Choose a style to apply to the sparkline.

4   Click to change sparkline color.

5   Click to change the color of the data markers that you added to your sparkline.

Click to edit the data used to create the sparkline

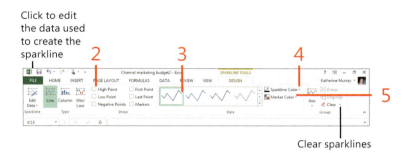

Clear sparklines

✓ **TIP**   For best results, create one sparkline for a specific range of data, edit the sparkline to appear as you'd like, and then copy and paste the sparkline to other cells in your worksheet. Excel 2013 adjusts the data ranges automatically for you, and you get the benefit of adding the sparkline style that you just created to each series you want represented. To copy the sparkline quickly through contiguous cells, drag the small rectangle in the lower-right corner of the sparkline cell in the direction that you want to add the sparklines.

✓ **TIP**   You can delete sparklines from your worksheet by simply selecting the cell containing the sparkline and clicking Clear in the Sparkline Tools Design tab. Choose whether you want to clear the individual sparkline or the entire sparkline group, and Excel does the rest for you.

Understanding Excel formulas and functions

Excel 2013 is a powerful worksheet program that gives you all kinds of tools for performing sophisticated calculations and data analyses. Depending on your needs, you might never need to do many high-end tasks in Excel, but having a working knowledge of formulas, functions, and cell referencing is an important part of getting Excel to perform even fairly simple calculations for you. This section introduces you to some of the basics you'll need as you use functions and cell references in the formulas you create.

the data in the cells specified, relative to its position on the worksheet. For example, with relative cell references, if you are summing the data in cells A1 to D1 and showing the total in E1, when you copy the formula in E1 to E2, the formula recalculates the data based on cells B1 to D2. If the cells in A1 to D1 are absolute references, the formula you copy to cell B2 will continue to reference the cells in A1 to D1. By default, cells use relative references, but if you want to make the references for cells absolute, select the cells you want to change in the formula bar and press F4 to switch from relative to absolute referencing. Excel adds a dollar sign ($) to the beginning of any reference that is treated as absolute in a calculation.

Learning about cell references

Each cell in your Excel worksheet has its own unique address that represents the intersection of the row and column where the cell is located; for example, C5 is an individual cell that falls at the intersection of column C, row 5. K23 is another, located in column K, row 23. You can easily determine the address of the cell by clicking in the cell. The Name box in the upper-left corner of the Excel window shows the cell reference of the selected cell.

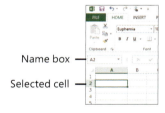

Name box

Selected cell

When you select a range of cells, Excel describes that range by separating the individual cell references with a colon; for example, B4:B20 describes a range of cells that begins with cell B4 and extends to cell B20, which happens to define a group of cells that are all in one column.

When you create formulas, the formula will behave differently depending on whether the cell has an *absolute* or *relative reference*. A formula with a relative cell address uses

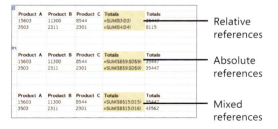

Relative references

Absolute references

Mixed references

Understanding formulas and functions

You'll need to understand cell references to use them properly in formulas. Formulas instruct Excel as to what calculations to perform on your worksheet. A formula might be very simple; for example =3*5+2. (Note that the equal sign [=] informs Excel that what follows is a formula or function and should be calculated as such, not treated as worksheet data.) A more common formula uses cell references to indicate to Excel where to find the data for the calculation, such as =D4+D5.

You use functions to perform common calculations on the cells you select in your worksheet. You include functions in your worksheet formulas. Some of the functions in Excel are very common and you'll be at home using them right off the bat. Using functions such as SUM, AVERAGE, and COUNT, you can total values, find an average value, and display the number of elements in a data range. You insert a function in a formula and specify to the function which cells you want to include in the calculation, as in the following example:

=SUM(B3:E3)

In this formula, SUM is the function. The cell reference (B3:E3) points Excel to the values you want to use to produce the formula result.

You'll use the Formula bar and the Insert Function tool to create and modify formulas in Excel. The Formulas tab also includes the tools you need to insert, manipulate, and modify formulas and functions on your worksheet.

Insert function tool   Formulas tab

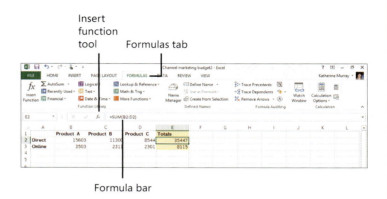

Formula bar

Performing common calculations

Excel 2013 knows that you'll use some calculations more than others, and for this reason, on the Home tab you have a tool within reach to help you perform some common calculations. Specifically, the Sum tool in the Editing group gives you access to functions you might use often: Sum, Average, Count Numbers, Max, and Min. You can also display additional functions by choosing More Functions in the Sum tool list and use the Subtotal tool on the Data tab to subtotal values on your worksheet.

Do a basic calculation

1 Click the cell in which you want to create the formula.

2 Type the equation you want Excel to perform, starting with the equal sign (=).

3 Press the Enter key.

Excel carries out the math and displays the answer in the cell.

Use the Sum tool for common calculations

1 Click the cell below the column that you want to summarize.

2 Click the Home tab.

3 Click the down arrow adjacent to the Sum button.

The Sum tool list offers the Sum, Average, Count Numbers, Max, and Min functions. You can also open the Insert Function dialog box by choosing More Functions.

4 Click the function that you want to use.

5 Press the Enter key or tap outside the cell to accept the suggested formula.

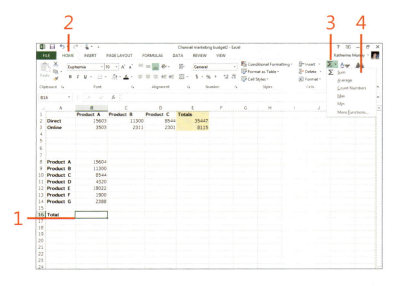

Subtotaling data values

Subtotaling cell values is another common calculation task that Excel can perform for you. You can find the Subtotal tool on the Data tab, in the Outline group.

Subtotal data values

1 Select the data, including column headers, for which you want a subtotal.

2 Click the Data tab.

3 Click Subtotal.

4 Select when you want the function to be applied.

5 Choose the subtotal function that you want to use.

6 Select what you want to subtotal.

7 Choose the check box to specify where you want the subtotal to appear.

8 Click OK.

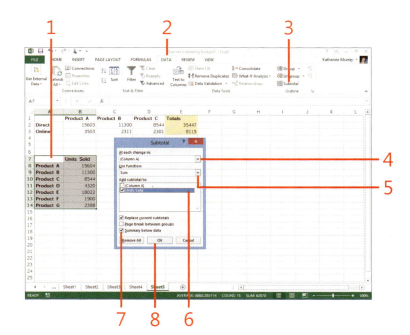

Entering formulas

A formula can be as simple as =2+2 or as complicated as you can imagine. Excel 2013 gives you all the tools you need, no matter how involved your calculation needs might be. You can type a formula directly in the Formula Bar at the top of the Excel worksheet area or you can type it in the selected cell. Along the way, you can also type or select the function you need and type or drag to select the cells you want to include. See how flexible Excel is when it comes to formulas? And, the program even provides you with on-the-spot error checking (the subject of the next task) to help ensure that your formulas are calculating properly.

Type a formula

1 Click the cell in which you want to enter the formula.

2 Type an equal sign (=).

3 Type the name of the function, followed by a left parenthesis character.

4 Type the cell addresses that you want to include in the formula.

You can also click the cells or range on the worksheet that you want to include in the formula and Excel will add it for you.

5 Type a right parenthesis character and press the Enter key or tap outside the cell.

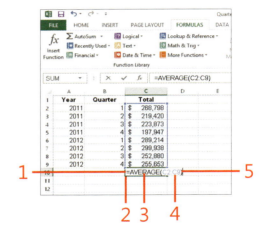

✓ **TIP** If you need to edit a formula that you've already added to the worksheet, you can make changes easily. Click the cell containing the formula you want to change, type the corrected formula on the worksheet, and then press the Enter key or tap outside the cell. Whether you make the edits in the cell or in the formula bar, after you press Enter, the edits are added to the worksheet and other cells depending on that formula are recalculated, as needed.

Troubleshooting formulas

Excel 2013 includes a number of tools to help you troubleshoot the formulas in your worksheet. If things aren't working out properly or you're questioning the accuracy of a formula (or Excel displays an error indicator, alerting you to a problem), you can use these tools to find the problem and correct it.

Check for formula errors

1 Click the Formulas tab.

2 In the Formula Auditing group, click the Error Checking tool.

The Error Checking dialog box opens.

3 Use the controls in the Error Checking dialog box to change the formula or ignore the error.

4 Click Previous or Next to view the preceding or ensuing error that Excel has found in the worksheet.

5 Click the Close box to close the Error Checking dialog box and return to the worksheet.

1   2

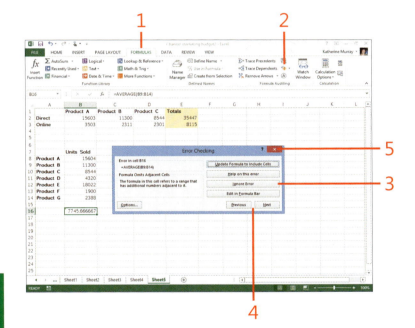

5

3

4

> **✓ TIP**   Excel has a comprehensive Help tool that can assist you in deciphering formula errors and correcting them. To get help with an error in a formula, click the Formulas tab and choose Error Checking. In the Error Checking dialog box that opens, click Help On This Error, which displays the Excel Help window.
>
> Read through the entries related to the problem you're having. Click the Pin tool in the upper-right corner of the Help window if you want to keep it open on your screen while you work through the problems. You can also search Help and read about related issues. When you're finished, click the Close box to exit Help and then click the Close box on the Error Checking dialog box.

Working with functions

As you've already seen in this section, functions are the engines that drive your formulas. They do the actual processing, whether the formula calls for simple or complex calculations. When you add a function to a formula, the function needs to know which cells to use in the calculation.

Find the function you want

1 Click the cell in which you want to add the function and then click the Formulas tab.

2 On the far left side of the Function Library group, click the Insert Function button.

The Insert Function dialog box opens.

3 Click the category down arrow to display the drop-down list and then select the function category that you want to view.

You can choose from All, Financial, Date & Time, Math & Trig, Statistical, Lookup & Reference, Database, Text, Logical, Information, Engineering, Cube, Compatibility, or Web categories. Upon choosing a category, the list of functions available in the Select A Function list changes.

4 Click the function that you want to examine.

5 Click OK to select the function

The Function Arguments dialog box opens, in which you can specify additional information for your formula. (Read on for more about working with function arguments.)

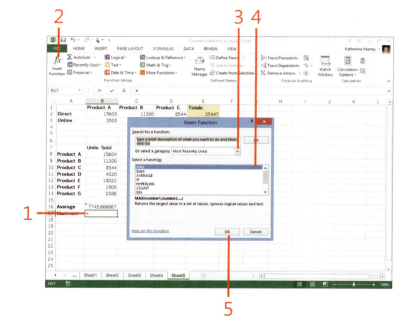

> ✓ **TIP** You can display the Insert Function dialog box by clicking the Insert Function tool to the left of the formula area in the Formula Bar at the top of the Excel worksheet area.

Add function arguments

1 When you click OK in the Insert Function dialog box to add a function to your worksheet, the Function Arguments dialog box opens.

The options you see in the Function Arguments dialog box will vary, depending on which function you have selected.

2 Enter or choose the range of cells that you want to include in the formula. Select any additional options that are required by the selected function.

3 Click OK to close the dialog box and add the formula to the selected worksheet cell.

2

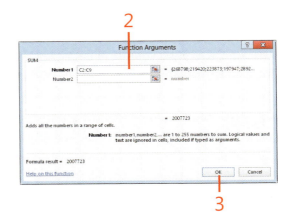

3

✓ **TIP** The Function Library group on the Formulas tab also displays the various categories of functions you can add to your formula. You can add a function without using the Insert Function dialog box by clicking the category of the function you'd like to add and then clicking the function in the displayed list.

Creating and modifying data tables

Instead of creating and formatting an entire worksheet, you might prefer to use a data table to store your Excel data. Excel 2013 includes a gallery of predesigned table formats that you can use to create the table. You can then work with table information and name and resize the table as needed.

Create an Excel table

1 Type your table headers in a single row.

2 Click any cell in the range from which you want to create a table.

3 On the Home tab, click Format As Table.

4 Click the desired table style.

5 Verify that Excel identified the data range correctly.

6 If your table has headers, select the My Table Has Headers check box.

7 Click OK.

Excel applies the data table format to your data.

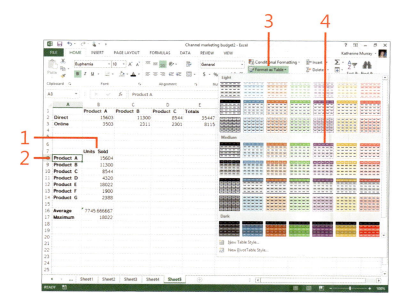

Name an Excel table

1 Click any cell in the Excel table.

2 Click the Table Tools Design tab.

3 In the Properties group, type a new name for your Excel table and press Enter.

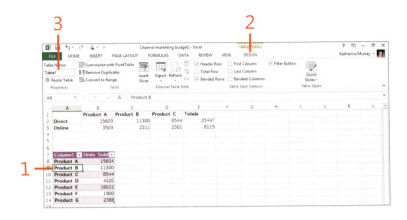

Resize an Excel table

1 Click a table cell.

2 Click the Table Tools Design tab.

3 In the Properties group, click Resize Table.

    The Resize Table dialog box opens.

4 Specify a new cell range for the table.

5 Click OK.

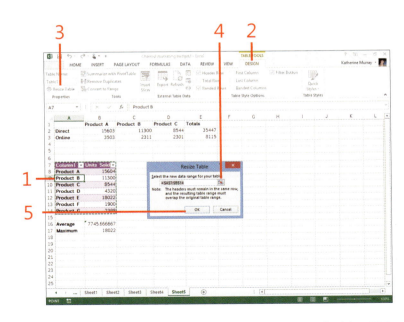

Sorting data

Because you can use Excel 2013 for more than just numbers, you might want to take advantage of it to store all kinds of information such as customer lists or inventory databases. You can use Excel's Sort tool to organize the information in your worksheet and sort it in a way that's meaningful for you.

Sorting is easy in Excel. You can choose an Ascending or Descending sort, or you can customize the process by sorting your information on the elements and in the order you specify.

Do a simple sort

1 Click any cell in the column of data that you want to sort.

2 Click the Data tab.

3 Follow either of these steps:

- In the Sort & Filter group, click the Sort Ascending button.
- In the Sort & Filter group, click the Sort Descending button.

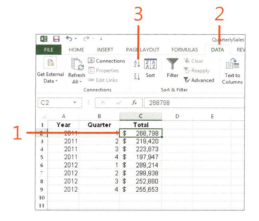

> ✓ **TIP** You can undo the sort by pressing Ctrl+Z immediately after sorting the data. You can also click Descending (if your first sort was Ascending) to reverse the order.

Create a custom sort

1 Select a cell in the data range or Excel table that you want to sort.

2 Click the Data tab.

3 Click Sort.

The Sort dialog box opens.

4 Click the Sort By arrow and select the criterion by which you want to sort.

5 Click the Sort On arrow and select the criterion by which you want to sort.

6 Click the Order arrow and then select the order in which the column's values should be sorted.

7 Click Add Level.

8 If necessary, repeat steps 4–7 to set the columns and order for additional sorting rules.

9 Click OK.

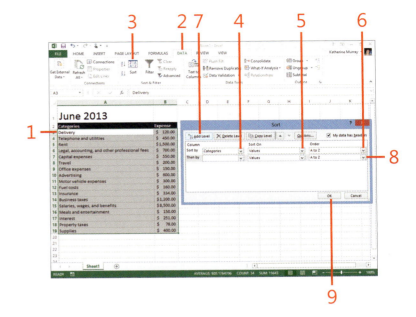

TIP If you want to include the headers in the sort range of the data you're asking Excel to order, select the My Data Has Headers check box in the upper-right corner of the Sort dialog box. If you want to exclude the headers, click to clear the check box if necessary.

Sorting data: Create a custom sort **223**

Filtering worksheet data

When you want to look at a subset of your data or display only data values related to a specific category of information, you can apply filters to that data. You use the Filter tool on the Data tab to instruct Excel 2013 as to how you want to filter the information on the worksheet. When you filter your data, the data items that don't meet the filter criteria are hidden temporarily so that you can view only the data you need.

You can also use *slicers* to filter your data in real time in a table format. Slicers are simple, graphical tables with which you can display your data in different ways without changing selections on the worksheet. Slicers are easy to add and can be an effective tool for showing how your data looks when filtered in different ways.

Filter selected data

1 Click any cell in the range that you want to filter.

2 Click the Data tab.

3 Click Filter.

4 Click the filter arrow for the column that contains the data you want to filter.

5 Select the check boxes adjacent to the values by which you want to filter the list.

6 Click OK.

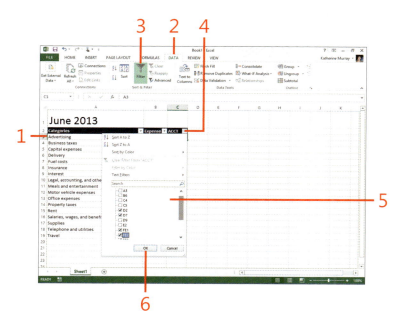

Use a slicer to filter a table

1 Click any cell in the Excel table that you want to filter.

2 Click the Insert tab.

3 Click Slicer.

The Insert Slicers dialog box opens.

4 Select the check boxes adjacent to the fields for which you want to create a slicer.

5 Click OK.

6 Do any of the following steps:

- Click an item to display just that item's values in the table.

- Ctrl+click a second item to add it to the list of displayed values.

- Click an item and then Shift+click another item to display every item between those two items.

- Click the Clear Filter button to remove all filters applied by the slicer.

- Right-click and hold the slicer and click the Remove menu item to delete the slicer.

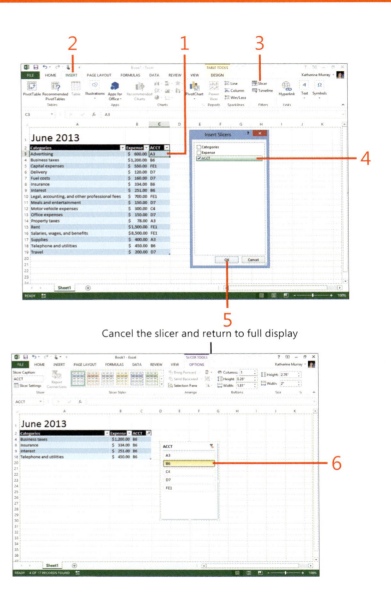

Cancel the slicer and return to full display

Creating PivotTables

PivotTables are powerful tools that can help you analyze your data in a variety of ways and from a variety of perspectives. You specify to Excel 2013 how you want to display the data in the PivotTable and then—here's the pivot part—you can easily change the data to display the information in different ways within the same table.

Create a recommended PivotTable

1 Click a cell within the range that you want to summarize.

2 Click the Insert tab.

3 Click Recommended PivotTables.

4 In the Recommended PivotTables dialog box that opens, click the PivotTable that you want to create.

5 Click OK.

Create a PivotTable

1 Click a cell within the range that you want to summarize.

2 Click the Insert tab.

3 Click PivotTable.

4 Verify that the proper data range appears in the Table/Range box.

5 Click OK.

6 Drag a field to the Values area.

7 Drag other field headers to the Rows and Columns areas, as needed.

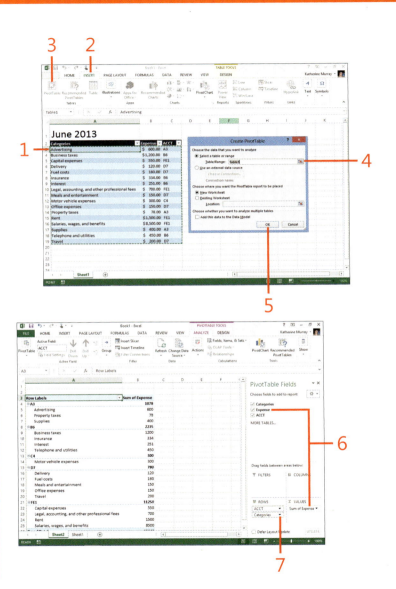

> **TIP** To change your PivotTable, click any cell in the data area of the PivotTable, and then on the PivotTable Tools Analyze tab, choose Field Settings. Choose Field Settings in the Active Field group, and the Value Field Settings dialog box appears. If you want to change the format of numbers in the PivotTable, click the Number Format button and choose a different format in the Format Number dialog box. If you want to change the data source the table is using to create the PivotTable, in the Data group, click Change Data Source and choose a different table to use as the basis for your PivotTable. When you're done making changes, test out the table to ensure that it shows your data to your satisfaction.

Viewing data instantly with Quick Analysis

Quick Analysis is a new feature in Excel 2013 with which you can apply different analysis tools to the data you've selected on your worksheet. It's easy to use and can show you at a glance what trends are appearing in the information you're gathering.

Apply Quick Analysis

1 In an open Excel workbook, drag to select the cell range that you want to analyze.

The Quick Analysis tool appears just below and to the right of the range you selected.

2 Click the Quick Analysis tool.

A palette of tools appears, showing you different options for analyzing the selected data. You can choose to apply conditional formatting tools, display the data as a chart, use Total functions, display the data in tables, or add sparklines to show data trends.

3 Click the desired category.

4 Click the analysis tool that you want to apply.

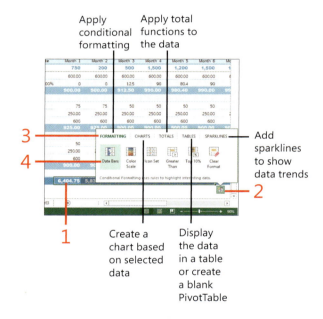

Apply conditional formatting

Apply total functions to the data

3

4

Add sparklines to show data trends

2

1

Create a chart based on selected data

Display the data in a table or create a blank PivotTable

Creating a presentation in PowerPoint 2013

12

Microsoft PowerPoint 2013 includes great new features that make it easier than ever for you to create professional presentations in a snap, share them easily with others, and customize the elements, animations, and transitions to achieve just the effect you want. From the new PowerPoint 2013 Start screen, you can begin a new or existing presentation in whatever way is convenient for you; search for a template, choose a template style, open a recent presentation, or navigate to a previously created presentation on your hard drive or in the cloud.

The new redesigned PowerPoint window is clean, bright, and open for easy use by mouse or by touch. You can work with the ribbon on the screen, unpin the ribbon so that it appears only when you point to a tab, or display Full Screen Mode to hide the ribbon, the scroll bar, and the status bar, and view only your slide in the work area. You can also apply themes to your presentations, enhancing them with coordinated colors, effects, and fonts. In addition, with PowerPoint 2013, you can work (by default!) with a 16:9 layout to accommodate high-definition, widescreen displays. (Though if you prefer, you can also reset the slide size to the standard 4:3 aspect ratio.)

In this section:

- Getting started with PowerPoint 2013
- Starting a new presentation from the Start screen
- Opening an existing presentation
- Choosing themes and variants
- Changing the slide background
- Adding text to slides
- Adding new slides
- Inserting and editing pictures
- Aligning elements with Smart Guides
- Merging shapes
- Adding and editing video
- Adding sound to your presentation
- Adding transitions
- Animating slide elements

Getting started with PowerPoint 2013

Your first task is to launch PowerPoint 2013 and begin to familiarize yourself with the PowerPoint window. You'll notice the clean design right off the bat, and find that the flexible ribbon

display (you can display it when you want it and hide it when you don't) offers you maximum room for working on your slides.

Launch PowerPoint in Windows 8

1 Scroll to display the app tiles that are beyond the right edge of the screen.

2 Click the PowerPoint 2013 tile.

The program opens on your Windows 8 desktop.

> ✓ **TIP** If you're using Windows 7, you can launch PowerPoint 2013 by clicking Start, choosing All Programs, selecting the Microsoft Office 2013 folder, and then clicking PowerPoint 2013.

> ✓ **TIP** You can pin the PowerPoint 2013 program icon to your Windows 8 Desktop taskbar by swiping down on (or right-clicking) the app tile and choosing the Pin To Taskbar icon on the apps bar at the bottom of the screen.

A look at the PowerPoint Window

The PowerPoint 2013 window has a new, clean design that maximizes your access to tools and gives you plenty of room on your screen in which to work. Here are the tools and elements in the PowerPoint window that you're sure to use regularly:

- Choose the task you want to accomplish by selecting a tab on the ribbon

- Click a tool to select it

- Unpin the ribbon so that it appears only when you point to a tab or tool

- Display the slide in Full Screen Mode

- See thumbnails of slides in your presentation

- Add slide notes

- Display the Comments pane

- Change the slide view

- Check slide spelling

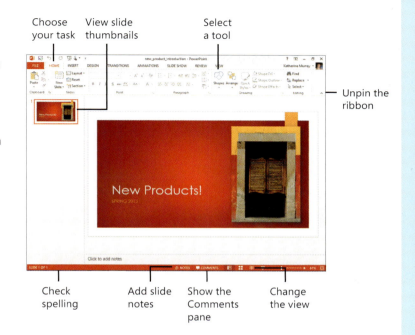

Choose your task

View slide thumbnails

Select a tool

Unpin the ribbon

Check spelling

Add slide notes

Show the Comments pane

Change the view

Starting a new presentation from the Start screen

PowerPoint 2013 gives you more choices for starting a new presentation than PowerPoint users have ever had before, and they all appear on the Start screen that displays when you first launch PowerPoint. You can choose from a sweeping array of templates to get a head-start on the type of presentation you want to create. Template categories include Business, Calendar, Charts and Diagrams, Education, Medical, Nature, and Photo Album. You can also search specifically for a template that matches a style or approach that you like. And, of course, if you want to begin with a blank slate, you can do that, too.

Start a blank presentation

1 Launch PowerPoint 2013.

The Start experience appears on your screen.

2 Click Blank Presentation.

The PowerPoint window opens, and the slide area is blank, except for the title and subtitle prompts, in which you can click to add text.

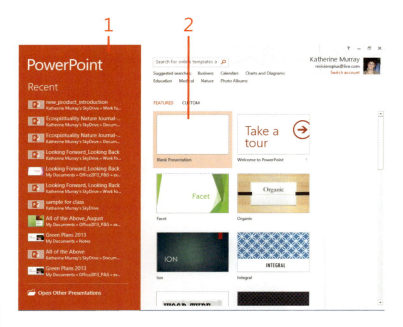

> ✓ **TIP** On the left side of the Start screen, you will see a list of recently opened presentations. If you want to open an existing presentation right off the bat, click the presentation file you want to use. If you don't see it listed in the Recent list, click Open Other Presentations to display the Open dialog box, in which you can navigate to the place and folder where the file is stored. Click the file to open it.

Start a presentation from a template

1 Scroll through the list to see all templates displayed by default.

2 Click the template that you want to use.

3 Alternatively, click a template category that reflects the type of template you're looking for.

4 Click the filter category to see the templates in that group.

5 Click the template that you want to use.

6 You can also click in the Search box and type a word or phrase that reflects the template you're trying to find.

7 Click the magnifying glass to start searching.

8 Click the template that you want to use.

9 Click the arrows to view the pages in the template.

10 Click Create to open a new file based on that template.

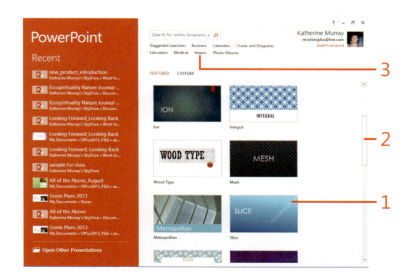

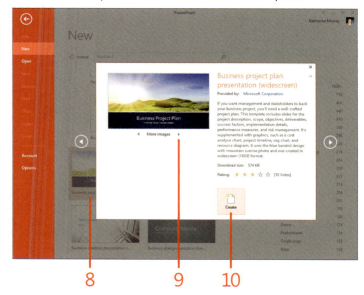

Click Home to return to the default templates view

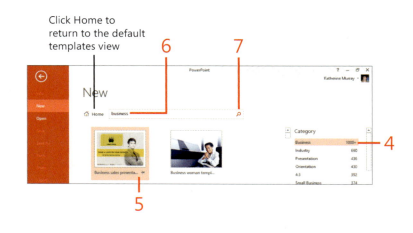

Opening an existing presentation

PowerPoint presentations typically aren't one-shot deals. You create a presentation file, work on it a while, save it, and close it. Tomorrow you'll return and work some more on the presentation, invite feedback from others, and maybe work on the animations. This means that you'll often be opening the same file—one you've already worked on—multiple times. You can easily open an existing presentation from the PowerPoint 2013 Start screen or by choosing Open from the Backstage view.

Open an existing file

1 Click the File tab to display the Backstage view.

2 Click Open.

3 Choose the location at which your file is located.

4 Click the folder that you want to access.

When the Open dialog box appears, click the file that you want and choose Open.

> **TIP** Depending on the place you choose in the Places area on the Open tab in the Backstage view, you might see either file names or folders in the panel on the right side of the screen. If files appear in the list, you can simply click the file that you want to open in the PowerPoint window.

> **TRY THIS!** To add a new place to look for files on the Open tab in the Backstage view, at the bottom of the Places list, click Add A Place. Choose the location you want to add from the list that appears on the right side of the screen.
>
> When you are prompted to sign in with your user ID and password, enter the information and click Sign In. The place you selected is added to the center list, and you'll be able to choose it as a location for the files you want to retrieve.

Choosing themes and variants

Themes in PowerPoint 2013 make it easy for you to apply a harmonious, coordinated look to the presentation you're creating. Each theme includes a number of design choices that control how the colors, fonts, and effects look in your presentation. You can get more specific with your design choices by choosing one of the new PowerPoint 2013 variants, which display the same theme in a variety of colors from which you can select.

Apply a theme

1 Open the presentation that you want to use.

2 Click the Design tab.

3 In the Themes group, click the arrow to display additional theme choices.

A gallery of themes appears.

4 Click the theme that you want to apply to the current presentation.

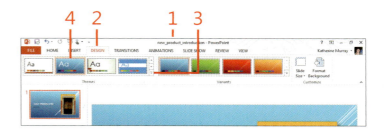

Choose a variant

1 Choose the Design tab, if necessary.

2 Click the variant that you want to apply to the presentation.

Your selection is applied and all slides in your presentation show the new color of the selected variant.

Changing the slide background

Your slide background might not seem too important at first glance, but think about the presentations you've seen recently. Have any been hard to read, boring, or uninspired? The background can have a lot to do with that.

Good presentations are interesting without being overpowering and provide a good contrast with respect to text color and size so that you can read what's on the slide without difficulty. You can change the slide background easily in your PowerPoint presentations or use the ones the program applies when you choose a theme. You can also modify an existing background to add your own special touches such as a company logo or an image that you want to appear on every slide.

Change the slide background

1 Click the Design tab.

2 In the Customize group, choose Format Background.

The Format Background pane appears on the right side of the PowerPoint window. The options displayed here vary depending on the type of background your slide currently displays.

3 Click to change the background fill style from solid to gradient to a pattern or a picture.

4 Click to hide any background graphics.

5 Choose the options that you want to apply to the fill setting you've selected.

Here you see the options related to a gradient fill. If you choose Solid Fill, there are options available with which you can change the color and transparency of the background.

6 If you want to abandon your changes, click Reset Background.

7 Click Apply To All; the background of all slides in your presentation are changed.

Adding text to slides

PowerPoint 2013 provides a number of layouts for your slides that already have different areas blocked out for you. Some slides include text areas and picture areas. Others include text and media. Whichever format you choose, you can easily add text to the slide by clicking in a text box and typing the content that you want to add. Once you add the text you can edit it easily or change the format to suit your preferences for the font, size, color, and alignment.

Add slide text

1 When you start with a new presentation, PowerPoint displays the title page by default.

2 To add the first text, click in the area labeled Click To Add Title (on touchscreen devices, this label reads Tap To Add Title).

3 Type the title of your presentation.

4 Click in the area labeled Click To Add Subtitle (Tap To Add Subtitle on touchscreen devices) and type a subtitle for the presentation.

5 Click outside the text box.

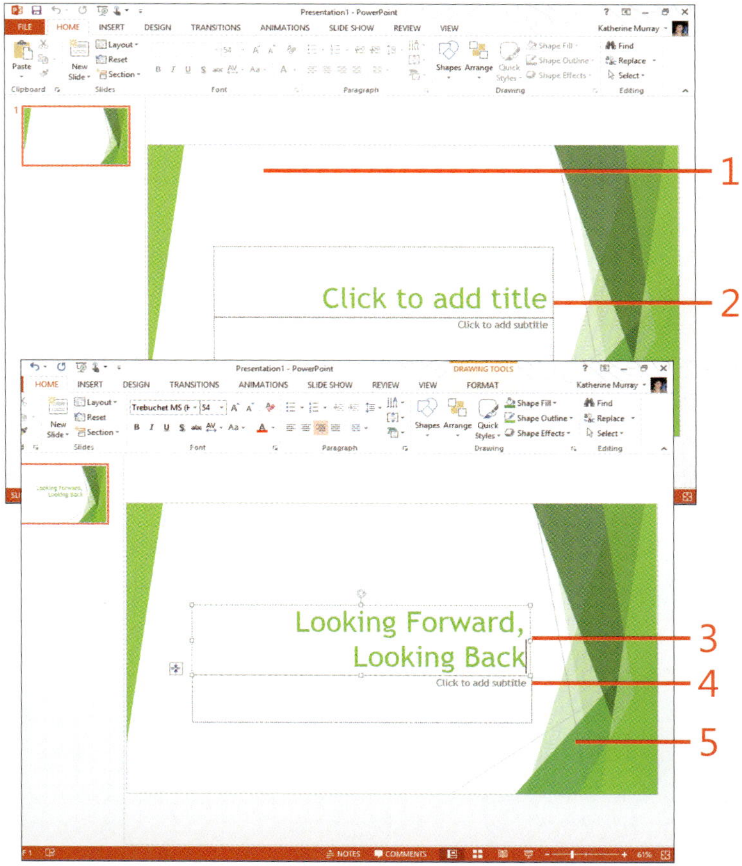

> ✓ **TIP**   To format your slide text, click the text box that contains the text you want to change and highlight the text. The formatting minibar appears next the selection. Simply click the formatting tool that reflects the change you want to make. (Also, you can choose the formatting tool you want to use from the Font group, on the Home tab.)

Adding new slides

You can add new slides easily with a single click and then choose the slide layout that you want to apply to the slide. If you decide after the fact to change the slide layout, no problem; just click the layout that you want and PowerPoint does the rest. (You might need to move the slide elements to where you want them on the new layout, though.)

Insert a new slide

1 Click the Home tab.

2 In the Slides group, click the New Slide arrow.

A gallery of slide layouts opens.

3 Choose the layout that you want to use for the new slide.

4 Alternatively, if you want to make a duplicate of a slide you've selected, choose Duplicate Selected Slides.

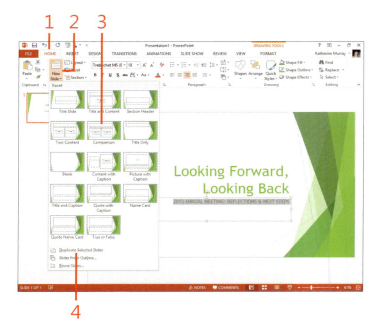

TIP You can reuse slides from another PowerPoint presentation by choosing Reuse Slides from the bottom of the New Slides gallery. In the Reuse Slides pane, choose Open A PowerPoint File and navigate to the folder in which the other presentation is stored, select it, and then click Open.

The slides that are part of that presentation appear in the Reuse Slides pane. Add them to your presentation by clicking the ones that you want to use. The theme used for your current presentation is applied to the reused slides, and you can edit the slides normally so that they integrate well with the current presentation.

Change a slide layout

1 If you're using the mouse, right-click the slide that contains the layout you want to change.

2 Hover the mouse pointer on the Layout option.

A gallery of layout choices opens.

3 Click the layout that you want to apply to the slide.

4 Alternatively, if you're using a tablet or touchscreen, tap and hold the slide with the layout that you want to change.

5 When a rectangle appears at the point of touch, release the touch and the slide minibar appears. Tap Layout to display the layout gallery.

6 Tap the layout that you want to apply.

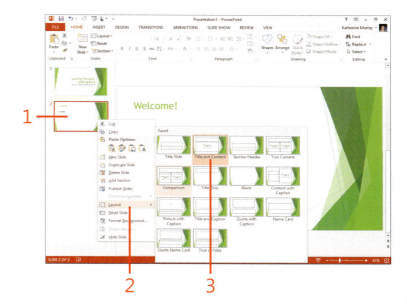

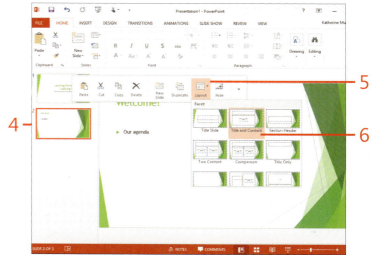

Inserting pictures

A long presentation full of bullet points is a pretty boring presentation. To liven things up and keep your audience interested, add some compelling pictures to your slides. You might include pictures of a beautiful landscape on the way to your offices, images of your key staff members, stylized photos of your newest products, or images that simply inspire and help you make your point, whatever that might be. You can add pictures from your computer, from cloud storage, or from other connected picture sharing sites without ever leaving your PowerPoint slide.

Add a picture from your computer or the cloud

1 Display the slide to which you want to add a picture.

2 Click the Picture icon on the slide.

3 Alternatively, click the Insert tab and select Pictures.

The Insert Picture dialog box opens.

4 Choose the Folder containing the picture that you want to use.

5 Click the picture.

6 Click Insert.

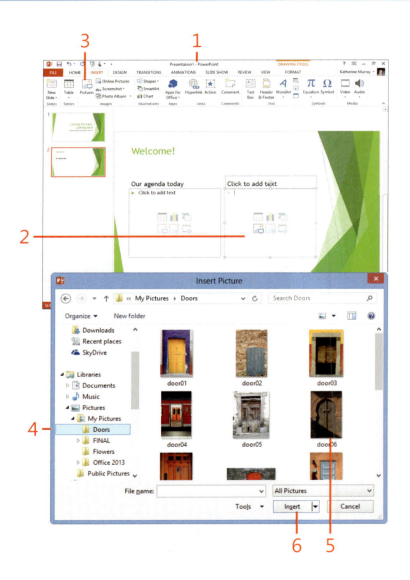

TIP If you want to add a picture that's stored in the cloud, in the Favorites area of the Insert Picture dialog box, click SkyDrive. Navigate to the folder containing the file that you want to add, select it, and then click Insert.

Add an online picture

1 Display the slide to which you want to add the picture from an online source.

2 Click the Insert tab.

3 In the Images group, choose Online Pictures.

The Insert Pictures window appears.

4 If you want to find clip art, type a word or phrase and click Search.

5 To search for an image using Bing, type a description and click Search.

6 Choose an image from a photo sharing site to which you connected Office 2013.

7 Browse your SkyDrive folders to locate the picture that you want to use.

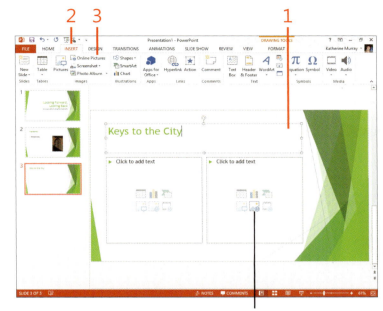

You can also click Online Pictures in the content block on the slide

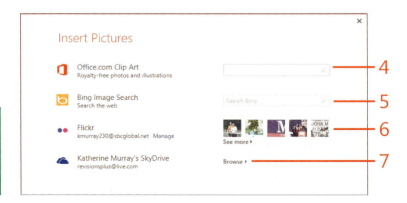

> **TIP** You can also go online to search additional folders and albums in your photo-sharing site by clicking See More beneath the photos displayed. If you want to change settings for the account connected to Office 2013, in the Insert Picture dialog box, click the Manage link to the right of the service name.

Editing pictures

Once you add your pictures to a slide, you can correct the images, add picture styles, and fine-tune them in a number of ways. You can use the image editing tools provided by PowerPoint 2013 to really make your pictures shine. By applying

artistic effects, you can make your images look like paintings, drawings, pen-and-ink etchings, and more. By using the built-in corrections, you can adjust the light balance, sharpen the image, and correct the color tone.

Apply a picture style

1 Select the picture to which you want to add the picture style.

The Picture Tools Format contextual tab becomes available.

2 Click the Picture Tools Format tab.

3 In the Picture Styles group, click the More arrow to display the full gallery of styles.

4 Click the style that you want to apply to the selected picture.

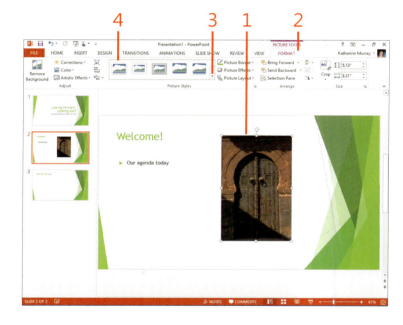

TIP   You can add special effects to the picture on your slide by choosing Picture Effects in the Picture Styles group on the Picture Tools Format tab. PowerPoint 2013 includes a number of special effects, including Shadow, Reflection, Glow, Soft Edges, Bevel, and 3-D Rotation.

Correct picture sharpness and contrast

1 Choose the picture on the slide.

2 Click the Picture Tools Format tab.

3 In the Adjust group, click the Corrections arrow.

The Corrections palette appears.

4 Click the thumbnail image that represents the sharpness you want to apply.

5 Choose the Brightness/Contrast example that you want to use for your picture.

TRY THIS! Now, when you're editing pictures in PowerPoint 2013, you can use the eyedropper tool to match colors between objects on your slide. Click the object with the color you want to select and click the Picture Tools Format tab. Next, in the Shape Styles group, click Shape Fill and click Eyedropper. Position the pointer over the color that you want to copy; PowerPoint displays a preview box of the color you've selected. Click to choose that color and then select the other object on your slide to apply the color to that item.

Aligning elements by using Smart Guides

Smart Guides is a new feature that appear when you need them and disappear when you don't. Smart Guides help you see at a glance how any object or text box you are moving aligns with other elements on the slide or with the center or sides of the slide itself.

Align elements

1 Drag an item on the screen.

A smart guide appears on the slide, showing you how the item aligns with the nearest object.

2 Position the item where you want it to appear and release the mouse button.

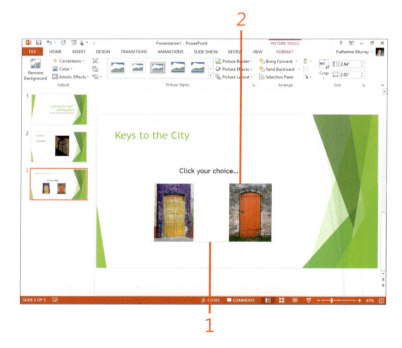

✓ **TIP** Smart Guides change as you move the item, showing how the object lines up at the top, center, or bottom of another element. Smart Guides might also show you the center of the page or the alignment with text boxes or titles.

Merging shapes

PowerPoint 2013 now makes it easy for you to combine a set of shapes into a single shape so that you can work with it as one item on the page. This means that you can animate it easily rather than having to make sure that each individual component in the drawing is selected. When you choose the Merge Shapes tool on the Drawing Tools Format tab, you can select Union, Combine, Fragment, Intersect, and Subtract to create just the kind of effect you want from the resulting merged shape.

Merge shapes on a slide

1 Select the shapes that you want to merge.

2 Click the Drawing Tools Format tab.

3 In the Insert Shapes group, click Merge Shapes.

4 Point to a merge option to preview it on the slide; click the one that you want to apply.

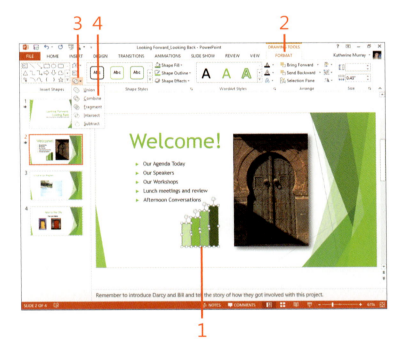

Adding and editing video

Using the Video tool, you can add video clips to your presentation, whether you're including an online video on your slide or adding a video file stored on your computer or tablet. Once you add the video to the slide, you can edit it to suit the topic and time you have available for it in your presentation.

Insert a video

1 Display the slide to which you want to add the video.

2 Click the Insert tab.

3 In the Media group, click Video.

4 Choose either the Online Video or Video On My PC option.

If you choose Online Video, the Insert Video dialog box opens, in which you can search for video by using Bing, locate your own video clip in your SkyDrive account, or use video Embed code from a favorite YouTube video. If you choose Video On My PC, the Insert Video dialog box opens.

5 Click the folder in which the video is stored.

6 Select the video that you want to add.

7 Click Insert.

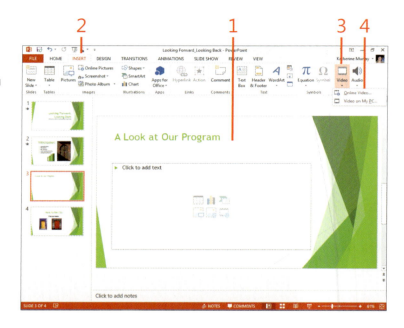

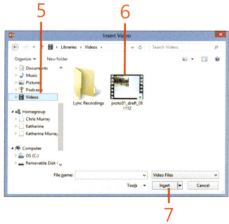

Edit your video

1 Click the video on the slide.

The Video Tools contextual tabs appear.

2 Click the Video Tools Playback tab.

3 In the Editing group, click Trim Video.

The Trim Video dialog box opens.

4 Adjust the Start slider to the point at which you want the video to begin.

5 Drag the End slider to the point at which you want the video to end.

6 Click to play the video clip.

7 Click OK to save your changes.

8 If you want the video to fade in, in the Fade In box, enter a value.

9 If you want the video to fade out, in the Fade Out box, enter a value.

10 In the Video Options group, set any additional video options.

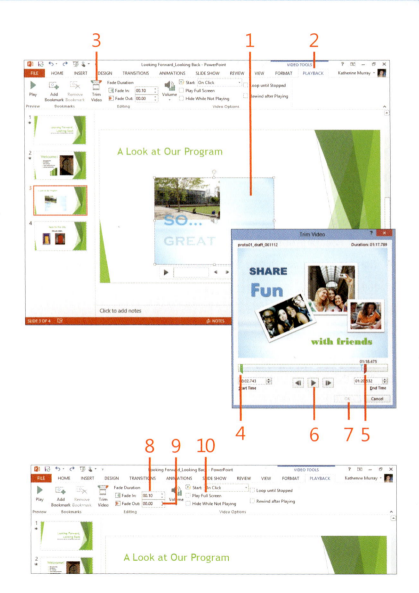

Adding sound to your presentation

With PowerPoint 2013, you can add sound to your presentation such as including narration or applying sound effects to specific slides. You can add audio to your presentation three ways: on the Insert tab, in the Media group, use the Audio tool; on the Slide Show tab, in the Set Up group, use the Record Slide Show tool to record narration and other settings for your slide show; or, on the Transitions tab, in the Timing group, add sound effects by using the Sound tool.

Record presentation audio

1 Display the slide for which you want to begin audio playback.

2 Click the Insert tab.

3 In the Media group, choose Audio.

4 Select Record Audio.

The Record Sound dialog box opens.

5 Type a name for the new sound clip.

6 Click Record and record the audio that you want to include on the slide.

7 Click Stop to end recording.

Repeat steps 6 and 7 to add to the recording if necessary.

8 Click OK to add the audio object to your slide.

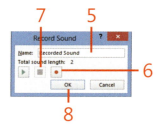

TIP To add a sound clip you've already saved, use the Online Audio or Audio On My PC options in the Audio tool on the Insert tab. Navigate to the site or the folder where your audio file is stored and click Insert to add it to the PowerPoint slide.

Adding transitions

You might be surprised how the way in which your slides change from one to the next can influence the feel of your presentation. A transition that has a dramatic effect—such as the Flip transition—shows a lot of movement and captures the attention of your audience. A transition that is more understated—such as Fade or Reveal—is a more subtle way to keep things flowing smoothly from one slide to the next.

Choose a transition

1 Click the Transitions tab.

2 In the Transition To This Slide group, click the More button to view the full gallery of transitions.

3 Click the transition that you want to apply.

4 Add a sound to the transition, if you'd like.

Built-in sound effects in PowerPoint include sounds like applause, a breeze, a chime, a drum roll, a typewriter, and more.

5 Choose how you want to advance the slide.

By default, On Mouse Click is selected, which means that you must click to display the next slide. If you want your slides to advance automatically, select the After check box and enter the number of minutes and seconds for which you want the current slide to be displayed before the next slide appears automatically.

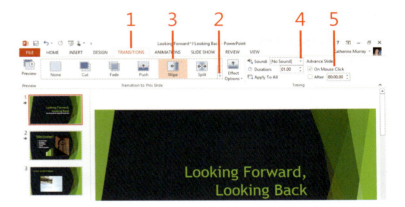

Animating slide elements

Animation in PowerPoint 2013 is easy to do, and you can create as simple or as elaborate an effect as you'd like. The process involves selecting the element on the page that you want to animate, choosing the animation you want to apply, and arranging the animated elements in the order in which you want them to appear. Getting your animation just right will probably involve a little trial and error because you'll be coordinating a number of elements on the slide and adjusting the timing to get it all right. But these minor tweaks are easy to make. And, the effect of a good animation? Priceless.

Animate a slide element

1   Click the text box, picture, or shape that you want to animate.

2   Choose the Animations tab.

3   Click Add Animation.

    The animation gallery opens.

4   Click the animation that you want to apply to the text.

    The object is displayed on the slide with the animation you applied.

5   To display additional entrance animations, click More Entrance Effects.

6   To see more exit animations, choose More Exit Effects.

> **TRY THIS!**   You can animate objects on your PowerPoint slide by choosing a motion path to control where they go on the slide. Now, PowerPoint displays where your object will end up when you apply a motion path animation. To add a motion path to your object, select the object, click the Animation tab, and then click Add Animation. Scroll to the Motion Paths area on the Animation gallery and click the motion path that you want to use. You can also view additional motion paths by selecting More Motion Paths at the bottom of the gallery.

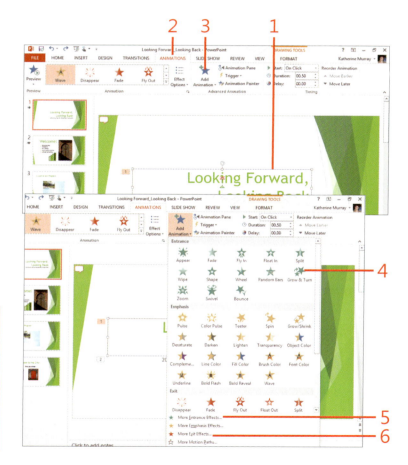

Set timing and reorder animations

1 Display the slide with the animations that you want to change.

2 Click the Animations tab.

3 Select the item that you want to change.

4 Click the Start arrow in the Timing group.

Choose whether you want the animation effect to be applied On Click, With Previous, or After Previous. On Click means that the item won't be animated until you click the mouse; With Previous means the animation will play with the animation of the previous object; and After Previous causes the animation to play as soon as that previous animation has completed.

5 Enter the duration for which you want to allow for the animation.

6 Specify a delay if you want a pause to be inserted before the animation plays.

7 Reorder the animation sequence by clicking Move Earlier or Move Later.

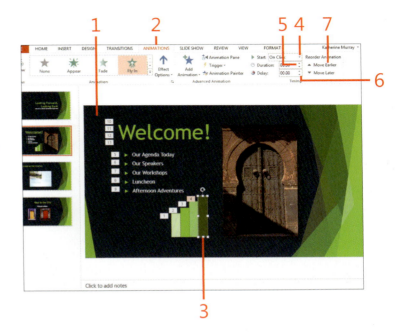

TIP Another way to control when the animation for an item plays is to set a specific trigger for the event. For example, in the Advanced Animation group, you can click the Trigger tool and choose to play an animation when you click one of the items on the slide.

Collaborating and finishing your presentation in PowerPoint 2013

13

Today more than ever, we're working together on projects. We share documents, look over each other's worksheets, and add comments, images, and content to team presentations. This kind of share-the-work ethic makes reaching deadlines easier (usually) and it also means that our favorite tools need to have collaboration features.

Microsoft PowerPoint 2013 makes it easy for you to work collaboratively on a presentation, whether you each have defined roles (as in, "I'll write the text; you do the pictures") or you are reviewing each other's work as you go. Moreover, you can collaborate easily, even if you don't all work in the same geographical location or you're scattered across the globe. This section introduces you to the collaboration features available in Power-Point and shows you how to put all the finishing touches on the presentation you are preparing.

In this section:

- Commenting on a presentation
- Sharing your presentation with colleagues
- Co-authoring presentations in real time
- Previewing your presentation
- Timing the presentation
- Incorporating speaker notes
- Printing presentation materials
- Presenting live
- Navigating your presentation
- Packaging your presentation
- Broadcasting your presentation online
- Saving your presentation as a video

Commenting on a presentation

Comments make it possible for you to add notes, ask questions, and make suggestions that might improve presentations you work on with your team. With PowerPoint, you can easily add, respond to, and move among comments in the Comments pane. Now, in PowerPoint 2013, the comment conversations are threaded so that replies indent within the original comment post, which makes it easy to see and respond to the comment you want.

Add a comment

1 Display the slide to which you want to add a comment.

2 Click the Review tab.

3 In the Comments group, click New Comment.

The Comments pane appears on the right side of the slide window.

4 Type the comment that you want to add.

Your profile picture appears to the left of the comment, making it easy for people to see at a glance who has added the comment. (PowerPoint uses the profile picture associated with your Microsoft Account.)

5 Close the Comments pane by clicking the Close tool.

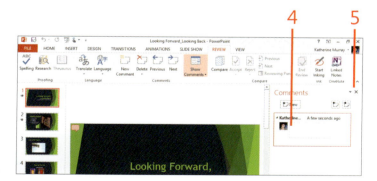

> **TIP** If you want to view the comments in the Comments pane you can display it (and alternately, hide it again) at any time by clicking Show Comments in the Comments group on the Review tab.

Respond to a comment

1 Navigate to the slide that has the comment to which you want to respond.

2 Click the Comment icon on the slide.

The Comments pane opens.

3 Click in the Reply box, type your response, and then press the Enter key or tap outside the comment.

PowerPoint indents the response within the original comment so that you can easily read through all conversations related to the initially posted comment.

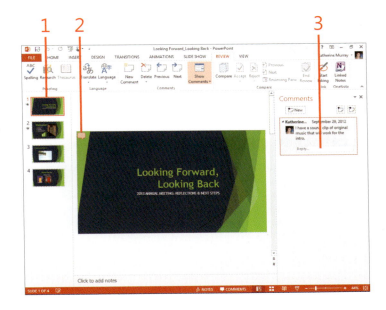

Navigate comments

1 Display the presentation that you want to use.

2 Click the Review tab.

3 Click Previous to move to a previous comment in the presentation.

The comment opens in the Comments pane on the right side of the PowerPoint window.

4 Click Next to move to the next comment in the presentation.

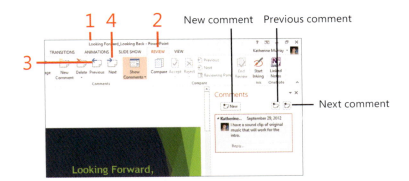

Sharing your presentation with colleagues

Sharing files is easy when you're working in the cloud. Because PowerPoint 2013 by default connects to your SkyDrive account, you can easily post and share files that you want others to review by inviting them to see the file in the cloud. You can also email a shared file to others, which stores the master copy of the file in the cloud so that you can all work on the file together online and then let PowerPoint synchronize all the changes for you.

Invite others to share your presentation

1 Open the presentation that you want to share and click File to display the Backstage view.

2 Click the Share tab.

3 Choose Invite People.

The Invite People pane opens on the right side of the Backstage view.

4 Type the name of people whom you want to invite to view the presentation.

5 Alternatively, click the Address Book icon, choose the names of contacts from the displayed list, and then click OK.

6 Click the arrow to choose whether you want to allow invited participants to view and edit or only to view your presentation.

7 Type a message to send to those you are inviting.

8 If you want your colleagues to sign in before they view your presentation, select the Require Users To Sign-In Before Accessing Document check box.

9 Click Share.

Email the presentation to others

1 Display the presentation that you want to email and click the File tab to display the Backstage view.

2 Click the Share tab.

3 Choose Email.

The Email pane appears on the right, offering you five different ways to email the presentation: Send As Attachment, Send A Link, Send As PDF, Send As XPS, and Send As Internet Fax.

4 Click your choice (for example, Send As Attachment).

A blank email message window opens with your presentation displayed as an attachment.

5 Enter the email address of the people to whom you want to email the presentation in the To line.

6 Add a message, if you'd like.

7 Click Send to send the message with your presentation attached.

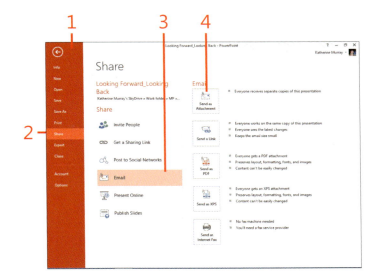

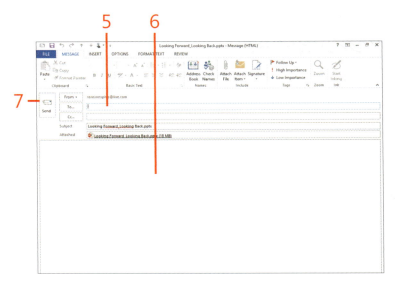

Co-authoring presentations in real time

When you invite others to share your presentation, they can open the file and work on it—even if you're already in there editing. You do this type of co-authoring in the cloud, and PowerPoint 2013 keeps track of the changes being made so no change you or your co-authors make is lost or overwritten.

Open a shared presentation

1 Click the File tab to display the Backstage view.

2 Click Open.

3 Choose the online location where your shared presentation is stored.

4 If necessary, click Browse to look through folders and files in your cloud space.

5 Click the folder containing the file that you want to use and select the file.

6 Click Open.

The presentation opens on your screen. The co-authoring indicator in the status bar shows you how many people are currently working on the presentation.

7 Hover the mouse over or tap the indicator in the status bar of the PowerPoint window to see who else is working on the presentation.

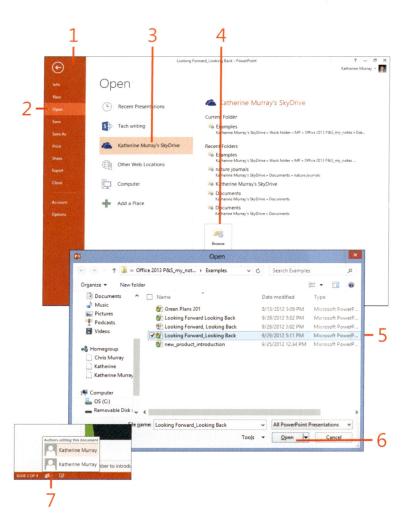

Co-author a presentation

1 Make any changes you want to make in the presentation.

When any other author saves changes, PowerPoint lets you know that updates are available.

2 Click Updates Available.

PowerPoint displays a message box alerting you that when you save the document, it will be updated with the changes others have made.

TIP You can contact a co-author while you're working by clicking the name of the person in the indicator on the status bar. Your co-author's contact information appears, and you can choose to send an instant message, email, or call the person directly.

Previewing your presentation

You can easily preview your presentation before giving it live by choosing From Beginning or From Current Slide in the Start Slide Show group on the Slide Show tab. You can choose to view the entire presentation or check out the slides from the current slide onward. You can also use Slide Sorter view to get a bird's-eye view of your slides and rearrange them as you like.

Preview your presentation

1 Open the presentation that you want to preview.

2 Click the Slide Show tab.

3 If you want to display the entire slide show, in the Start Slide Show group, click From Beginning.

4 To view the presentation from the current point onward, choose From Current Slide.

The presentation begins to play. The slides will advance depending on the method you selected: timed advancement or advancing only when you click the mouse.

5 Move the mouse pointer or swipe in the lower-left corner of the preview window.

You can use the navigation controls to move among the different slides and change the way the presentation is viewed and annotated.

6 Press the Esc key to end the slide show and return to normal view (not pictured). If you're using a touch device, end the slide show by tapping the screen and then tapping the Exit Presentation tool in the far right side of the presentation toolbar.

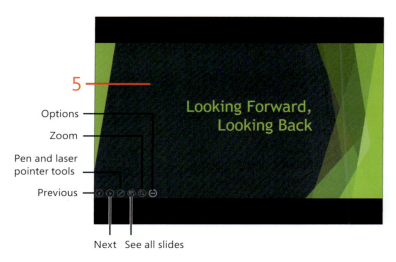

Options
Zoom
Pen and laser pointer tools
Previous

Next   See all slides

Reorder slides in Slide Sorter view

1 Click the View tab.

2 In the Presentation Views group, choose Slide Sorter.

3 Alternatively, click Slide Sorter in the view controls area.

4 Drag the slide that you want to move to a new location.

The other slides in your presentation adjust to accommodate the moved slide. Release the slide when it positioned where you want it to appear.

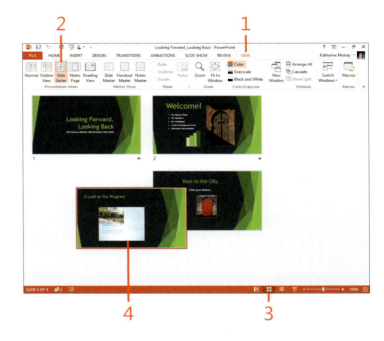

TIP If you're using the mouse, you can move multiple slides by pressing and holding the Ctrl key while you click additional slides. When you drag the selection to a new area, all of the selected slides are moved together to the new location.

Timing the presentation

For some presentations, you might want to control the advance of every slide by clicking. For other presentations, you might want slides to advance automatically after a predefined amount of time. You can use the Rehearse Timings tool in PowerPoint 2013 to practice the timing of your presentation and record the advance of your slides as you go.

Time the presentation

1 Open the presentation that you want to time and click the Slide Show tab.

2 In the Set Up group, choose Rehearse Timings.

The presentation begins to play, and the Recording toolbar appears in the upper-left corner of the screen.

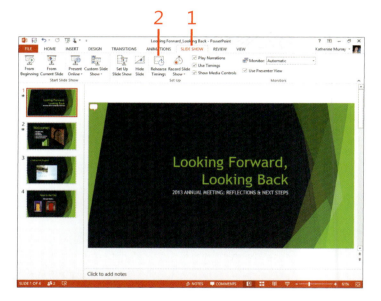

3 Click Next when you are ready to advance either to the next animation or, if there are no animations on your slide, to the next slide.

4 Click Pause to suspend recording.

A message box appears indicating that the recording has been paused. When you're ready to continue, click Resume Recording.

5 Click the Close button when you're done recording timings.

PowerPoint displays a message box asking whether you want to keep the new slide timings. Click Yes to save your new settings or No to cancel the timing values.

> ⚠ **CAUTION**   If you choose to save the timings you recorded during the rehearsal, any timing values you entered manually in the Timing group of the Transitions tab will be replaced with the new values.

Incorporating speaker notes

Most of us want some kind of notes—either printed or electronic—when we have to give a presentation, lead a meeting, or give a speech. PowerPoint 2013 gives you two ways to add notes to your presentation. First, in normal view, you can add notes beneath the slide to remind you of points that you want to cover when that slide is being displayed. You can also use Notes Pages view to display a page that shows the slide at the top of the page and notes at the bottom. When you enter notes in either view, the notes you add appear in Presentation View when you're presenting live.

Add speaker notes

1 In Normal view, display the slide to which you want to add notes.

2 In the status bar at the bottom of the screen, click Notes.

   The Notes area opens at the bottom of Normal view.

3 Type the notes that you want to add to the slide.

TIP To print the notes you added in Notes Pages view, click File to display the Backstage view and choose Print. In the Settings area of the Print screen, choose the arrow to the right of Full Page Slides. A gallery opens, listing the different layout options you have for slide and handout printing. Click Notes Pages; PowerPoint displays the notes pages you created in the preview area on the right side of the Print screen. Finish setting print options and click Print to print your notes pages.

Create notes pages

1 Click the View tab.

2 In the Presentations Views group, choose Notes Page. PowerPoint displays a message box alerting you that your notes will be lost when saved to the server (meaning your SkyDrive or SharePoint cloud storage).

3 If you want to Check Out the file (this is for SharePoint cloud storage only), click Check Out.

4 If you want to save the file to your computer, click Save As and choose the folder on your computer in which you want to save the file and then click Save.

5 On the Notes page, type the notes that you want to add for the current slide.

6 Click to increase the size of the page if necessary.

7 Display additional slides in Notes Page view by scrolling down through the file.

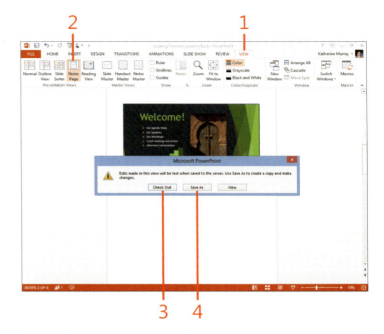

 TIP In Presenter View, you can see the notes you added in the notes area so that you can refer to them as you present.

Printing presentation materials

As you're preparing the materials you need for the final presentation, you will probably want to print handouts for audience members. You might also want to have some printed slides available to share with people who request them. You can easily print all slides or a range of slides and produce handouts that share the essence of your presentation with those who want to see it in printed form.

Print slides

1 Save the presentation that you want to print and click File to display the Backstage view.

2 Click Print.

3 Choose the printer that you want to use.

4 Choose which slides you want to print.

5 Alternatively, enter the range of slides that you want to print (for example, 4–5).

6 If you're printing multiple copies of your slides, choose how (or whether) you want the pages to be collated.

7 Select whether you want to print the slides in color, grayscale, or black and white.

8 Preview your slides in the print preview area.

9 Browse through the various slides.

10 Change the size of the previewed slide.

11 Scroll through the presentation.

12 Click Print to send the slides to the printer.

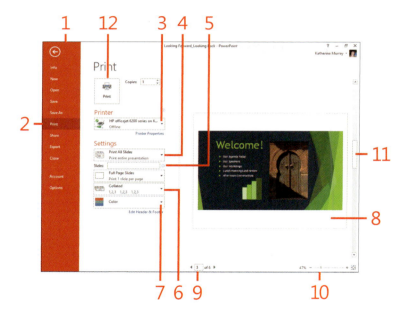

Prepare handouts

1 Click File to display the Backstage view.

2 Click Print.

3 Click the arrow to the right of Full Page Slides.

A gallery of options opens.

4 Select the way you'd like your handouts to display the slides in your presentation.

You can choose to have one, two, three, four, six, or nine slides on a printed page.

5 Choose whether you want to print the handouts in color, grayscale, or black and white.

6 Click Print to print the handouts.

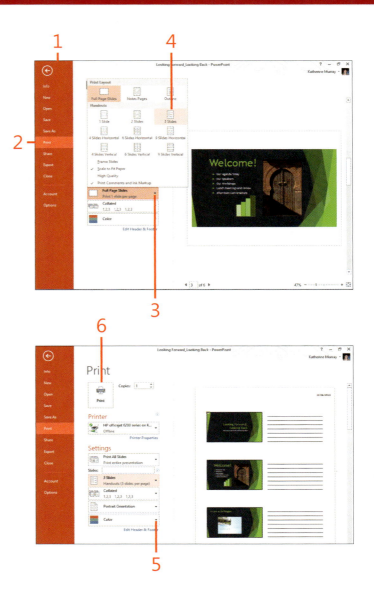

Presenting live

PowerPoint 2013 makes it easier than ever to present with the introduction the new Presenter View feature. Presenter View brings together all the elements you need in one handy dashboard interface that is visible only to you, the presenter. You can see the slide your audience is viewing and write on the slide using pen and laser tools. Also with Presenter View, you can move among all your slides easily, see which slide is next in queue, and read your slide notes while you present.

Display Presenter View

1 Open the file that you want to present.

2 Click the Slide Show tab.

3 In the Start Slide Show group, click From Beginning to start the slide show.

4 Move the pointer to the lower-left corner of the display to reveal the navigation controls. Click the Options tool.

5 Click Show Presenter View.

Presenter View opens on your screen, but it is not visible to your audience.

Use Presenter View

1 Click to select the pen tool and draw on the current slide.

2 Pause the presentation.

3 Display the next slide.

4 Display the previous slide.

5 See the next slide that will be displayed.

6 Review your presentation notes.

7 Enlarge the font used to display slide notes.

8 Show the Windows taskbar so that you can switch between programs.

Navigating your presentation

Presenter View gives you an easy way to move through your presentation while keeping all the information you need right there in one dashboard on your screen. You can easily move forward or back through your presentation and even display a navigation grid that lets you move directly to the slides you choose. If you want to call special attention to an area on the slide you are presenting, you can use Slide Zoom to focus your audience's attention on specific slide elements.

Use the navigation grid

1 Click the Slide Show tab, and then in the Start Slide Show group, choose From Beginning.

2 Move the pointer to or tap the lower-left corner of the screen to reveal the navigation tools.

3 Click the Navigation Grid tool.

Your slides appear in a grid format.

4 Click the slide that you want to display next.

5 Use the Zoom control if necessary to make the slide grid larger or smaller.

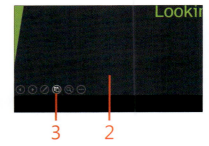

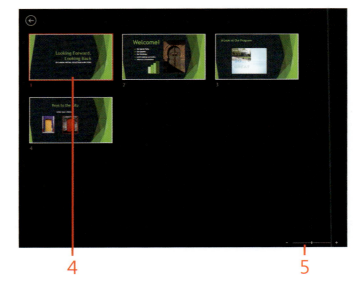

Focus audience attention with slide zoom

1 Click From Beginning to start the slide show and then display the navigation tools in the lower-left corner of the screen.

2 Click the Zoom tool.

A rectangular area appears on your screen that you can move to frame the area you want to enlarge.

3 Drag the selection rectangle to the portion of the slide that you want to zoom in on and click the screen.

PowerPoint magnifies that area of the slide.

4 To return the slide to normal display, right-click anywhere on the magnified area.

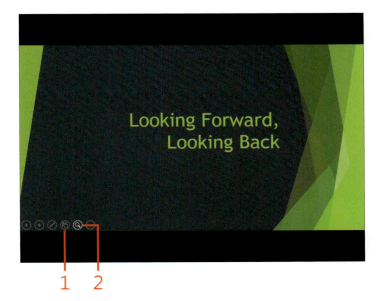

> ✓ **TIP** The Navigation Grid is not visible to your audience. You can use it as needed to move back and forth among slides in your presentation.

> ✓ **TIP** The Zoom tool is available to you only if you're using the mouse during the presentation. If you're in touch mode, you can zoom the presentation and return it to normal display by using the pinch gesture on your touchscreen device.

Packaging your presentation

When all is said and done, you probably want to save all the good work you did on a stellar presentation. You can package your presentation and save it to a CD-ROM to be used again at a later date. You can also publish your slides to a folder of your choosing so that you can use the slides, or the entire presentation, again in the future.

Package your presentation

1 Choose the presentation that you want to package for CD and click the File tab to display the Backstage view.

2 Click the Export tab.

The Export options appear in the Backstage view.

3 Click Package Presentation For CD.

4 Click Package For CD.

The Package For CD dialog box opens.

5 Enter a name for the CD.

6 Click Options if you want to choose whether to link or embed files or assign a password to the packaged presentation. Click OK after you enter your choices.

7 Click Copy To Folder if you want to copy the packaged files to a folder on your computer.

The Copy To Folder dialog box opens, in which you can choose a location and click OK.

8 Click Copy To CD to copy the files to the CD.

PowerPoint displays a message box asking whether you want to include the linked files in the presentation. Click Yes to complete the copy procedure.

9 Click Close to close the Package For CD dialog box.

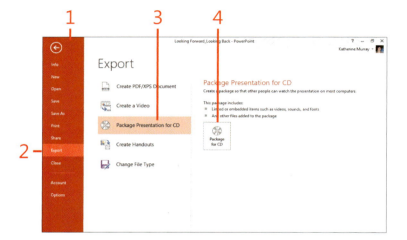

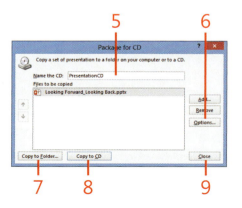

Publish your slides

1 Click the File tab to display the Backstage view.

2 Click the Share tab.

3 Choose Publish Slides.

The right panel appears, describing what you can do with published slides.

4 Click the Publish Slides button.

The Publish Slides dialog box opens.

5 Select the check boxes of the slides you want to publish. Alternatively, click Select All to select all slides in the presentation.

6 Click Browse to choose a location to which you will publish the slides. In the Select A Slide Library dialog box, choose the folder in which you want to save the slides and then click Select.

7 Click Publish to publish the files to the location you specified.

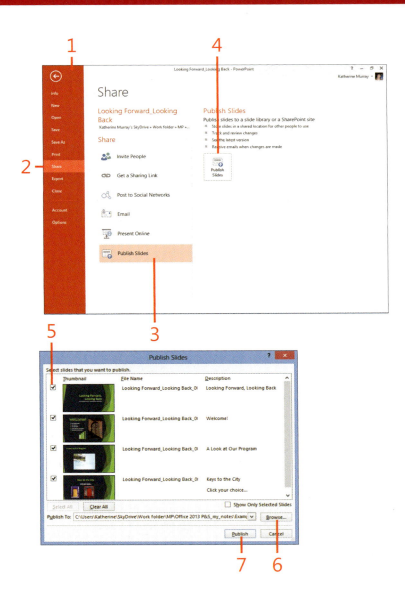

Saving your presentation as a video

A great way to create an auto-playing presentation for others is to create a video of the presentation itself. This is great for those times when you can't be there in person to give the presentation. Instead, people can watch your presentation as a video they access online or on CD.

Create a video

1 Save all changes in your presentation and click File to display the Backstage view.

2 Click Export.

3 Choose Create A Video.

The Create A Video pane appears on the right side of the Backstage view.

4 Click to choose the format for the video.

You can select Computer & HD Displays, which saves the file so that it can be viewed on a computer or other high-definition display; Internet & DVD, which saves the presentation in a form suitable for the web or a standard DVD; or Portable Devices, which saves the presentation in a form optimized for devices running Microsoft Zune.

5 Click to choose whether you want to use the timings and narrations you've included with the presentation.

6 If you opt not to use the timings saved with the presentation, you can specify the amount of time that you want to assign to the display of each slide.

7 Click Create Video.

PowerPoint displays the Save As dialog box, in which you can choose the folder where you want to store the video.

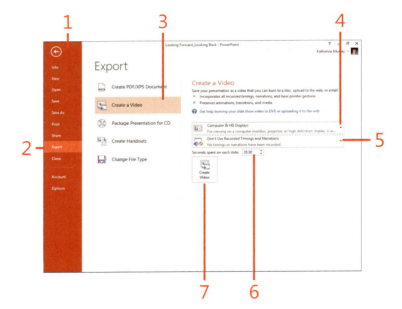

8 Choose the folder for the video.

9 Enter a new name for the file, if necessary.

10 Click Save.

PowerPoint saves the video to the folder you selected.

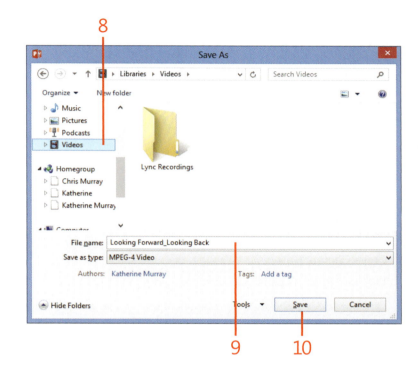

Broadcasting your presentation online

Another great way to share your finished presentation is to broadcast it live online. The great thing about this feature is that the people viewing your presentation don't even need Office 2013 in order to participate. Because the presentation is displayed on the web, anyone with a web browser can use the link you sent and view the live presentation.

Present your presentation online

1 Display the presentation that you want to use and click File to display the Backstage view.

2 Click the Share tab.

3 Choose Present Online.

    The Present Online panel opens on the right side of the screen.

4 Click the arrow to choose the presentation service that you want to use.

    Choose Microsoft Lync if the colleagues with whom you want to share the presentation are all Lync contacts; choose Office Presentation Service if people viewing your presentation will be viewing your presentation in their browser windows.

5 Click Present Online.

6 If you choose the Office Presentation Service, the Present Online dialog box asks you to agree to the service's agreement. Click Connect.

> ✓ **TIP** If you choose Office Presentation Service, others will be able to view your presentation on the web, even if they don't have Office 2013 installed.

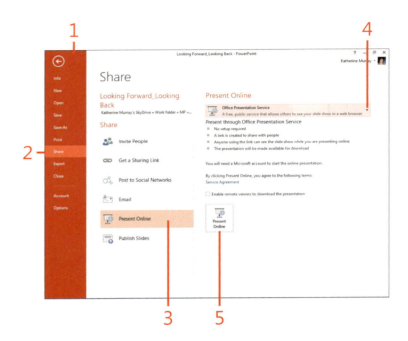

Managing and sharing notes in OneNote 2013

14

Microsoft OneNote 2013 would be glad to be a master organizer of all your great ideas if you're willing to let it help. The program, which was included with Microsoft Office 2010 as a standard application, has a dedicated but fairly small following, mostly because many people simply haven't tried it yet. But, you can use OneNote to capture notes in basically any form they occur to you—you can easily save text, pictures, audio, video, and drawings. It gives you a simple but effective way to manage all the information you collect: with just a few clicks, you can create notebooks, add sections, and create all the notes pages you need. Moreover, you can base those notes pages on templates so that you can collect information in the form that makes the most sense to you. As an added bonus, once you save your notes, you can use them seamlessly in other Office apps, such as Microsoft Word and PowerPoint, or share them online with your team.

In this section:

- Getting started with OneNote 2013
- Creating a notebook
- Opening existing notebooks
- Setting up your notes pages
- Adding notes
- Formatting notes
- Tagging notes
- Inserting pictures
- Recording audio and video notes
- Inviting others to share your notebook
- Sharing notebooks in a meeting
- Searching for notes

Getting started with OneNote 2013

Do you brainstorm? Do you love to gather with your team and toss out ideas on the fly? Or, maybe you're a more orderly thinker: you'd rather open your notebook, add notes, and file the entries as they occur to you. No matter which style suits you best, you can use the tools in the OneNote window to create a new note and add the content you want to store away for later.

Launch OneNote 2013

1 Scroll to display the app tiles that are beyond the right side of the Start screen.

2 Click the OneNote 2013 tile.

   The program opens on your Windows 8 Desktop.

> **✓ TIP** You can change the OneNote display so that the page tabs appear on the left side of the display if you prefer. Click the File tab to display the Backstage view and then click Options. In the Options dialog box, choose Display and click to select the Page Tabs Appear On The Left check box. Click OK to close the Options dialog box. All page tabs for the current section are now listed down the left side of the OneNote window instead of on the right.

> **✓ TIP** If you're using Windows 7, you can start OneNote 2013 by clicking Start, choosing All Programs, and then selecting the Microsoft Office 2013 folder. Then, click OneNote 2013 to launch the program.

Explore the OneNote window

- Display the Backstage view to change notebook settings, share the notebook, print note pages, and more.

- Find common tools such as Undo, Print, and Touch Mode in the Quick Access toolbar. You can also customize this toolbar to display the tools you use most often in OneNote.

- By default, the OneNote ribbon is hidden so that you can view the Show Notebooks tool and the section tabs. When you click a tab, the ribbon appears so that you can choose the tool you want to use. After you click the tool, the ribbon is hidden again.

- Click the + tab to add a new section to the current notebook. You can then add a title to the new section and add note pages by clicking Add Page.

- The note pages you create are listed in the panel on the right side of the OneNote window. If you haven't added a note page title, the first line of text is displayed to give you an idea of what the note contains.

- Click the Insert tab to see the various items you can add to your note pages, including tables, spreadsheets, files, pictures, audio, video, the date and time, equations, symbols, and more.

- Enter a word or phrase in the Search box, and OneNote's powerful search tool finds and displays results instantly.

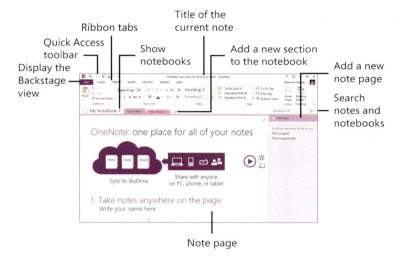

Note page

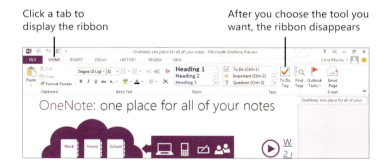

Creating a notebook

When you first start OneNote 2013, the app displays a notebook that is already created for you called My Notebook. You can easily add your own notebook by clicking the File tab and then choosing New or by clicking the Notebook selector in the tab row and choosing Add Notebook.

Start a new notebook

1 Start OneNote.

Your most recent notebook opens on the screen.

2 Click the Show Notebook arrow.

3 Choose Add Notebook.

The Backstage view opens, in which you can enter information about the new notebook you're creating.

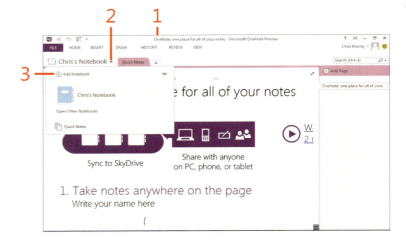

4 Click the location where you want to store the new notebook. You can choose a SkyDrive or SharePoint folder, which saves your notebook in the cloud, or a folder on your computer.

5 Type a name for the new notebook.

6 Click Create Notebook.

A pop-up message box informs you that the notebook has been created and asks you whether you want to invite others to share the notebook.

7 Choose I Am Done For Now and the new notebook opens in the OneNote window.

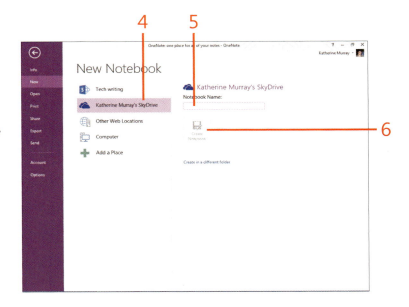

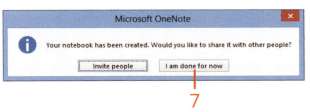

TIP You can use any combination of letters and numbers to name your new notebook, except a space or any of the following characters: * ?" | < > : or /. If you use any of these, Microsoft will prompt you to remove them before the file name can be saved.

Opening existing notebooks

OneNote 2013 makes it easy to open existing notebooks, no matter how many notebooks you might have. You can access notebooks saved online in your cloud storage or stored in a folder on your computer. You'll find the existing notebooks by choosing the File tab and clicking Open or by selecting Open Other Notebooks in the notebook selection list at the top of the notes area.

Open a notebook from SkyDrive

1 Start OneNote and click the File tab to display the Backstage view.

2 Select a notebook saved on SkyDrive that you want to open.

3 Click the refresh icon to refresh the folder display from your cloud storage.

4 Click to display your SkyDrive folder so that you can manage the files and folders stored there.

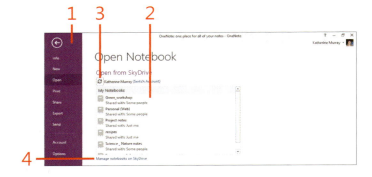

> ✓ **TIP** OneNote displays the notebooks that are connected with the Microsoft Account that you used to log on to your computer, but you can change to a different account by clicking Switch Account at the top of the Open From SkyDrive list. In the Microsoft Account dialog box, enter the user name and password you want to use to sign in to the other account and then click Sign In. The notebooks saved in the cloud space connected to that account then appear in the Open Notebook list.

Open a notebook from your computer

1 In the Backstage view, click Open.

2 In the Recent Notebooks list, scroll through the notebooks.

3 Click the notebook that you want to open.

4 Alternatively, choose another location. The list on the left changes to show the notebooks in that location. Click the notebook that you want to open.

Setting up your notes pages

Our preferences are important to us. This might be because when things are set up the way we like them, we can more easily focus on the task at hand. For whatever the reason, though, you can set up your notes pages by using a specific template if you want to configure a specific look. For example, you might choose a template designed to help you capture class notes or choose a specific style for a to-do list.

In addition to templates, you can change the color and line style of your notes page by choosing the View tab, and then in the Page Setup group, click the Page Color and Rule Lines buttons. Page Color displays a palette of 16 soft shades, and Rule Lines offers choices for adding rule lines or grid lines to your pages.

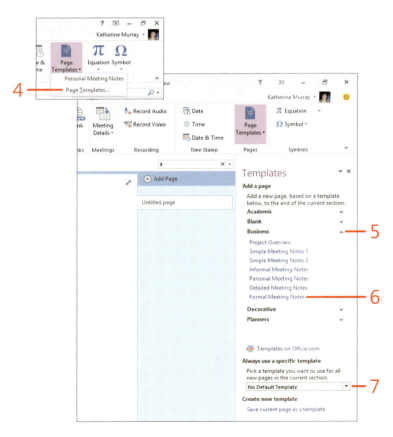

Create a new page based on a template

1 Open the OneNote notebook that you want to use.

2 Click the Insert tab.

3 In the Pages group, click Page Templates.

A list appears showing any templates that you've previously selected, and offering the choice of Page Templates.

4 Click Page Templates to display the Templates pane.

5 Click the category of templates that you'd like to view.

A list of templates appears.

6 Click the template that you want to open.

7 Click the down-arrow to display a list of templates that you can choose as a default template for all of your new notes pages.

Add lines to the page

1 Display the note page on which you want to add lines.

2 Click the View tab.

3 Click the Rule Lines down-arrow.

A palette of line styles and options opens.

4 Click the line style that you want.

You can choose Narrow Ruled, College Ruled, Standard Ruled, and Wide Ruled.

5 Click the grid style you that want if you choose to display a grid instead of horizontal lines.

You can select Small Grid, Medium Grid, Large Grid, or Very Large Grid.

6 If you want to choose a new line color, click Rule Line Color.

A list of color options appears.

7 Click the color that you want to apply to the lines.

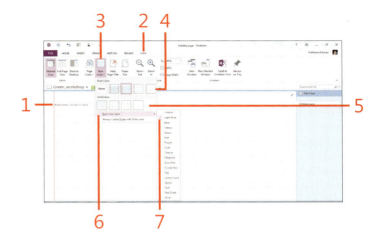

> **TIP** If you want to instruct OneNote to always use your line selection when creating new notes pages, at the bottom of the Rule Lines list, click Always Create Pages With Rule Lines. A check mark appears to the left of the option name, and new note pages will include lines. If you want to turn off the lines feature at a later time, display the Rule Lines list again and click the option to clear the check mark.

Adding notes

One of the best things about OneNote 2013 is that you can add notes in whatever method that suits you best. Whether you prefer to click and type your notes or sketch your ideas out on the page, your doodles and jottings are safe on the One-Note page. If you choose to sketch your notes or write them freehand, you can use the tools on the Draw tab to choose the color and thickness of your pen. And, whether you use a drawing pad or tablet or not, you can draw out your ideas in a way that feels comfortable to you and highlight existing notes easily.

Add a note

1 Click anywhere on the notes page and type your note.

As you type, OneNote expands the text box to make room for your text.

2 Press the Enter key to move the cursor to the next line.

3 Drag to increase or decrease the width of the note box.

4 Drag to move the note box to another position on the page.

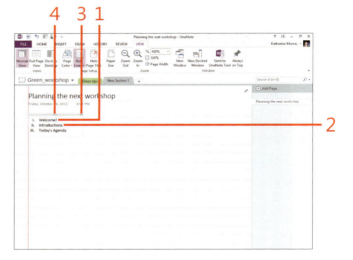

Draw notes

1 Click the Draw tab.

The ribbon displays the drawing tools that you can use to change the pen width and color, add shapes, erase lines, and arrange elements on the page.

2 Select the pen style that you want to use.

3 Click Color & Thickness to choose the color.

The Color & Thickness dialog box opens.

4 Choose whether you want to apply the settings to a pen or highlighter.

5 Click the thickness of the line that you want to use to draw the note.

6 Click the line color.

7 Click OK to save the settings.

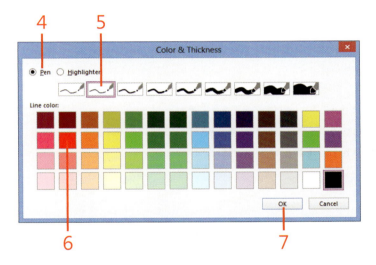

Formatting notes

You'll probably recognize the formatting tools in OneNote because they resemble the formatting tools you've seen in other Office applications. You can select text and add styles, such as Heading 1 or a Quote style, or change text characteristics like font, size, style, and indention.

Add simple formatting

1 Highlight the text to which you want to add the format.

The Formatting toolbar appears.

2 Use the formatting tools to make changes to the selected text.

✓ TIP You can also use the formatting tools in the Basic Text group on the Home tab to apply formatting changes to selected text on your notes page.

✓ TIP To change the default font OneNote uses to display all text on your notes pages as you enter it, click the File tab and choose Options. The OneNote Options dialog box opens, with the General tab displayed. Click the Font arrow in the Default Font area and click the font you want to set as the default. You can also change the size of the font and the font color. Click OK to save your changes and close the OneNote Options dialog box.

Apply styles

1 Select the text to which you want to apply the style.

2 Click the Home tab.

3 Click the Styles arrows to scroll through the styles.

4 Alternatively, click the More arrow to display a list of styles. Click the style that you want to apply.

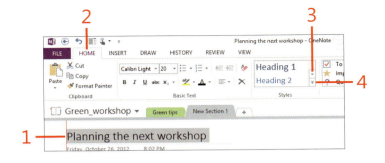

> **TIP** You can remove all formatting from selected text by clicking the Styles arrow, and then at the bottom of the Styles list, choose Clear Formatting.

Tagging notes

You can opt to tag your notes so that you can find them easily later. Simply choose the text you want to tag, click the Home tab, and then choose the tag in the Tags group that fits your needs. Whenever you want to locate notes that have a certain tag, all you need to do is use the Find Tags.

Tag your note content

1 Click in the line of text that you want to tag, or highlight the text to which you want to apply the tag.

2 Click the Home tab.

3 In the Tags group, choose the More arrow to the right of the tags gallery.

A list of available tags appears.

4 Select the tag that you want to apply to the text.

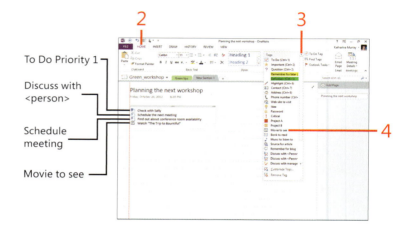

To Do Priority 1

Discuss with <person>

Schedule meeting

Movie to see

TRY THIS! You can customize the tags you use with OneNote by clicking the More button in the Tags gallery and choosing Customize Tags at the bottom of the list. In the Customize Tags dialog box, click New Tag to open the New Tag dialog box. You can type a name for the tag, choose the symbol you want to assign to the tag, and choose the font and highlight color. The Preview area shows you how the tag will look. Click OK to save the new tag. Then, you can apply it to the notes on your page as normal.

Find tagged notes

1 Display the notebook that you want to use.

2 Click the Home tab.

3 In the Tags group, choose Find Tags

The Tags Summary page opens. Tags are listed by tag name by default.

4 Change the way tags are grouped by clicking the Group Tags By down-arrow and choosing another option (Section, Title, Date, or Note Text).

5 Choose where you want to search for tags, ranging from All Notebooks to Last Week's Notes to This Page Group or This Section.

6 Click Refresh Results to summarize tags again.

7 Choose Create Summary Page to display a page of tag results.

A new notes page is added to the current section with the results of the summary.

TRY THIS! OneNote includes a clipping tool that you can use to grab content from the screen, no matter what you happen to be viewing. To use the clipping tool, click the View tab, and then in the Window group, choose Clipping Panel. The OneNote Clipping Tool appears at the bottom of the window, offering you three options. You can use the Screen Clipping tool to clip a portion of the current screen and save it to your notes, you can use Send To OneNote to send the current page to your notebook, or you can choose New Quick Note to create a new note that OneNote will save in a section of your notes called Quick Notes. You can later file the notes wherever you want them to be stored by clicking the Show Notebooks arrow and choosing Quick Notes at the bottom of the list. You can then cut and paste the notes you've saved as Quick Notes to other sections—or even other notebooks—as you'd like.

Inserting pictures

A picture's worth a thousand words, so think how many words you're saving when you add pictures to your OneNote pages. You might capture a picture of a diagram on your mobile phone and add it to a note page, insert a photo of a new product you want to share, or search for a logo you really like and paste it to the page so that you can use it to inspire your own creative ideas.

You can use the Insert tab to add pictures to your notes pages, or you can simply drag an image from your computer onto the page. Once the image is on the page, you can rotate or resize it to fit the space you have available.

Insert pictures

1   Open the note to which you want to add the picture.

2   Click the Insert tab.

3   In the Images group, click Pictures.

    The Insert Picture dialog box opens.

4   Choose the folder that contains the picture you want to add to your note page.

5   Select the picture.

6   Click Open.

    The picture is added to the page.

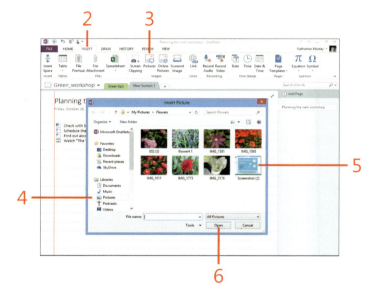

Insert online pictures

1 Open the note to which you want to add the picture and then click the Insert tab.

2 In the Images group, click Online Pictures.

The Insert Pictures dialog box opens.

3 Type a word or phrase to search for clip art that fits your needs.

4 Search Bing for images related to a topic you enter.

5 Click to add a picture from a file sharing account you've connected to Office 2013.

6 Choose a picture that you've saved in your cloud storage online.

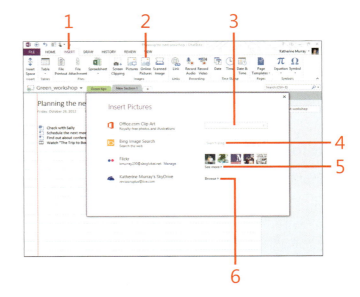

TRY THIS Right-click a picture on your note page and then point to Rotate. A list of options appears with which you can rotate the picture to the right or left or flip it vertically or horizontally. Click the option that you want to apply, and your picture adjusts accordingly.

TIP If you have a number of items on your note page, you can arrange them in the order you want by using the Order tool in the picture options list. Right-click the picture, point to Order, and then choose the item that reflects how you want to order the selected picture.

Recording audio and video notes

If you prefer to dictate your notes or capture video of an event that you want to include in your notebook, you're in luck: with OneNote 2013, you can record both audio and video and add them to your notes pages. You'll find the tools you need on the Insert tab, in the Recording group. You can easily record whatever you like and OneNote will place it on the current page. You can play the audio or video note at any time by double-clicking the media icon to display the options list and clicking Play.

Record audio

1 Open the note to which you want to add audio.

2 Click the Insert tab.

3 In the Recording group, click Record Audio.

   The Audio & Video Recording contextual tab appears, and recording has begun. Record your content as needed.

4 Click Pause to suspend recording.

5 Click Stop when you're finished and want to discontinue recording.

   The Audio & Video Playback contextual tab appears so that you can play back the recording you've captured.

6 Click Play to listen to the recording.

Record video

1 Open the note to which you want to add video.

2 Click the Insert tab.

3 In the Recording group, click Record Video.

The Audio & Video Recording contextual tab appears and OneNote begins recording video using the webcam that is connected to your computer or the on-board video camera in your computer.

4 Click Pause if you need to suspend recording.

5 Click Stop to end the recording.

You can then play back the video clip by clicking Play on the Audio & Video Playback contextual tab.

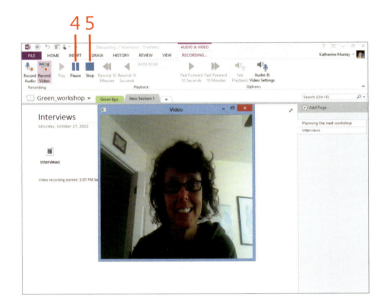

Inviting others to share your notebook

Like all the other apps in Office 2013, you can easily share the OneNote notebooks you create. You can do this by saving it to the cloud (either SkyDrive or SharePoint) and then inviting others to share the notebook or sending a link. Begin on the Share tab of the Backstage view. If you haven't yet saved the notebook to the cloud, OneNote will prompt you to save it before you can share it with others.

Invite others to share your notebook

1 Click the File tab to display the Backstage view.

2 Click Share.

3 In the Share area, click Invite People.

   The Invite People fields appear on the right side of your screen.

4 Type the names or email addresses of those with whom you want to share the notebook.

5 Enter any message that you want to send with the invitation.

6 Click Share.

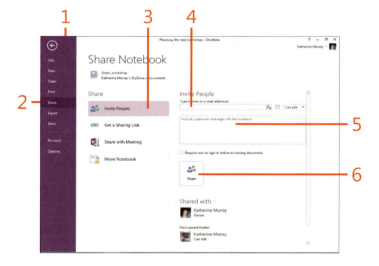

Send a link to your notebook

1 Click the File tab to display the Backstage view.

2 Click Share.

3 Click Get A Sharing Link.

The Get A Sharing Link options appear at the right side of the Back-stage view.

4 If you want others to be able to only view (but not change) the notebook, in the View Link area, click Create Link.

5 For notebooks you've shared previously, you can also click Disable Link to stop sharing if you choose.

6 The Shared With area shows what sharing permissions are in effect for the current notebook.

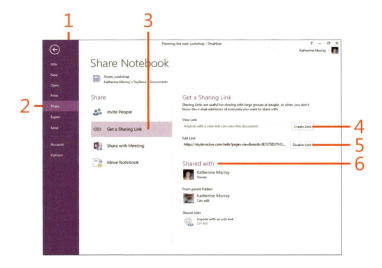

Sharing notebooks in a meeting

If you're meeting with others online and want to discuss something in your OneNote notebook, you can easily share it with those in attendance. You can start the meeting from within OneNote if you want to share your notes on the fly, or you can add your notebook to an online meeting that is already in progress.

Share your notebook in a meeting

1 Click the File tab to display the Backstage view.

2 Click Share.

3 Click Share With Meeting.

4 Click Share With Meeting.

The Share Notes With An Online Meeting dialog box opens, in which you can choose a current conversation or meeting or launch a new meeting.

5 Click your choice.

6 Click OK.

The meeting information is added to your notes page, and others who have the necessary permissions will be able to share your notes.

Searching for notes

OneNote 2013 has a great, fast search tool that brings you instantly the results you're seeking, whether you've typed a single character or a word or phrase. You can use search criteria to locate notes within a specific page, section, or notebook, and you can choose to search all notebooks at once if you like. If you think you'll be using a certain search regularly, you can set it as the default search so that you can use it again easily in the future.

Search for note content

1   Click in the Search box on the right side of the OneNote window and type a word or phrase that you want to find.

2   OneNote instantly shows you where the word or phrase is found.

3   The word is also highlighted if found on the current note page.

4   Narrow your search by clicking the Change Search Scope arrow.

A list of options lets you choose to find what you're searching for on the current page, in the current section, in a group of sections, in the current notebook, or in all of your OneNote notebooks.

5   Select the scope that you want to define for the search.

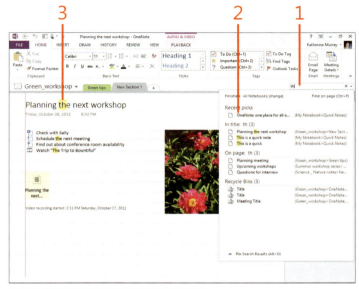

Stay in touch with Outlook 2013

15

Microsoft Outlook 2013 provides a broad set of features for managing your contacts, calendar, and tasks. The most common thing people use Outlook for, however, is sending and receiving email. You can use Outlook to send relatively simple messages in plain text, or you can use it to send highly structured messages containing different font types and formatting, images, and other elements. In fact, you can create HTML content in an email message that makes the message look just like a webpage.

After you have configured at least one email account in Outlook, you can begin creating and sending email, setting up email signatures (text and graphics that are added to the bottom of each new message you create), and customizing the Outlook window to better suit the way you work. Outlook also provides a wealth of features to help you sort, filter, and organize your email by using folders, rules, and other methods.

In this section:

- Launching Outlook 2013
- Looking around the Outlook window
- Tweaking the Outlook window
- Setting up mail accounts
- Reading and responding to messages
- Using Quick Steps to manage mail
- Flagging mail for follow-up
- Categorizing your mail
- Working with mail folders
- Creating email signatures

Launching Outlook 2013

When you install Office 2013, Setup places an Outlook 2013 icon on the Start screen (in Windows 8) or on the Start menu (in Windows 7). Starting Outlook is a simple matter of choosing it from the Start menu or clicking its icon on the Start screen. The first time Outlook starts (or if no Outlook user profile exists), you are prompted to set up an email account, and a wizard steps you through the process of connecting Outlook to your mailbox.

Start Outlook

1 On the Windows 8 Start screen, click the Outlook 2013 icon.

The first time you launch Outlook, the Welcome To Outlook 2013 screen appears. Click Next; Outlook asks you whether you want to add an email account.

> ✓ **TIP** When you first launch Outlook, the program will prompt you to add your first email account so that you can receive and send email. You can add other email accounts later if you like, so that you receive email from web-based accounts, your work account, and any additional email accounts you may have. It will be nice to have them all in one place, right? Outlook 2013 will help you keep all your messages straight, no matter how many accounts you have.

2 Click Yes.

3 Click Next.

The Add Account page of the wizard opens, in which you can provide information about your account.

4 Type your name.

5 Type your email address.

6 Type and confirm your password.

7 Click Next.

Outlook sets up the account and displays a final wizard page informing you that the task is complete.

8 Click Finish to open your new email account in Outlook.

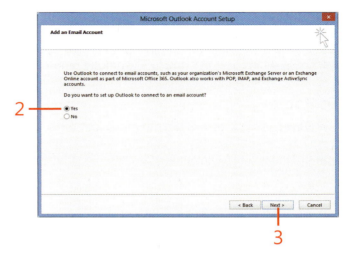

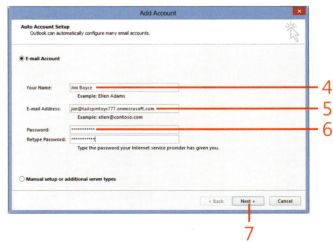

Looking around the Outlook window

Outlook 2013 offers many of the same interface elements as the other Office 2013 apps, such as the ribbon. However, Outlook's interface is also a bit different from the other apps in some ways. These differences are due to the unique nature of

Outlook as a tool for managing different types of information, such as email, calendar items, contacts (which Outlook now calls "people"), and so on. Fortunately, the Outlook interface is easy to navigate and use.

Mail

The Mail window gives you access to your Inbox and other email folders as well as the commands you commonly use to send, receive, and organize email, view and work with the Address Book, and work with email in other ways.

Calendar

The Calendar window gives you access to your calendar items. You can create new meetings and events in the Calendar folder, view the calendars of other people, share your calendar, and perform other tasks associated with your schedule.

Quick Access Toolbar   Messages in the Inbox   Currently selected mailbox   Ribbon   Minimize Ribbon

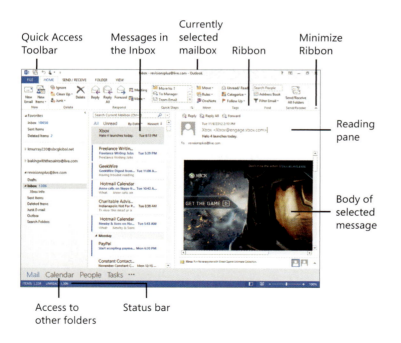

Reading pane

Body of selected message

Access to other folders   Status bar

Ribbon   Select day(s) to show   Create or open calendar groups

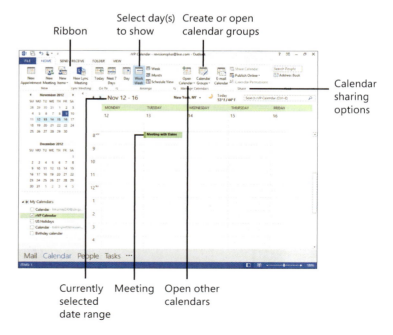

Calendar sharing options

Currently selected date range   Meeting   Open other calendars

People

The People window works much like the Contacts window in previous versions of Outlook. You use the People window to view and manage your contacts.

Selected task

Assign follow-up or due date

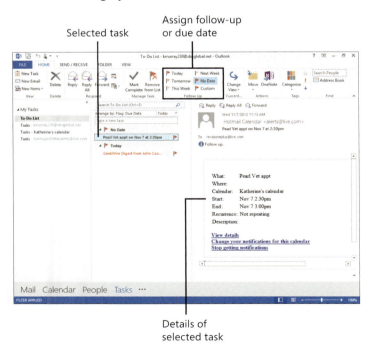

Details of selected task

Tasks

The Tasks window lets you create and manage tasks in Outlook. In addition to working with your own tasks, you can also create and assign tasks to others (if you are using Exchange Server as the backend for Outlook).

Selected contact

Start new email to contact

Contacts

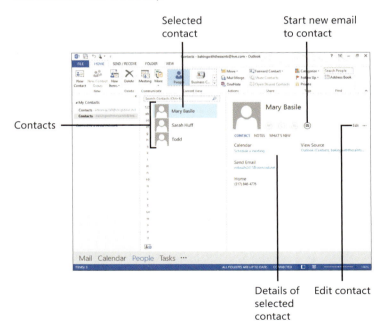

Details of selected contact

Edit contact

Tweaking the Outlook window

By default, Outlook 2013 displays all the tools you're likely to need as you read and respond to messages or add items to your calendar. You can customize the look of the window, however, to display the Folder pane, change where the Reading pane appears, and control the ribbon's display on the screen.

Change the Outlook window

1 Click the arrow to expand the Folder pane.

2 Click the View tab.

3 Click the Reading Pane button and choose Bottom.

4 Click Message Preview and choose Off.

5 Click This Folder.

6 Click the up arrow to minimize the ribbon.

7 Click a tab to show the ribbon.

8 Click the Pin icon to pin the ribbon in place.

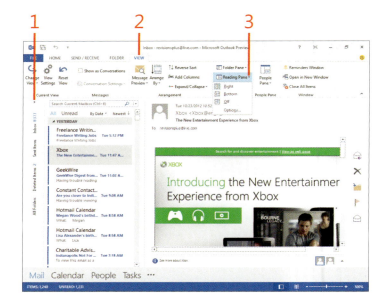

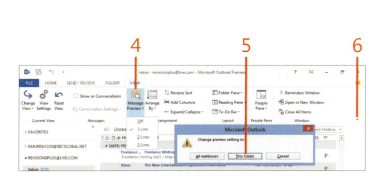

Setting up mail accounts

Outlook 2013 makes it simple for you to add multiple email accounts so that you can access your email all in one place. You use the Info tab in the Backstage view to start the process.

Set up a mail account

1 Launch Outlook and click the File tab to display the Backstage view.

2 Select the Info tab.

3 Click Add Account.

The Add Account Wizard opens.

4 Type your name.

5 Type your email address.

6 Type and then retype your password.

7 Click Next.

Outlook configures the new account using the information you provided, logs on to the mail server, and the wizard displays a Congratulations screen when everything is complete. Click Finish to complete the process.

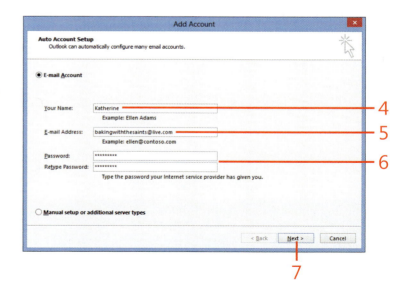

Reading and responding to messages

The most basic task you'll probably want to accomplish with Outlook 2013—and right away, no doubt—is checking and responding to your email. Outlook makes it very easy for you to read your messages quickly and respond to them in kind.

Read and reply to a message

1 Click the Inbox folder.

2 Click a message header.

3 Preview the message in the Reading pane.

4 Either at the top of the Reading pane or on the ribbon, on the Home tab, click Reply.

5 Type your reply.

6 Click Send to send the message.

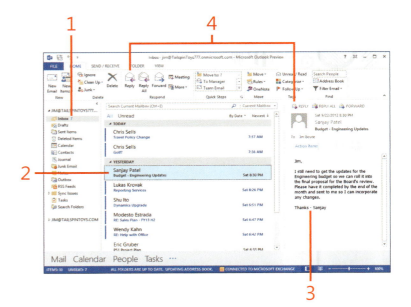

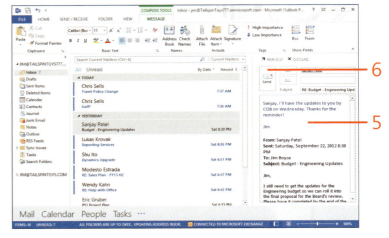

> **✓ TIP** If you prefer to open an email message and work with it in its own window, in your Inbox, double-click the message that you want to view . The message opens on the screen and you can click Reply and respond to it as you like. When you're finished writing your response, click Send to send the message.

Using Quick Steps to manage mail

Quick Steps give you a convenient way to manage the volume of mail that, if you're like most of us, threatens to bury you during the course of a day. Quick Steps help you to create, send, reply to, and organize your mail quickly, with a minimum of steps.

Set up and use a Quick Step

1 In your Inbox, click the email message that you want to use.

2 In the Quick Steps box, click Move To.

The First Time Setup dialog box opens.

3 Click the Move To Folder down arrow.

4 Click Other Folder if you want to specify a folder where the mail will be stored automatically when you choose the Move To Quick Step.

5 Click Always Ask For Folder if you want Outlook to prompt you to choose the folder each time you select the Move To Quick Step.

6 If you choose Other Folder, the Select Folder dialog box opens. Click the arrow if necessary to show the folders in the email account that you want to use.

7 Click the folder to which you want to move the mail.

8 Alternatively, click New if you want to add a new folder, type a name for the new folder, and then click OK.

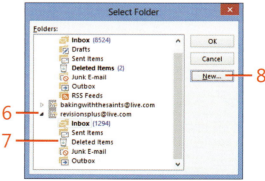

Flagging mail for follow-up

Here's an easy way to ensure that you don't miss a message to which you need to follow up. You can flag the message so that you can easily return to it later and take whatever action is needed. And, if you're concerned that you might miss it anyway, you can set a reminder so that Outlook alerts you that it's time to take on that flagged message.

Flag mail

1 Select a message that you want to flag for follow-up.

2 Click the Home tab.

3 In the Tags group, click Follow Up.

4 Choose the time that you want to assign to the flag.

5 Alternatively, click No Date if you don't want to set an end date for the message.

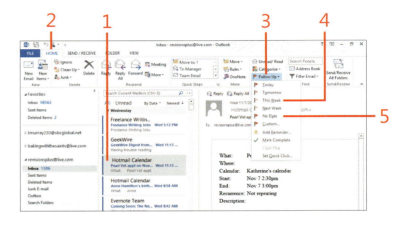

> **✓ TIP** If you want to mark a message as complete—for example, if you've responded to a customer's technical question—in the Tags group, click Follow Up and click Mark Complete. Outlook adds a green checkmark to the message in your Inbox so that you know the message requires no further action by you.

Add a reminder

1 With the flagged message still selected, click Follow Up a second time.

2 Choose Add Reminder.

The Custom dialog box opens

3 Verify that the Reminder check box is selected.

4 Choose a date for the reminder.

5 Choose a time for the reminder.

6 Click OK.

The reminder is added in your Tasks list and will prompt you according to the date and time you specified.

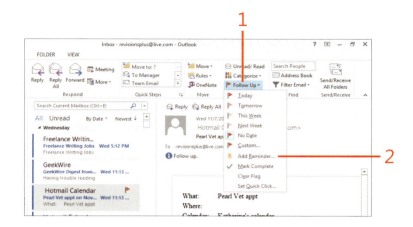

TIP You can view the reminders as well as the messages you've flagged for follow up by clicking the Tasks selection along the bottom of the Outlook window. This displays Tasks view, where your flagged items appear in the center column of the window.

Categorizing your mail

Chances are good that your Inbox collects email messages from many different sources and covering many different topics. You might receive mail from your workplace, your favorite non-profit organizations, friends and family, your children's schools, and so on. How can you keep all the mail straight so that you can be sure to respond to the ones that are most important? One answer is to categorize mail from senders who matter most to you. You can do this by assigning a color category to messages so that you can see at a glance which ones are the most pressing items in your Inbox.

Categorize your email

1 On the Home tab, in the Tags group, click Categorize .

2 Choose All Categories.

3 Click New.

   The Add New Category dialog box opens.

4 Type a name for the new category.

5 Choose a color for the new category.

6 Click OK.

7 Click OK to close the Color Categories dialog box and save the new category.

   You can now assign the category to email by choosing it from the Categorize list.

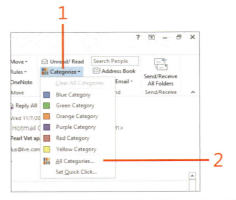

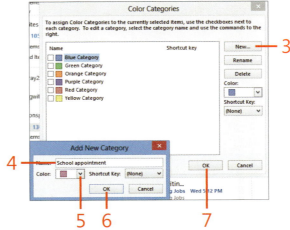

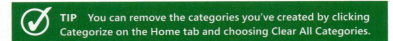

TIP You can remove the categories you've created by clicking Categorize on the Home tab and choosing Clear All Categories.

Use Quick Click categories

You can also create a Quick Click category for messages if you want to be able to categorize messages with a single-click while you scan your messages.

You can display the Categorize list in either of two ways: on the Home tab, in the Tags group, click Categorize, or right-click the message that you want to categorize. Choose Set Quick Click, which opens the Set Quick Click dialog box. Choose the category that you want to apply when you click and choose OK.

Now, you'll be able to categorize your mail by using the category you just selected when you click the Categories column in your Inbox. If you have the Reading pane displayed in the right side of your Outlook window, you might not be able to see the Categories column by default. To display it, move the Reading pane to the bottom of your window or turn it off completely. To do that, click the View tab, and then in the Layout group, click Reading Pane and select Bottom or Off. In the Categories column, click the open box of the messages that you want to categories, Outlook adds the color category you selected.

Working with mail folders

If you receive a steady stream of email during the day, you'll realize very quickly that leaving all your messages in your Inbox isn't a very convenient way to organize the ones that you might need later. Outlook makes it simple for you to add mail folders so that you can organize messages by project, by who sent the message, or by using any other organizational structure that makes sense for you.

Organize your mail by using folders

1 Click the Folder tab.

2 In the New group, click New Folder.

The Create New Folder dialog box opens.

3 Type a name for the new folder.

4 Select the folder in which you want the new folder created.

5 Click OK.

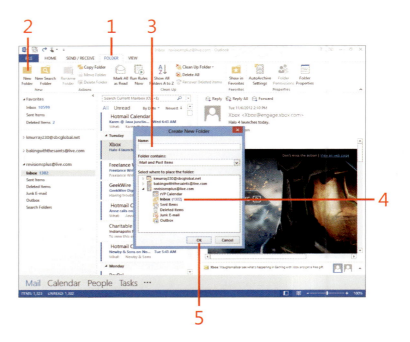

Move mail to the new folder

1 Click the Home tab.

2 Select a message to move.

3 Click Move.

4 Choose the destination folder.

Outlook moves the message to the folder you select.

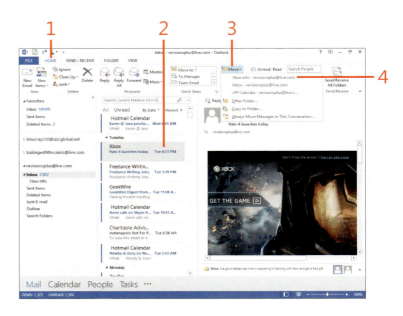

✓ **TIP** You can also use a Quick Step to move mail to a specific folder. Tap the message you want to move and tap Move To ? in the Quick Steps list. Outlook prompts you to choose the name of the folder you want to move the message. Choose the folder name and click Save.

✓ **TIP** If you're feeling adventurous with Outlook, you may want to create a rule to help you manage mail that you know you'll want to file right away. For example, you might create a rule to move all the email messages from your son's school to your Family folder. To create a rule, click the Home tab and click Rules in the Move group. Choose Create Rule and choose the action you want Outlook to take, along with the folder where you want the message to be stored. Click OK to save your settings.

Creating email signatures

What do you want to include in the signature of your email messages? You might list your name, city and state, your blog address, a favorite motto, or a book that you're trying to sell (wherever did I get that idea from??). Whatever you want to include in your signature, Outlook 2013 makes it easy to create and add signatures to your messages.

Create a signature

1 Click File to display the Backstage view.

2 Click the Options tab.

The Outlook Options dialog box opens.

3 Click the Mail tab.

4 Click the Signatures button.

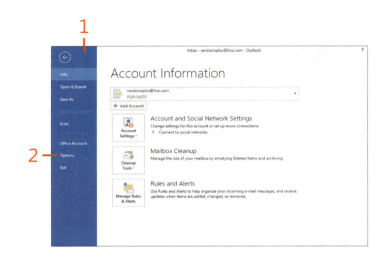

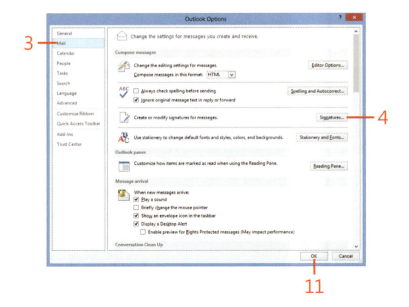

5 Click New.

6 Type a name for the signature.

7 Click OK.

8 In the Edit Signature text box, type the desired signature text.

9 Use the formatting tools to format the text.

10 To have the signature used for all new emails, choose the signature from the New Messages list.

11 Click OK. Click OK in the Options dialog box to close it.

Add the signatures to a message

1 Click New Email to open the new message window.

2 Enter the recipient in the To line.

3 Type a subject.

4 Add the content for the body of the message.

5 On the Message tab, in the Include group, click Signature .

6 Click the signature that you want to add to the email.

Outlook inserts the signature at the bottom of the message.

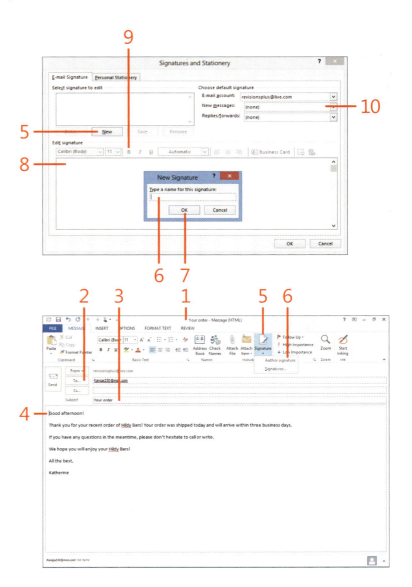

Keeping your calendar current

16

The busier our lives become, the more we need a calendar to keep it all straight. Microsoft Outlook 2013 includes a great calendar that makes it easy for you to schedule meetings, set up recurring appointments, share calendars with others, view your team calendars, and much more. You can choose the view you're most comfortable using and tweak the calendar so that you can see at a glance what you have coming up.

This section shows you how to use the Calendar tool in Outlook 2013. You'll find out how to set up appointments and meetings, update your calendar, share your calendar with others, and set calendar options so that your calendar looks and feels the way you want it to.

In this section:

- Working in the calendar window
- Creating appointments
- Creating meetings
- Scheduling recurring appointments
- Creating and joining online meetings
- Working with calendar views
- Using the To-Do Bar
- Working with team calendars
- Creating and using calendar groups
- Setting calendar options
- Sending your calendar by email

Working in the calendar window

Along the bottom of the Outlook 2013 window, you'll notice four large links: Mail, Calendar, People, and Tasks. To the right of those links is an ellipsis icon (three dots) that you can click to access additional Outlook tools, like Notes, Folders, and

Shortcuts. We're going to be exploring the Calendar tool, so go ahead and click the Calendar link. You can then navigate the view to display the day or days that you want to view.

Navigate the calendar

1 Click Calendar.

   The Calendar view appears.

2 On the Home tab, click Day to show only one day.

3 Click a date to display that day in the calendar area.

4 Click Month to show the entire month.

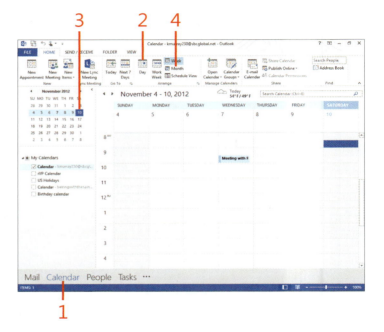

Search your calendar

1 Click in the Search box and type the word or phrase that you want to find.

2 Click the Search tool.

Outlook displays the results in a results list.

3 Double-click an item to display it in an appointment window.

4 At the right end of the Search box, click the close icon (x) to exit search and return to the calendar window.

Choose search options

Select a recent search

Creating appointments

You can easily add an appointment to your calendar for the time, place, and duration you need. You can also add notes about the meeting or even attach files to use during the appointment such as a sales brochure that you want to share with your manager or an invoice you plan to pass along to a client.

Add a calendar entry quickly

1 Click a time slot on your calendar.

2 Type a word or phrase describing the appointment.

3 To extend the duration of the appointment, drag one of the handles in the direction that you want to extend the time.

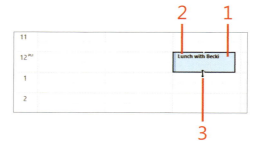

> ✓ **TIP** If you want to add more information about your appointment, simply double-click it in the calendar window. The appointment window opens, in which you can add the location, change the start and end times, or include notes or files that you want to cover during the meeting.

Create an appointment

1 Click a segment in the calendar to choose a block of time for the appointment.

2 On the Home tab, click New Appointment.

3 Type a subject for the appointment.

4 Type or choose a location.

5 Choose the start date and time.

6 Choose the end date and time.

7 Add notes as desired.

8 Click Save & Close.

Outlook closes the appointment window and displays the calendar window.

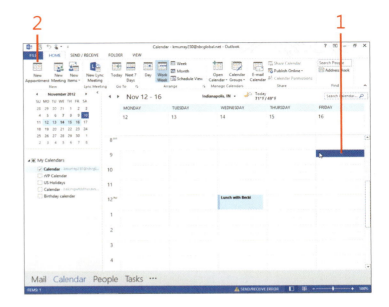

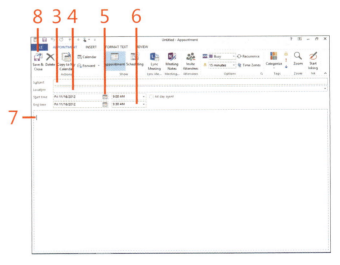

Creating meetings

The calendar in Outlook 2013 makes it very easy to set up meetings and send out an invitation that includes the time and place of the meeting as well as any notes or agenda items.

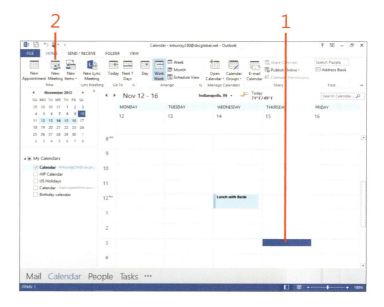

Create meeting invitations

1 Select a time slot for the meeting.

2 On the Home tab, click New Meeting.

3 Type a subject for the meeting.

4 Type a location.

5 Enter notes or agenda topics for the meeting.

6 Click To.

The Select Attendees and Resources dialog box opens.

7 Click the names of those whom you want to attend the meeting.

8 Click Required, Optional, or Resources, depending on the role the person will play in the meeting.

9 Select additional attendees if necessary.

10 Click OK to close the dialog box.

11 Click Send.

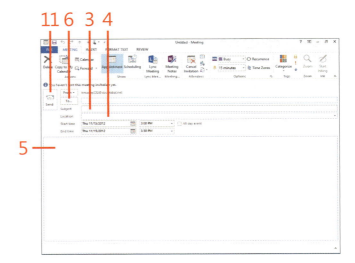

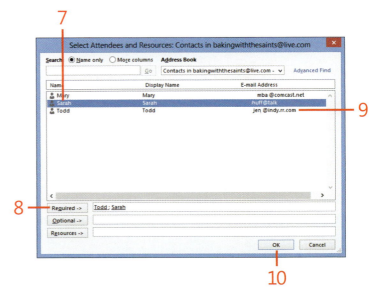

Scheduling recurring appointments

In addition to adding appointments and meetings to your calendar, you can set up scheduled events that occur on a regular basis. You can choose to repeat an appointment daily, weekly, monthly, or yearly. If you prefer you can select the day of the week on which you want the appointment to recur, and you can choose the start and end date for the recurrence, as well.

Create a recurring item

1 Select the entry on your calendar that you want to turn into a recurring item.

2 On the Calendar Tools Meeting contextual tab, click Recurrence.

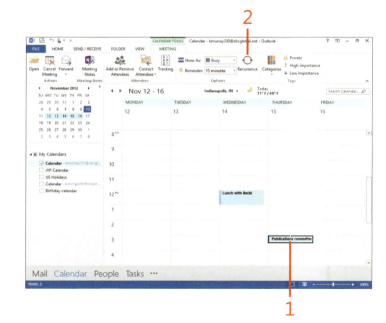

TIP If you want to change the specifics of a recurring item later, simply click the item on the calendar and click Recurrence. In the Appointment Recurrence dialog box, change the settings you need to change and click OK to save your changes.

3 Choose how often you want the event to recur.

4 Enter the number of weeks for which you want the recurrence to continue.

5 If you want the item to recur on a particular day of the week, click your choice.

6 Choose a start date for the recurrence.

7 Choose when you want the recurrence to end.

8 Click OK to save the settings.

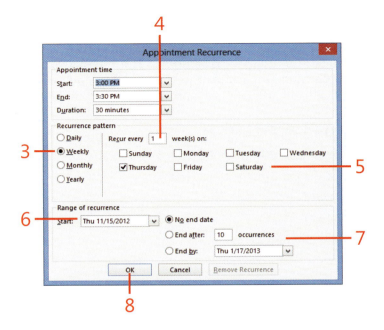

Creating and joining online meetings

From within the Outlook calendar, you can create and host online meetings by using Microsoft Lync 2013. You can also join in meetings that are already in progress.

Create online meetings

1 Select a time slot for the meeting.

2 On the Home tab, click New Lync Meeting.

3 Add attendees.

4 Add a subject.

5 Note the online meeting information added to the body of the message.

6 Click Send.

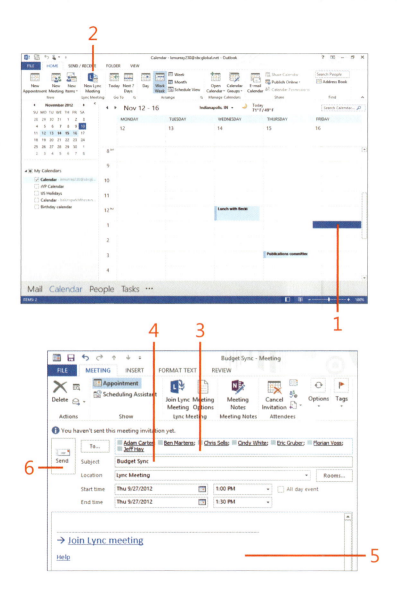

Join an online meeting

1 Right-click the online meeting.

2 In the shortcut menu that appears, choose Join Lync Meeting.

The Join Meeting Audio dialog box opens.

3 To use Lync for voice, choose Use Lync.

4 To have Lync call your phone, choose Call Me At and enter your phone number in the text box.

5 Click OK.

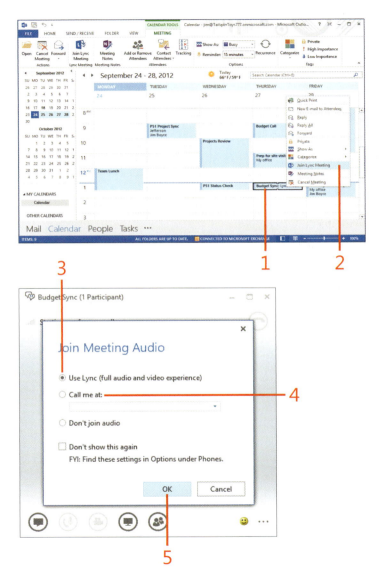

Working with calendar views

You can change the appearance of the calendar to include more information in a single window. By minimizing the Folder Pane along the left side of the window, you allow yourself more room for appointments on your calendar.

Customize the calendar display

1 Click the View tab.

2 Click Color.

3 Choose a color.

4 Click Time Scale.

5 Choose the time increment that you want to show in the calendar window.

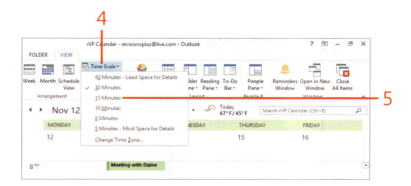

Change the layout of the calendar window

1 On the View tab, in the Layout group, click Folder Pane.

2 Click Minimized.

The Folder Pane shrinks in size to a vertical bar along the left edge of your Calendar window.

3 Click Daily Task List.

4 Click Normal.

The task list—and any tasks you've already entered—appear at the bottom of the Calendar window.

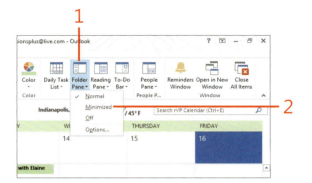

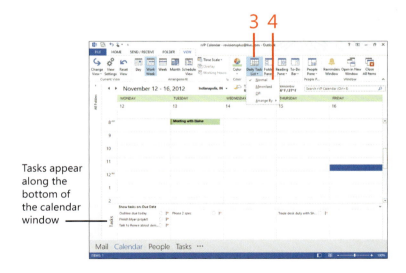

Tasks appear along the bottom of the calendar window

Using the To-Do Bar

The Outlook 2013 To-Do Bar can remind you about upcoming tasks and meetings during your day and provides a way for you to easily connect with favorite people.

Use the To-Do Bar

1 Click the View tab.

2 Click To-Do Bar.

3 Click Calendar.

4 Click People.

5 Click Tasks.

The To-Do Bar shows all of the information you have saved in each of these categories.

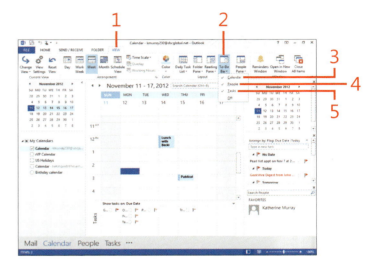

Add favorites to the To-Do Bar

1 Open an existing meeting with attendees (or create one).

2 Click the Meeting tab and then right-click a contact.

3 Choose Add to Favorites.

4 Click Close.

5 The contact is added to the Favorites area of the To-Do Bar. Click the contact to display the ways in which you can communicate with that person in real time.

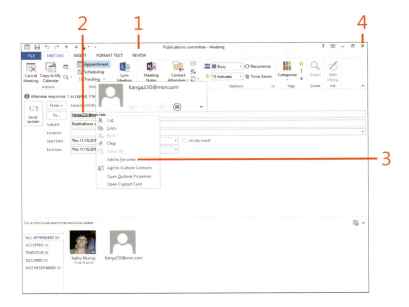

Working with team calendars

You can easily add the calendars of members of your team to your own Calendar window so that you can see at a glance when you can gather everybody in the same spot (virtually or physically). You can open the calendars shared with you by team members and even merge the calendars into a single view.

Open a calendar

1 Display the Calendar window. In the Manage Calendars group, click Open Calendar.

2 If you want to add the calendar of a team member in your Address Book, click the first option.

    The Select Name dialog box opens.

3 Click the Address Book down-arrow and choose the name of the contact list that you want to use.

4 Click the names of those whom you want to include.

5 Click Calendar.

    Outlook adds the name to the list.

6 Click OK.

    The names of the calendar owners are displayed in the Shared Calendars list at the bottom of the left pane, and the calendars are added to the Calendar window alongside your displayed calendar.

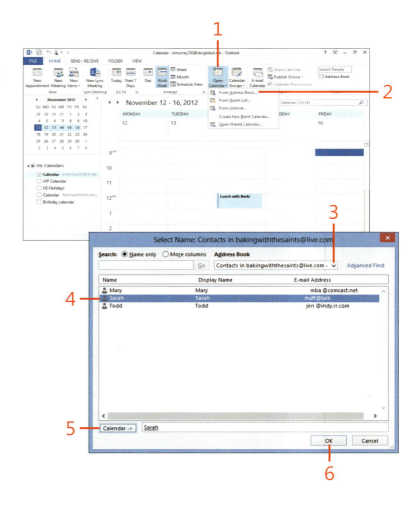

Merge shared calendars

1 In the Shared Calendar area, click the team member who owns the calendar that you want to merge.

Review that team member's calendar availability.

2 Click to merge together the calendars. Add other team members as needed.

3 Click your calendar to bring it to the front.

Creating and using calendar groups

You can create a calendar group that displays multiple calendars together so that you can easily compare dates and appointments and schedule events at a time that everyone has available.

Save a calendar group from existing calendars

1 Display the Calendar window. In the My Calendars area, select the check boxes of the calendars that you want to display.

2 On the Home tab, in the Manage Calendars group, click Calendar Groups.

3 Choose Save As New Calendar Group.

4 Type a name for the calendar group.

5 Click OK.

The new group appears in the Folder pane on the left side of the Calendar window.

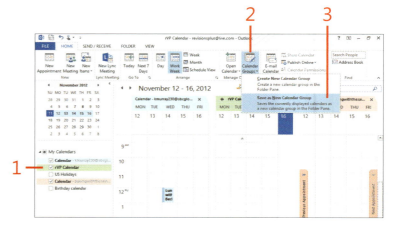

Create a new calendar group

1   On the Home tab, in the Manage Calendars group, click Calendar
    Groups.

2   Click Create New Calendar Group.

3   Type a name for the new group.

4   Click OK.

    The Select Name dialog box opens.

5   Click the names of members whom you want to include in the new
    group.

6   Click Group Members.

7   Click OK.

    Outlook creates the new calendar group and displays the group
    members in the pane on the left side of the Calendar window.

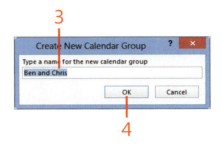

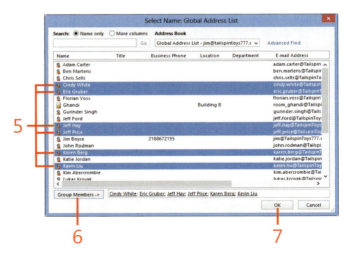

Setting calendar options

You can use the Outlook Options dialog box to choose some of the basic settings that control how Outlook behaves. You can choose how you want your calendar to appear and choose your default time zone so that your appointments and meetings are scheduled properly.

Set calendar options

1 Click the File tab to display the Backstage view.

2 Click Options.

The Outlook Options dialog box opens.

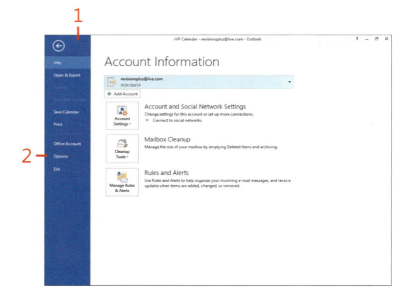

3 Click Calendar.

4 Set the options for work day start and end, days in your work week, and other options that define your work schedule.

5 Set the default reminder and other general calendar options.

6 Set the calendar display options.

7 Scroll down to display additional options.

8 Label your default time zone.

9 Select your default time zone.

10 Optionally, add another time zone to show in the Calendar.

11 Choose whether you want to automatically accept or decline meeting requests from others.

12 Set up your weather preferences.

13 Click OK when finished.

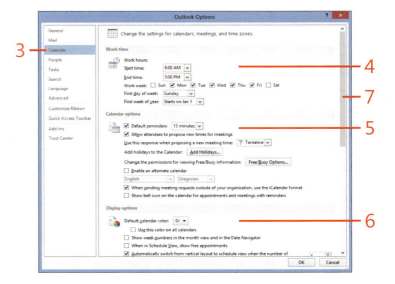

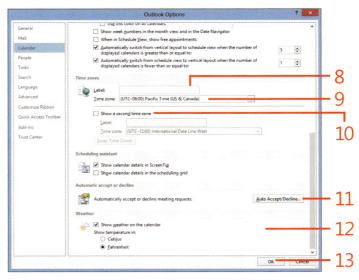

Sending your calendar by email

You can easily email the calendar you create in Outlook 2013 so that others can see at a glance what your schedule looks like. You'll find the E-mail Calendar tool on the Home tab, in the Share group.

Send a calendar by email

1 On the Home tab, click Email Calendar.

2 Choose a date range.

3 Choose the level of calendar detail to share.

4 Click OK.

5 Address the email.

6 Add a note, if desired.

7 Click Send.

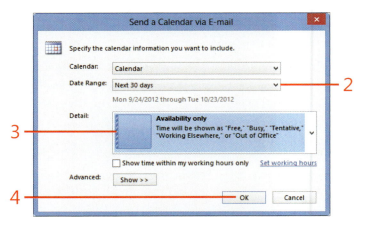

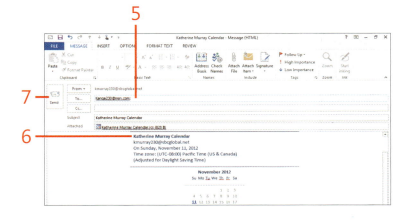

Managing people, tasks, and notes in Outlook 2013

17

You've probably noticed that Microsoft Outlook 2013 is much more than a program that you use to read, respond to, and manage your email and calendar. You can also organize and manage your contacts, which is a big job in and of itself. Plus, you can easily keep track of the various tasks you need to accomplish throughout the week and leave notes for yourself to help along the way.

The first portion of this section focuses on adding, editing, and managing contacts in Outlook 2013, which you will do via the People folder at the bottom of the Outlook window. You'll also learn how to create new tasks, assign tasks to others, and mark tasks as complete when they're done. Finally, you'll find out how to create, organize, and share notes using Outlook.

In this section:

- Adding new contacts
- Editing contacts
- Adding contact groups
- Working with people views
- Finding contacts
- Creating a new task
- Assigning a task
- Marking a task completed
- Creating and viewing notes

Adding new contacts

Once upon a time, if you're like most folks, you added contacts slowly, one at a time. Today it's possible to add entire lists of contacts from your social media accounts like Facebook and

LinkedIn with just a few clicks. When you want to add a new contact manually, Outlook 2013 makes it easy for you.

Add a new contact

1 At the bottom of the Outlook window, click People.

2 On the Home tab, click New Contact.

3 Type the contact's full name.

4 Type the contact's company name.

5 Type the contact's job title.

6 Type the contact's email address.

7 Type the contact's website address.

8 Add phone numbers as needed.

9 Add a physical address.

10 Add optional notes for the contact.

11 Click Save & Close.

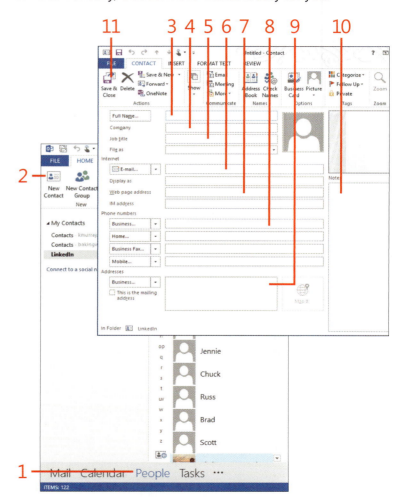

Editing contacts

The nature of working with people is that things are forever changing. We're constantly adjusting something—whether it's you or your colleagues, someone is always getting a new email address, changing a mobile phone number, moving to a different job or different position, or even just updating profile pictures. You can edit the contacts you've added to Outlook so that you're always working with the most accurate information available.

Edit a contact

1 Click the contact that you want to edit.

2 Click Edit.

3 Edit the contact name as needed.

4 Edit other fields as needed.

5 Click to add a new email address.

6 Click to add phone or Instant Message (IM) information.

7 Click Save to save the changes.

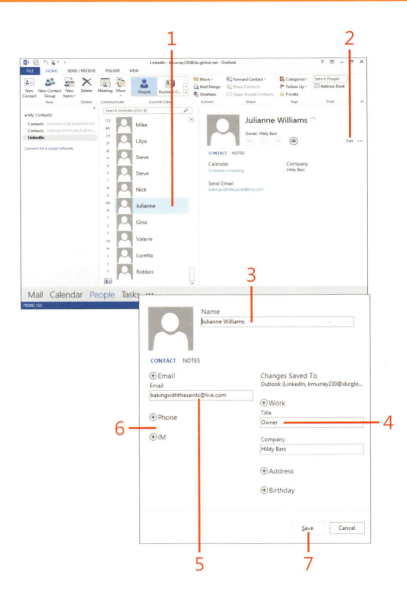

Adding contact groups

In Outlook 2013, you can create a contact group that collects the email addresses of the people you specify and then adds them all to the To line when you send an email message to the group.

Add a contact group

1 On the Home tab, click New Contact Group.

2 Click Add Members.

3 Type a name for the group.

4 Choose From Outlook Contacts or From Address Book.

The Select Members dialog box opens.

5 Select existing contacts by clicking the names of those whom you want to include.

6 Click Members.

7 Click OK.

The new members are added to the group listing in the Contact Group dialog box.

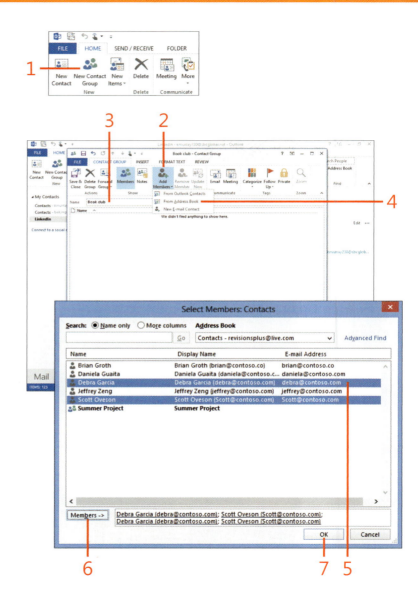

Add new members to the group

1 Display the contact group by locating the group name in your people list and double-clicking it.

2 In the Members group, click Add Members.

3 Choose New E-Mail Contact.

The Add New Member dialog box opens.

4 Type the contact's name.

5 Type the contact's email address.

6 Click OK.

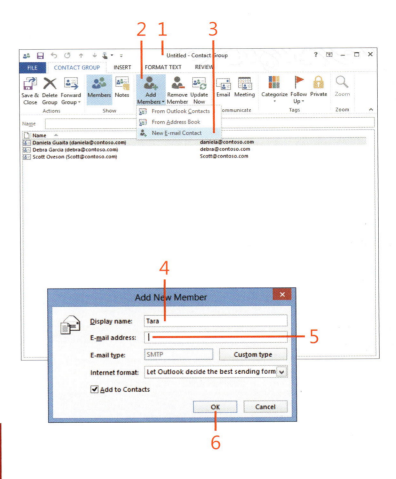

TRY THIS! To remove a group member, select a contact to remove from the group, and then on the Contact Group tab, in the Members group, click Remove Member. Click Save & Close to remove the contact from the group. Be forewarned: Outlook doesn't ask you to confirm the deletion; the contact is removed immediately. So, before you get carried away deleting folks from your group, be sure to double-check the ones you plan to delete. (But, if you do delete someone accidentally, don't worry—you can always use Add Members to return them to the group.)

Working with People view

When you're working with your contacts in Outlook 2013, you can choose a view from the Current View group in the Home tab to view your contacts in different ways. By default, contacts are shown in People view. You can also choose to display your contacts in Business Card view, which shows each person's name, picture, title, and email address, as well as the social media account on which the contact is listed, if applicable.

Display contacts in People view

1 On the Home tab, in the Current View gallery click the More button to display your view options.

2 Click the Business Card view.

Your contacts appear as though formatted for traditional business cards.

3 In the Current View gallery, choose List.

4 Click in the Company field of any contact that doesn't have a Company value.

5 Type a company name and press Enter or tap outside the field.

The contact is added to the Company group automatically.

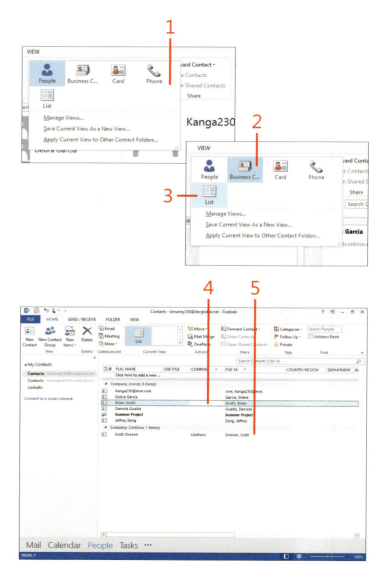

Finding contacts

Locating the contacts you need is a simple task in Outlook 2013. You can use the search Contacts box to locate contacts by typing just a few characters of a name. You can also use the search tools and Advanced Find to further narrow the focus of your search.

Find a contact

1 Click in the Search Contacts search box. Type the text you'd like to find.

The center pane shows results that match the search criteria.

2 On the Search tab, in the Options group, click Search Tools.

3 Choose Advanced Find.

The Advanced Find dialog box opens.

4 Type your search criteria.

5 Specify where to search.

6 Click Find Now.

7 Double-click the found item to open it (if desired).

8 Click to close the Advanced Find dialog box.

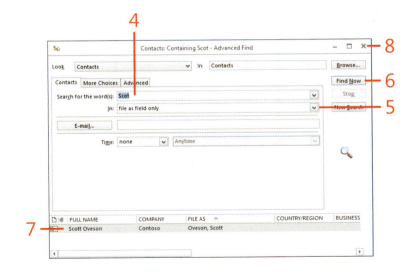

Creating a new task

If you're a list maker, you will love the task tools in Outlook 2013. You can easily add the items you need to accomplish and display the tasks in your To-Do bar, in Tasks view, or in the Quick Task list.

Create a task

1 At the bottom of the Outlook window, click Tasks.

2 On the Home tab, in the New group, click New Task.

3 Type a subject for the task.

4 Choose a start date.

5 Choose a due date.

6 Choose a status.

7 Add optional notes.

8 Click Save & Close.

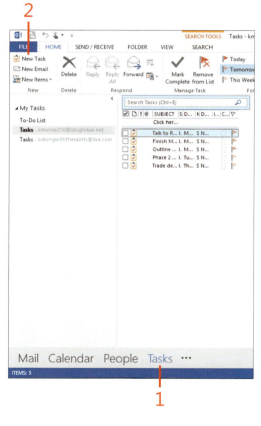

Set task properties

1 Select the task that you just created.

2 View the properties for the selected task.

3 Click the lock icon to mark the task as private and prevent others from seeing it.

4 Click the exclamation point icon to set the task priority to High.

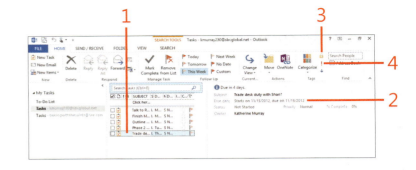

> ✓ **TIP** You can change the way your tasks are displayed by clicking Change Views in the Home tab in Task view. Choose from Detailed, Simple List, To-Do List, Prioritized, Active, Completed, Today, Next 7 Days, Overdue, Assigned, or Server Tasks. You can also choose Manage Views to display the manage All Views dialog box and apply the views you want to use with different task folders. You can also modify existing views or create your own.

Assigning a task

Luckily, you don't have to do all the tasks you create yourself.
You can assign tasks to others, as well, so that your team can
accomplish what it needs to get done and you can share the
workload.

Assign a task

1 Double-click a task to open it in the task window.

2 On the Task tab, in the Manage Task group, click Assign Task.

3 Type a recipient for the task or click To and choose a recipient.

4 Adjust the due date if needed.

5 Select Keep An Updated Copy Of This Task On My Task List check
box to keep an unassigned copy of the task in your own Tasks
folder.

6 Select Send Me A Status Report When This Task Is Complete check
box to receive a status report when the assignee marks the task as
Completed.

7 Click Send.

The person you sent the assignment to receives the notification
as an email message. When he clicks Accept, you will receive a
notification by email of the acceptance. Outlook then records the
assignment in your task list.

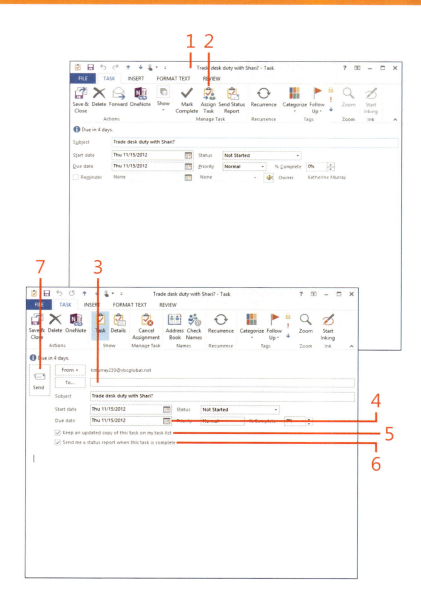

Marking a task completed

After you've finished a task, you can easily mark it as completed. That will remove the task from the active task list and show you that you're crossing items off your list.

Mark a task as complete

1 Click to select a task.

2 On the Home tab, in the Manage Task group, click Mark Complete.

3 Alternatively, right-click a task and then choose Mark Complete.

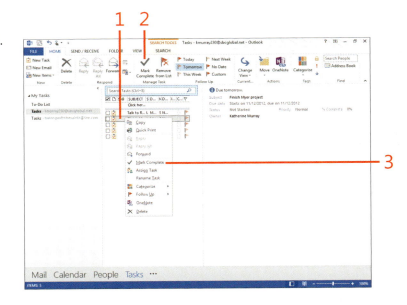

✓ **TIP** You can also select the check box to the left of the task to mark the task as complete in the task window.

Creating and viewing notes

Using the Notes tool in Outlook 2013, you can add brief text notes for any need you might have. Perhaps want to add reminders for an upcoming project, store information about an online account, or make a note to yourself about a question that

you want to ask a colleague tomorrow. You'll find the Notes tool by clicking the More control (the three dots) to the right of the Tasks selection at the bottom of the Outlook window.

Create a note

1 Click the More icon to open the navigation menu.

2 Choose Notes to open the Notes folder.

3 On the Home tab, in the New group, click New Note.

4 Enter a title for the note.

5 Add some text for the body of the note.

Outlook will use the first line as the title.

6 Click to close the note window.

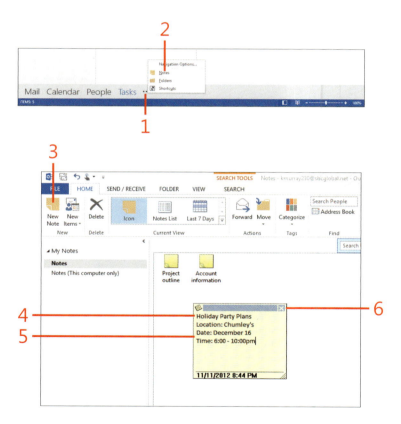

Change the way notes are displayed

1 Click the View tab.

2 Click to display the notes with small icons.

3 Click to show the notes in a list.

4 Choose View Settings to set your preferences for the way notes are displayed.

You can choose whether notes are displayed in ascending or descending order. You can also select the font to use for your notes. Click OK when you're finished entering settings.

5 Click Reset View if you want to return the notes display to the default view.

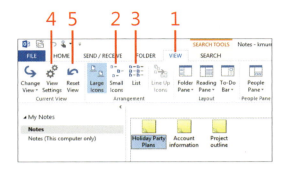

Make contact now with Lync 2013

18

Microsoft Lync 2013 is the real-time communication tool that helps tie together all your collaborative and in-the-cloud work. Whether you're engaged with with colleagues down the hall or around the world, with Lync, you can have conversations, hold meetings, share files, and work jointly.

The new features in Lync 2013 span across all its communications capabilities, from new ways of viewing your contacts, such as by group or relationship, to new ways of working in meetings. You can use Lync via a Windows Phone, iPhone, iPad, or Android device with a Lync client app, or stay in contact online via the Lync Web app. You can also place a video call and preview your own video before placing the call.

With Lync 2013 you also can take advantage of a host of new meeting features, including one-click responses to meeting invitations, the ability to create your own meeting room, and predetermine settings such as whether participants' audio will be muted and video will be blocked. Other settings also allow for a more organized meeting space. You also can now share Microsoft OneNote notes during a meeting. All of these new features make Lync an even more effective communications platform for your large or small business.

In this section:

Signing in to Lync

The first time you start Lync, you'll need to enter your user name and password, but if you select the Save My Password check box, Lync will log you on automatically for subsequent uses. You launch Lync from the Windows 8 Start screen (in Windows 7, you can use the Start button).

Start Lync 2013

1 Display the Windows 8 Start screen and scroll to the far right.

2 Click the Lync 2013 tile.

 Lync opens on your Windows 8 Desktop.

3 Type your user ID email address in the Sign-In Address text box, if needed. Usually, after you sign in the first time, you can skip this step.

4 Type your password in the Password text box. Again, if you later save your sign-in information, you also will be able to skip this step.

5 Click Sign In.

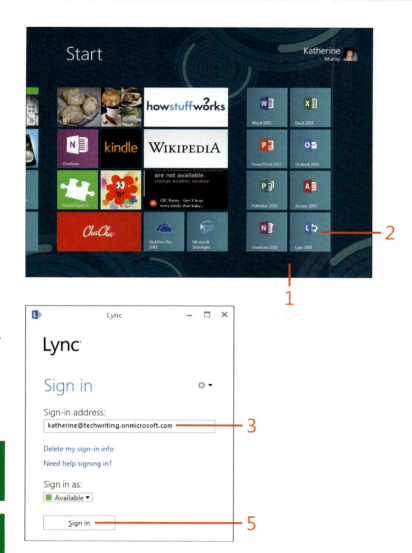

> ✓ **TIP** If you're using a Windows 7 computer, you can start Lync by clicking Start, choosing All Programs, pointing to the Microsoft Office 2013 folder, and then selecting Microsoft Lync 2013.

> ✓ **TIP** Sometimes another pop-up box or the Lync 2013 window prompts you to enter your credentials again. This is not a sign of malicious activity. Respond to the prompt and continue working.

Personalize your sign in

1 Start Lync 2013.

2 Click the status shown to the right of Sign In As.

3 Select the status to use when signing in.

Lync starts the sign-in process. If it prompts you to enter your password again, type it and click Sign In. And, if Lync asks you whether you want your sign-in information saved, click Yes.

TIP Having your password information entered automatically can be less secure in some environments. To delete saved password information, in the sign-in window, click the Delete My Sign-In Info link. When prompted to confirm that you want Lync to forget the sign-in information, click Yes.

Getting started with Lync

Lync 2013 looks and works a bit differently than the other Office 2013 applications. For one thing, Lync takes up only a portion of your screen. This is by design; that way you can view other files on your desktop while Lync is open along the left side of the screen. Lync also does not use the ribbon. Instead, it features its own variety of tools and settings, optimized for communicating. From the top down in the window, you can do the following:

- Manage various functions of your account such as your status and availability.

- Choose what action you want to perform in Lync, including setting options.

- Find contacts and choose how Lync lists contacts, such as arranging the list by groups, status, or relationships.

- Make setup choices for some features.

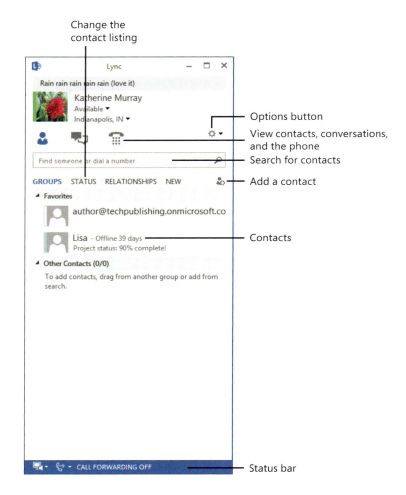

Change the contact listing

Options button

View contacts, conversations, and the phone

Search for contacts

Add a contact

Contacts

Status bar

Display and work with the Lync menu bar

1 To the right of the Options button, click the Show Menu arrow.

2 Click Show Menu Bar.

3 Click a menu name; in this case, Tools.

4 Click a setting that you want to change.

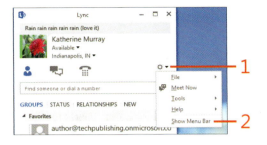

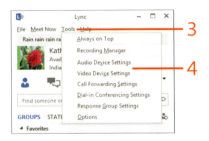

Use the Quick Lync bar

1 In your contacts list, move your mouse pointer over the picture of the contact with whom you want to interact.

2 Click the button for the activity that you want to perform: start a chat, start a call, start a video call, or view a contact card (from left to right).

Personalizing your Lync information

One of the fun aspects of Lync 2013 is its social nature; you can share what's going on with you in the What's Happening Today status area, customize your profile picture, share your location, and set your preferences for the way Lync behaves.

Update your status

1 In the Lync window, click in the status thought bubble above your picture.

Initially, it displays What's Happening Today?

2 Type your new status and press the Enter key.

Set your availability

1 Click the availability setting displayed below your user name in the Lync window.

2 Select a different availability setting.

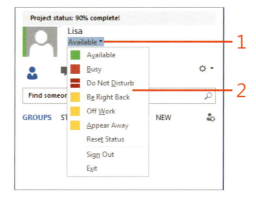

> ✓ **TIP** The bottom of the status menu offers the Sign Out and Exit choices for disconnecting from Lync and shutting down Lync completely.

Specify your location

1 In the Lync window, click the location displayed below your user name and availability.

2 Type another location and press the Enter key.

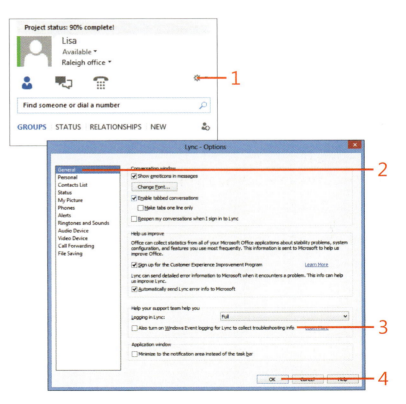

Set your Lync preferences

1 In the Lync window, click the Options button.

The Lync – Options dialog box opens.

2 Select a category.

3 Change the desired settings among those that appear in the dialog box.

4 Click OK to apply your changes.

Adding contacts

Lync 2013 makes it convenient for you to grow your contacts list and assign contacts to groups so that you can always easily find who you're looking for. You can add new contacts and assign those contacts to groups.

Create a contact group

1   In the Lync window, click the Add Contact icon.

2   Click Create A New Group.

3   In the text box that appears at the bottom of the Lync window, type the group name.

4   Press the Enter key or click outside the text box.

Add a new contact

1 In the Lync window, click the Add Contact icon.

2 Click Add A Contact That's In My Organization.

3 Begin typing the contact's name.

Lync automatically enters what you type in the search text box and displays a list of matching contacts.

4 Right-click the contact to add.

5 Choose to copy the contact to a particular group or add the contact to your Favorites list.

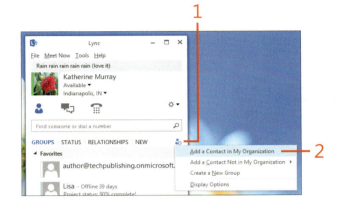

TIP After you add a contact to your Favorites list, Lync displays that contact at the top of your contact list in the Lync window so that you can easily find the contacts you work with most often.

Adding external contacts

In addition to adding contacts from your own workgroup, Lync 2013 makes it easy to add contacts that are external to your company, if the right permissions are in place.

Add an external contact

1 In the Lync window, click the Add Contact icon.

2 Click Add A Contact That's Not In My Organization.

3 Click the service the contact uses, such as Lync.

The Add Lync Contact dialog box opens

4 Type the contact's messaging ID in the IM Address text box.

5 Select a group.

6 Select a privacy relationship.

Lync suggests External Contacts by default when you add a contact via this method.

7 Click OK.

✓ **TIP** When you instruct Lync to add external contacts, messages are sent to the contact, inviting him to join your Contacts list. The recipients must respond to finish the process.

✓ **TIP** If you decide you'd rather not be in contact with someone on your list, you can block the contact. Right-click the contact name, choose Change Privacy Relationship, and then click Blocked Contacts. Click OK to confirm the operation. The contact will no longer be able to see your updates or contact you by using Lync.

View a contact card

1 Locate and right-click the contact in your Contacts list.

2 Click See Contact Card.

A contact card window for the selected individual opens.

3 Click a choice here to view a different category of information about a contact.

4 Click a choice here to instant message, voice call, video call, or send an email to the contact.

5 Click the Close button to exit the contact card window.

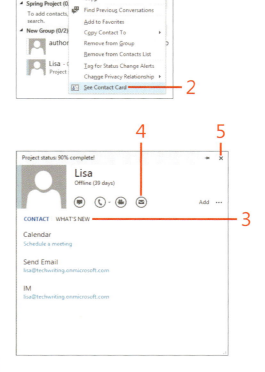

TIP By default, Lync tracks your conversations with your contacts. In the Lync window, click the Conversations icon below your location. Scroll down if needed, right-click the name for the contact with whom you had a prior conversation that you want to find again, and then click Find Previous Conversations.

Viewing and finding contacts

Being able to view your contacts as a group—or moving right to a contact with whom you want to have a conversation—gives you options for communicating in real time. You can easily see all the contacts that are currently online or sort your contacts in other ways so that you can easily find the people you need.

View your contacts

1 In the Lync window, click the Status tab.

Your Contacts list updates to display contacts grouped by status.

2 Click the Relationships tab.

Your Contacts list updates to display contacts grouped by relationship.

3 Click the New tab.

Your Contacts list updates to display contacts who have recently added you as contacts so that you can be sure you add them to your Contacts list.

4 Click the Groups tab.

Your Contacts list returns to the default display by group.

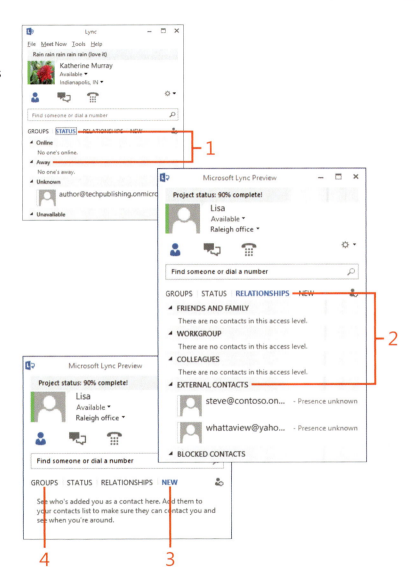

Find a contact

1 Click in the Find Someone Or Dial A Number text box.

2 Begin typing the contact name. Alternatively, you can move your mouse pointer over the contact name to display the Quick Lync toolbar.

3 Right-click a found contact to view options for working with that person.

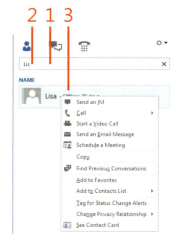

✓ **TIP** You can instruct Lync how you prefer to display contact information by clicking the Options button in the Lync window, and then in the Lync Options dialog box, choose the Contacts List category. Change any settings you'd like to modify. For example, under Display My Contacts With, you can control whether pictures display in the Contacts list. Under Order My list, you can choose either By Name or By Availability to control how Lync sorts the Contacts list. And, under Show This Information, select the details about the contact that appear in the list.

Having instant conversations

If you've used any kind of instant messaging (IM) program, like Windows Live Messenger or the Messaging app in Windows 8, you'll feel comfortable using the IM feature in Lync 2013. The process is simple: Just choose a contact, send a message, and reply to the messages you receive.

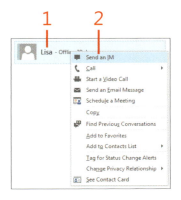

Send an instant message

1 In your Contacts list, right-click a contact.

2 Click Send An IM.

A conversation window opens.

3 Type your message text in the conversation window and press the Enter key.

Your message text appears in your conversation window as well as your contact's conversation window. Your contact's typed response will appear below the latest text you sent.

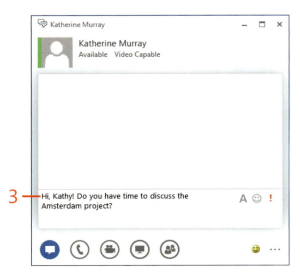

4 Scroll the conversation as needed by using the scroll bar at right.

5 Click the conversation window Close button to conclude the IM session.

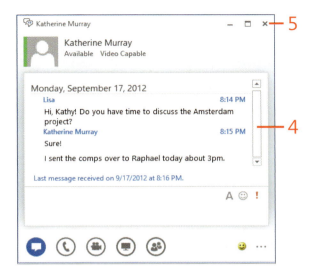

Making phone calls with Lync

Another natural and easy task in Lync 2013 is making calls. Whether you want to make audio calls or video calls, both are equally simple to do. Before you can make a video call, of course, you'll need a web camera connected to your computer.

You'll be able to determine whether your contacts are able to participate in a video call because you will see Video Capable listed in the contact information to the right of the contact name.

Set up your audio device

1   After installing your audio device hardware on your system, in the Lync window, click the Options button.

The Lync – Options dialog box opens.

2   In the categories pane on the left, click Audio Device.

3   Use the sliders to adjust the volumes for Speaker, Microphone, and Ringer.

4   Click OK.

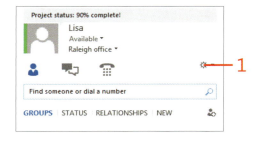

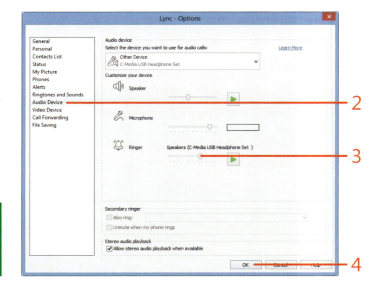

> ✓ **TIP**   If more than one audio device is installed on your computer, ensure that the correct audio device is selected from the Select The Device You Want To Use for Audio Calls drop-down list, above the Customize Your Device Sliders.

Make a Lync call

1 In your Contacts list, right-click a contact.

2 Click Call to display a submenu.

3 Click Lync Call.

A conversation window opens.

4 Talk normally, using the volume and mute controls on your audio device as needed.

5 Click the Hang Up button to conclude the call.

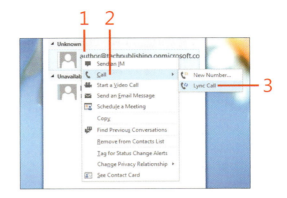

Making video calls with Lync

Lync makes participating in a video call as simple as sending an instant message. After you set up your video device and get your sound set, engaging in a video call is as simple as clicking a button and making contact.

Set up your video device

1 After installing your webcam device hardware on your system, in the Lync window, click the Options button.

The Lync – Options dialog box opens.

2 In the categories pane on the left, click Video Device.

3 Click Camera Settings.

The Properties dialog box for the video device opens.

4 Use the sliders on the two tabs of the Properties dialog box to adjust various camera settings.

5 Click OK to close the Properties dialog box.

6 Click OK.

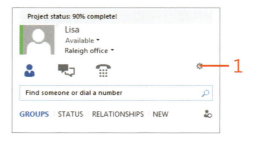

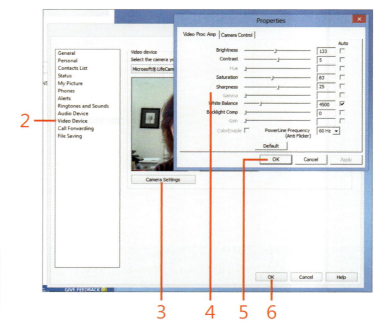

> ✓ **TIP** If more than one video device has been installed on your computer, ensure that the correct video device is selected from the Select The Camera You Want To Use For Video Calls drop-down list, above the camera picture preview.

Make a video call

1 In your Contacts list, right-click a contact.

2 Click Start A Video Call.

3 Talk normally, using the volume and mute controls on your audio device as needed.

4 Click the Hang Up button to conclude the call.

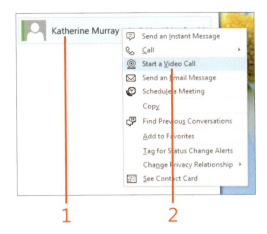

> **TIP** You might occasionally see error messages such as "Your mic is picking up a lot of noise" in a yellow bar in the conversation window. Click the Close button at the right end of the warning, and make any needed adjustments such as changing the position of your microphone.

> **TIP** To record a call, click the More Options button in the conversation window and then click Start Recording. This adds the recording controls to the bottom of the conversation window. Click the Record button and then click the Stop button when you are finished recording. After the recording, it might take a while for your system to finish building the file for the recording. Check the Recording Manager to ensure that your system has finished creating and saving the recording file.

Creating publications with Publisher 2013

19

Microsoft Publisher 2013 is an easy-to-use publishing program with which you can create all sorts of documents you might otherwise pay a designer or print shop to do for you. With Publisher, you can create simple projects like greeting cards, labels, and invitations, or more complex publications like reports, brochures, and catalogs.

You can easily arrange the text and pictures on the page just as you want them, creating a mutlticolumn effect, adding special text enhancements, and controlling the way the text flows from column to column or page to page. You can start by choosing a ready-made design and then add in your own context to produce a professional-looking publication in a snap. And, you can control the way all the items on the page appear by layering and arranging objects exactly as you want them. This section shows you how to get started creating a new Publisher project and how to add text, pictures, and tables along the way.

In this section:

- Launching Publisher 2013
- Choosing a template
- Modifying the publication
- Setting up pages
- Adding and importing text
- Linking text boxes
- Formatting text
- Adding pictures
- Editing and adding style to pictures
- Inserting tables
- Arranging and grouping page elements
- Finalizing your publication

Launching Publisher 2013

Just like all the other apps in Microsoft Office, starting Publisher 2013 is quick and easy, whether you're running in Windows 8 or Windows 7. Either way, after the program launches, you will notice the new, clean look of the Publisher 2013 window.

Launch Publisher

1 In Windows 8, swipe or scroll to display the app tiles that are out of view, beyond the right side of the screen.

In Windows 7, click the Start button, click All Programs, and then in the Microsoft Office 2013 folder, choose Publisher 2013.

2 Click the Publisher 2013 tile. The program opens on your Windows 8 Desktop.

Create a blank publication

1 Launch Publisher from the Windows 8 Start screen or by using the Start button in Windows 7.

The Publisher Start screen appears.

2 Click Blank to open a blank publication.

The new blank publication opens in the Publisher work area.

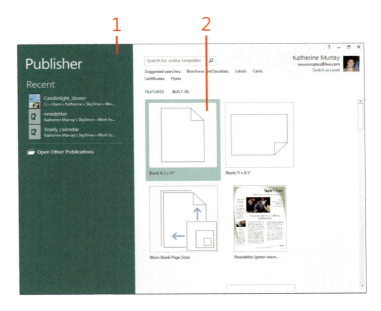

Choosing a template

Whether you want to create a simple invitation, a flyer for your garage sale, or an elaborate, four-color business plan that you will have printed by a commercial printer, Publisher 2013 makes the entire process of starting a publication easy. You can choose from a wide variety of professionally designed templates to get a good start on the look you want for your project.

Start a new publication based on a template

1   Click File to display the Backstage view.

2   Click the New tab.

3   Scroll down and choose the template that you want to use to start a new publication.

4   Alternatively, click in the Search box and type a word or phrase for the type of template you'd like to find.

5   Click Search.

   The results page shows you templates found that match the text you entered in the Search box.

6 Select the template that you'd like to use.

7 You can also select a Category in the Filter By column to search for additional templates in the categories listed.

8 Review the description of the template.

9 If you want to cancel the template and return to searching, click the close icon.

10 To open a new publication based on the selected template, click Create.

The file opens in the work area, using the color scheme, font, and layout of the template file.

TIP Remember to click Save in the Quick Access Toolbar to save your publication. The Save As screen of the Backstage view appears. Select a location to save the file, and then in the Save As dialog box, enter a name for the file and click Save.

Modifying the publication

After you open the file based on the template, there probably will be lots of changes that you want to make to the publication. You might want to choose your own color scheme, select fonts, or add or change a page background for your file, even before you start adding any text and pictures.

Modify the publication

1 Click the Page Design tab.

Publisher displays tools with which you can set up the page, add layout guides, work with pages, and customize the color scheme, fonts, and background used for your file.

2 Click the Schemes arrow.

A gallery of color schemes appears.

3 Scroll through the list to see all the available color schemes.

4 Click the color scheme that you want to use.

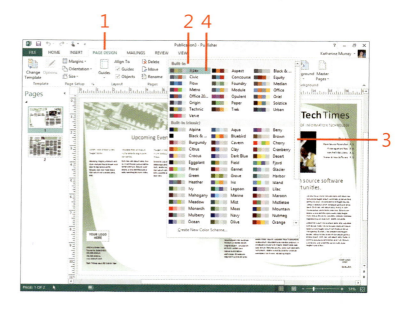

5 Click Fonts to display a gallery of font selections.

6 Click the font selection that you want to apply to the publication.

7 In the Page Background group, click Background.

8 Click the background style that you want to add to the publication.

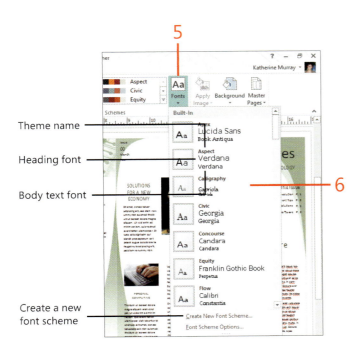

Theme name

Heading font

Body text font

Create a new
font scheme

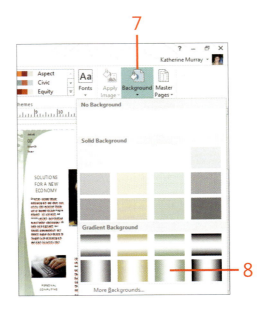

TIP For non-touchscreen users, if you're not sure which color scheme you want to select, hover the mouse over the one you're considering and Publisher previews it in the publication for you. You can simply click the one you want to keep, and Publisher does the rest.

Setting up pages

The settings you use to set up your page indicate to Publisher a number of important things about the document you're creating, including the page size, orientation, and margins. You can also choose the overall layout type for your publication, whether you want a traditional one-page-per-sheet selection, or whether you are creating a booklet, envelope, website, or other project.

Choose page setup options

1   With your document open in Publisher, click the Page Design tab.

2   In the Page Setup group, click the dialog box launcher to display the Page Setup dialog box.

3   Click the Layout Type arrow to display a list of layout choices for the current publication.

4   Select the layout that fits the type of publication that you are creating.

5   Click the Page arrows to change the width and height of the page.

6   Click to change the placement of margin guides along the top, bottom, left, and right sides of the page.

7   Review your changes in the Preview area.

8   Click OK to save your changes.

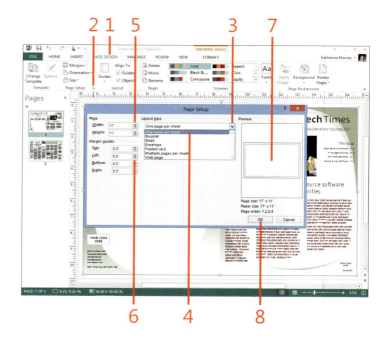

Insert pages

1 Click the Insert tab.

2 In the Pages group, click the Page arrow.

3 Click Insert Page.

4 Type the number of pages that you want to insert.

5 Choose whether you want to add the pages before or after the current page.

6 Choose whether you want to add a completely blank page, a page with a text box, or duplicates of objects on the currently selected page.

7 Click OK to add the page(s).

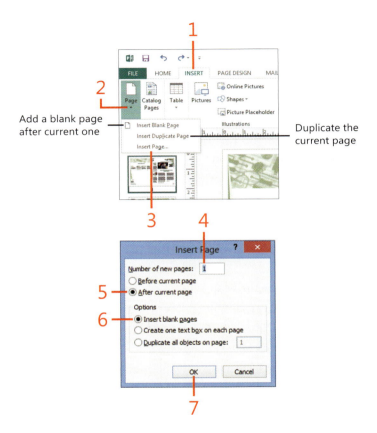

Add a blank page after current one

Duplicate the current page

Adding and importing text

You add text in Publisher inside text boxes that you can move, resize, and link as you'd like. This makes it easy for you to flow text around various elements on your page without a lot of fuss and bother. You can type directly into Publisher or import text from another program such as Microsoft Word. Additionally, Publisher keeps track of information about your business that you've entered, and you can insert it or edit it as you'd like.

Add new text

1 Click the Home tab.

2 In the Text group, click Draw Text Box.

    The pointer changes to a cross-hair cursor.

3 Drag a rectangle on the page. When it is the size you want, release the mouse button.

    Publisher displays the text box on the page.

4 Type the text that you want to add to the text box. When you're finished adding text, click outside the box.

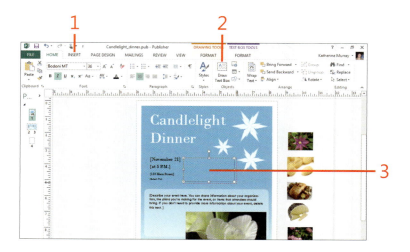

Import text

1 Display the page on which you want to add the new content.

2 Click the Insert tab.

3 In the Text group, click Insert File.

Publisher adds a text box on the page and displays the Insert Text dialog box.

4 Navigate to the folder that contains the file you want to import.

5 Click the file.

6 Click OK.

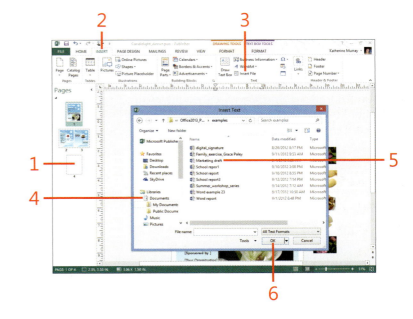

 CAUTION Depending on the format of the text you import, you might have some reformatting to do after you insert the file.

Linking text boxes

When you have text that needs to flow from box to box or column to column, you can easily link the text boxes so that the text flows appropriately when you make changes to it. You might have already created a text box in the task "Add new task," earlier in this section. If not, follow the steps in that task to add the first text box to your page. Enter enough text that not all of it can be displayed in that first text box.

Link text boxes

1   Create a second text box into which the overflow text will flow.

2   Click the first text box to select it.

The overflow indicator appears, letting you know that the text box contains more text than it can fit.

3   Click the overflow indicator.

The pointer changes to resemble a pitcher.

4   Click in the second text box to flow the text into that frame.

The remaining text flows into the space.

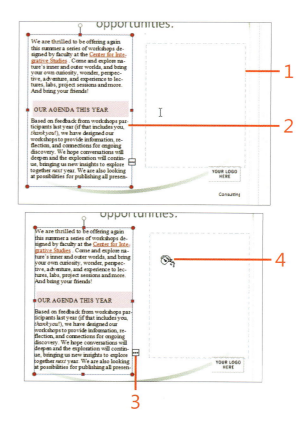

> ✓ **TIP** To control how your text flows around the pictures and shapes in your publication, in the Text Box Tools Format contextual tab, use the Wrap Text tool. Publisher offers a number of wrapping styles. You can also use Edit Wrap Points to create a unique shape for the text flow around the images on your page.

Formatting text

Formatting text in Publisher isn't much different from formatting text in Word or Microsoft PowerPoint; you can select the text and use the formatting toolbar to make simple changes. You can also use the tools in the Text Box Tools Format contextual tab to apply quick styles, change text color, adjust spacing, and employ higher-end typographical tools to fine-tune the appearance of your text.

Format text

1 Display the page with which you want to work.

2 Highlight the text that you want to change.

The formatting toolbar appears.

3 Change the font and size.

4 Change text color.

5 To view other formatting choices, click the Text Tools Format contextual tab.

6 To apply a style to the selected text, click Quick Styles.

7 Click to add special effects to the highlighted text.

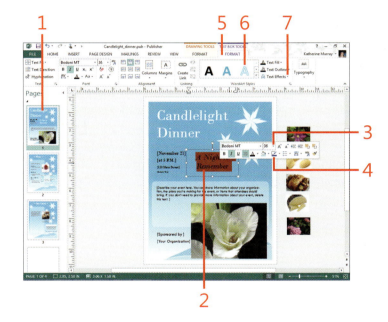

Adding pictures

The picture capabilities in Publisher 2013 have been enhanced, giving you the ability to work with multiple pictures more easily as you choose and place them in your document. In earlier versions of Publisher, whenever you added multiple pictures, they were clumped together in a pile in the center of your publication and you had to drag them to where you wanted them to appear. Now, Publisher places your pictures in the scratch area alongside your publication so that you can easily view and select the ones you want to use on the different pages in your document.

Insert a picture

1 Display the page on which you want to add a picture.

2 Click the Insert tab.

3 Click the tool in the Illustrations group that you want to use.

Choose Pictures if you have a picture on your computer that you want to add; select Online Pictures to download pictures from Bing, Office.com, your own picture-sharing sites, or your SkyDrive account. Click Shapes to display a gallery of shapes that you can add to your publication.

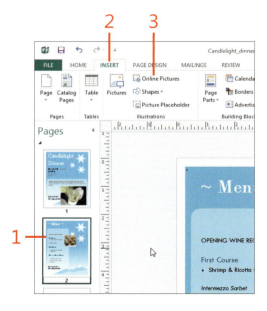

4 For example, click Online Pictures.

The Insert Pictures dialog box opens.

5 Enter a word or phrase to search Office.com for art related to that topic. Select the image that you want to use and click Insert.

6 Search the web for the images that you want to include. When you find a picture that fits your needs, select it and click Insert to add it to the page.

7 Choose a picture from an online picture sharing site to which you've connected Office 2013.

8 Click to select a photo from your SkyDrive account.

After you make your choice, Publisher downloads the file and inserts it at the cursor position.

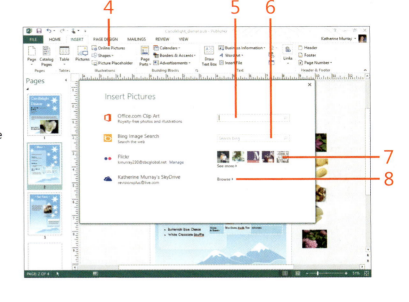

TIP Choose Picture Placeholder if you want to add a picture placeholder box on the Publisher page so that you can add a picture at a later time.

TIP One new feature in Publisher 2013 makes things easier when you'd like to open a number of pictures that you plan to place on your Publisher pages. In the Insert Picture dialog box, you can navigate to a folder containing all the photos you need. Select all the files you want to open and then click Insert. Publisher places the images as thumbnails along the right side of your page, in the scratch area. You can then move the pictures to the places in the document you want them to appear by simply dragging them to the new location.

Editing and adding style to pictures

Publisher 2013 includes some easy-to-use editing tools with which you can correct and enhance the pictures you place in your publication. Publisher displays convenient visual galleries that show the actual image on the page you've selected. This makes it possible for you to see at a glance which color brightness looks best or preview the styles you're considering adding to your images.

Edit a picture

1 Click the picture that you want to edit.

2 Click the Picture Tools Format contextual tab.

3 In the Adjust group, click Corrections.

4 Click the selection that offers the brightness and contrast that you feel looks best.

5 If you want to change the color of the image, click Recolor.

6 To choose a different color scheme for your image, click More Variations.

7 Click the color that you want to apply to the picture on the page.

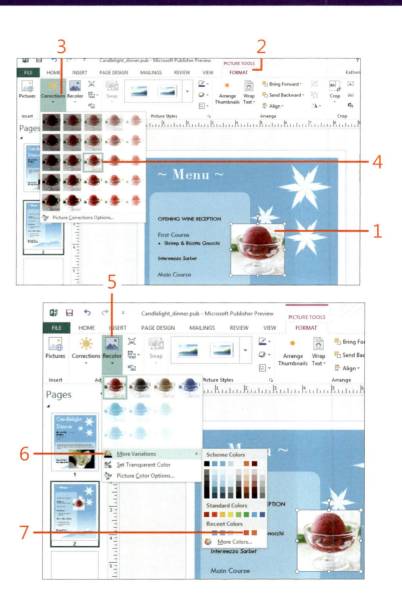

Add a picture style

1 Select the picture that you want to change.

2 Click the Picture Tools Format contextual tab.

3 Click to display the Picture Styles gallery.

You can preview the different styles in the gallery by pointing to the styles you like; Publisher shows the effect on your picture.

4 Click the style that you want to apply to the selected image.

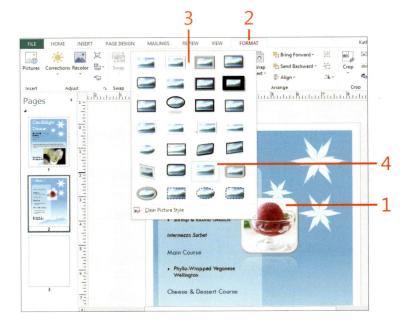

Inserting tables

You can use tables to showcase information in an easy-to-understand format for your readers. You might use a table to compare new products, to list the features of a new service, or to give your readers information about upcoming workshops. Publisher includes an intuitive Table tool that you can use to create and then customize the tables you need.

Add a table

1 Display the page on which you want to add the table.

2 Click the Insert tab.

3 Choose Table.

The Insert Table grid appears, in which you can choose the number columns and rows you want to create in your table.

4 Highlight the number of rows and columns you want to include.

When you release the mouse button, Publisher adds the table to your page, and you can add content to the table as needed.

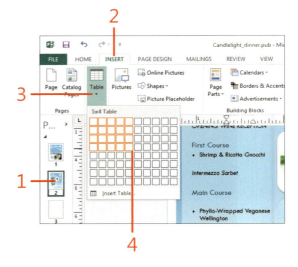

Format a table

1 Click the table on the page.

2 Click the Table Tools Design contextual tab.

3 In the Tablet Formats group, click the More button.

4 Position the pointer over the formats you'd like to preview; Publisher applies that format to the table on your page. When you find the format you like, select it to add it to your table.

5 If you want to change the background color of your table, select it by clicking the table border.

6 In the Table Formats group, click Fill.

7 Click the color that you want to apply.

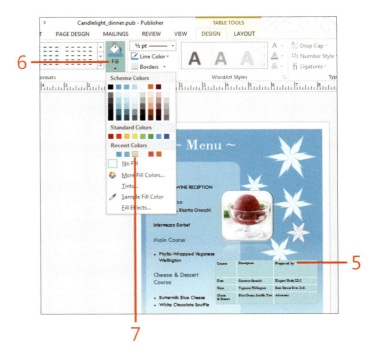

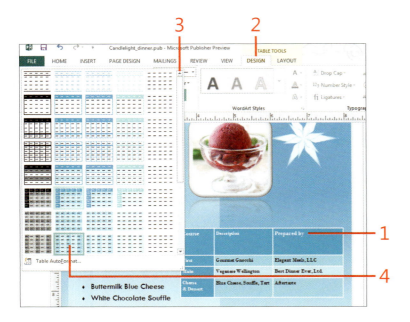

Arranging and grouping page elements

Some designs are simple and straightforward; others are more elaborate, requiring a little design finesse. If you have numerous objects on your page, the chances are that you'll have to deal with some overlap. You might, for example, want to position a picture slightly behind a headline, or group a picture and caption together so that text flows around them both. You can use the Arrange tools in Publisher to layer and arrange page elements just the way you want them.

Arrange objects

1   Click the object that you want to reorder.

2   Click the Picture Tools Format contextual tab.

3   Choose either Bring Forward or Send Backward.

A list of options appears. If you choose Bring Forward, you can choose Bring To Front, which brings the selected element to the front of the page, or Bring Forward, which moves the object one layer forward in the layers of objects on the page.

4   If you choose Send Backward, you can select Send Backward, which moves the object one layer down, or you can select Send to Back, which moves the object behind everything else on the page.

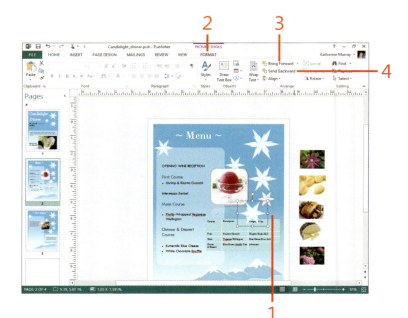

> ⚠ **CAUTION**   If you choose Send To Back and you have added a page background, your object might disappear completely! Don't panic: you can reverse the process by pressing Ctrl+Z to Undo your last action or by clicking Bring Forward and selecting Bring Forward.

Group page elements

1 Select the first object that you want to group.

2 Click additional objects that you want to include in the group.

3 Click the Picture Tools Format contextual tab.

4 In the Arrange group, click Group.

The outlines of the objects combine so that you can easily see that they have been grouped together.

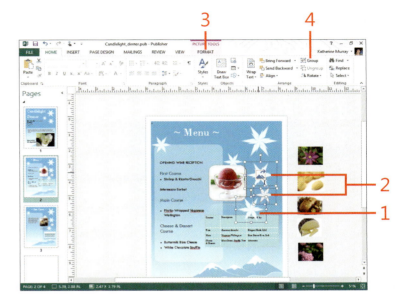

TIP If you decide later than you want to separate the items back to individual objects, click the grouped object, click the Picture Tools Format contextual tab, and then choose Ungroup (just beneath the Group tool). The objects are separated into their original configurations.

Finalizing your publication

Before you share your publication with others or release it to the wild, you should preview the document to ensure that it looks in its final form as you expect it to. You can use Publisher's Print tools to get a good last look at the publication, and you can run the Design Checker to ensure that your project is ready to be completed.

Run the Design Checker

1 Click the File tab to display the Backstage view.

2 Click Run Design Checker.

The Design Checker opens in a pane along the right side of the Publisher window.

3 Position the mouse pointer over the item in the list that you want to fix and click the arrow that appears. A list of options displays, offering ways to deal with the issue.

4 Choose Go To This Item to move to the object in your publication that triggered the issue.

5 Click Explain to see Help information on the topic.

6 Select this option to run another check for other formats (final publishing, website, or email checks).

7 Click to close the Design Checker.

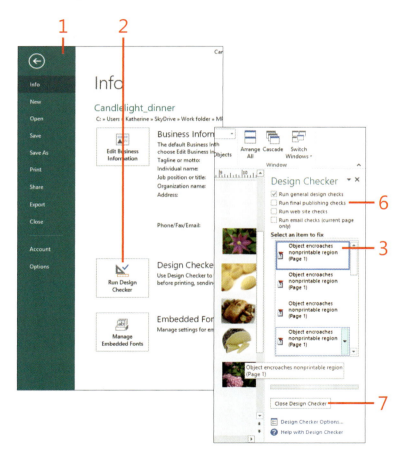

Preview and print your publication

1 Click the File tab to display the Backstage view.

2 Click the Print tab.

3 Review the publication in the preview window.

4 Browse through the pages in your document.

5 Increase or decrease page size.

6 Hide or redisplay the horizontal and vertical rulers.

7 Choose the printer that you want to use.

8 Choose print settings.

9 Enter the number of copies that you want to print.

10 Click Print.

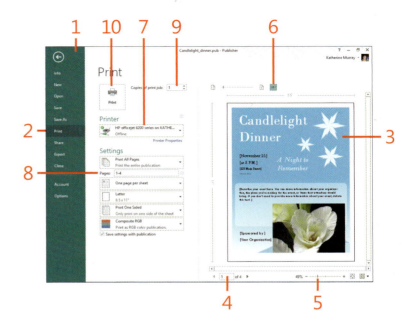

Creating a desktop database with Access 2013

20

If you remember Microsoft Access as the program in the Microsoft Office suite that you couldn't imagine yourself ever needing, you might want to take a new look at Access 2013. The new features it offers make it possible for you to create apps that you can use over the web to collect and work with the data you need to keep things moving. Now, Access distinguishes between the types of databases you create for use on your local computer (meaning they don't need to live online) and the apps you post and use online. According to Access terminology, the data you gather and store on your computer is stored in a *desktop database*, and the data you gather and store online is managed by using *web apps*.

One of the interesting things about this release of Office is that it is available to you through different channels. You can get it through Office 365 (*www.office365.com*), the subscription-based, in-the-cloud model. In Office 365, Access is available to you if you've subscribed to the Office 365 plans E3 or E4. If you have subscribed to a different plan—for example, the small business plan—you can add Office Professional Plus, which includes Access 2013, to your plan. If you would rather purchase the traditional, in-the-box version of the Office suite, be sure to get Office 2013 Professional if you want to use Access 2013.

In this section:

- Starting Access 2013
- Creating a new desktop database
- Preparing your data table
- Adding your data
- Importing data
- Creating table relationships
- Creating a simple form
- Creating reports

Starting Access 2013

When you start Access 2013, the app opens by presenting the Access Start screen, where you can choose a template or start a new blank desktop database or custom web app.

Start Access

1 On the Windows 8 Start screen, scroll or swipe to the right end of the Start screen to display the Office 2013 app tiles that are out of view.

   In Windows 7, click the Start button, click All Programs, and then in the Microsoft Office 2013 folder, choose Access 2013.

2 Click the Access 2013 tile.

   The Access 2013 Start screen appears.

✓ **TIP** For non-touchscreen users, when working on the desktop, if you hover over the lower left of your screen on the taskbar and click the miniaturized Desktop tile, you will be able to quickly return to the Windows Desktop tile where other Office 2013 apps can be started.

Use the Start screen

1 Click to create a new blank desktop database.

2 Alternatively, click to begin a new custom web app.

3 Scroll through the available templates.

4 If you want to start a new project based on a template, click the template that you want to use.

5 To search for a specific type of template, you can type a word or phrase and click the Search tool.

6 Open a recent project by clicking the file in the Recent list.

7 Click Open Other Files to display the Open screen, in which you can select a file from another location.

TRY THIS! Display the Access 2013 Start screen and browse through the templates available to you. Notice the desktop templates as well as the templates that you can use to create web apps. This is a new feature in Access 2013.

Creating a new desktop database

If you already have in mind what data you want to collect and how you want to do it, you can create your own blank desktop database. Creating the database is a simple process. After you create the desktop database, you can begin to add data in a manner that fits your needs.

Create a blank desktop database

1 On the Access 2013 Start screen, click Blank Desktop Database.

2 Enter the file name for your database.

3 Click Create.

The blank desktop database opens on your screen, ready to accept the data you want to enter.

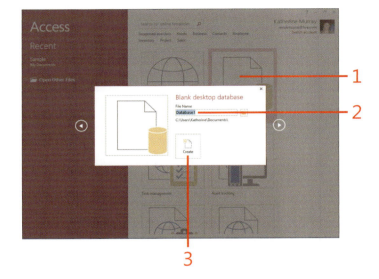

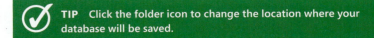

TIP Click the folder icon to change the location where your database will be saved.

Start a database from a template

1 Click the Access 2013 tile to display the Access Start screen.

2 Scroll down through the templates in the list.

Note that the templates that begin with the word "Desktop" (such as Desktop Asset Tracking or Desktop Issue Tracking) are the templates with which you create a new desktop database file. If you choose one of the other templates (such as Project Management), you will be creating a web app that shares data with SharePoint online.

3 Alternatively, type a word or phrase to search for a particular type of template.

4 Click the Start Searching icon.

5 Click the template in the list that fits the type of database that you want to create.

A dialog box opens, giving you more information about the template.

6 Type a new name for the database.

7 Click Create.

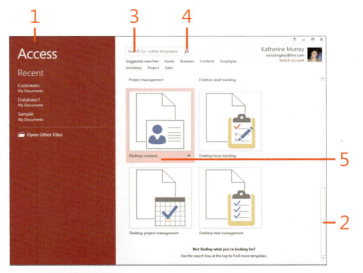

Preparing your data table

It's a pretty simple task to add data to your database. You can click a blank spot and type the information that you want to go there. After that, you press Tab to move to the next column. Easy, right? But, to manage your data effectively, you need to ensure that you set up your tables to store the data in the manner that you need it stored. This means that you might need to add new tables (especially if you've created a blank database), add fields (or rename the ones you have), and get your tables ready for the data you'll add. If you have just created a blank desktop database, your blank file will include a default table called Table 1. If you've used a template, tables will already be included in the new file you create.

Create a new data table

1   Open your database file.

2   Click the Create tab.

3   In the Tables group, click Table.

The new table appears in the Objects pane along the left side of Datasheet View.

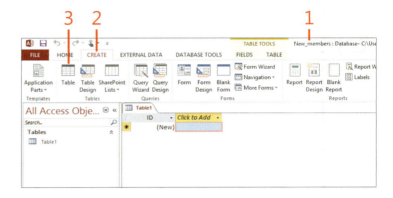

Add fields to your table

1 Click the field in the table after which you want to add the new field.

2 Click the Fields tab.

3 In the Add & Delete group, click the type of field that you want to add.

4 If you don't see the data type you want, click More Fields to display a list of data types and then click the one you want.

Access adds the new field to the column list and highlights the name of the new field.

5 Type the name that you want to assign the new field. Click outside the field to save your changes.

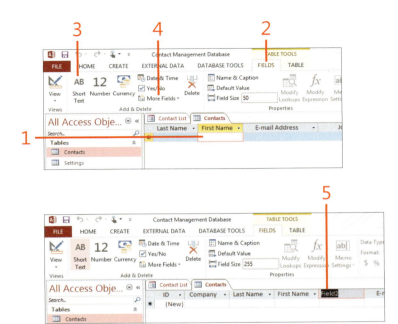

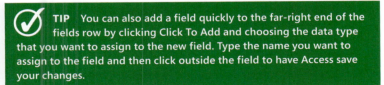

TIP You can also add a field quickly to the far-right end of the fields row by clicking Click To Add and choosing the data type that you want to assign to the new field. Type the name you want to assign to the field and then click outside the field to have Access save your changes.

Adding your data

Entering data in your database is simple, depending on the type of database you've chosen to create. If you've created a blank database, you'll need to add fields so that Access knows how to categorize the data you add in the data tables. If you created your database based on a template, the fields will have already been created for you.

Add data to a datasheet

1 In the Navigation pane, open the table that you want to use by double-clicking it.

2 Click the new record icon.

3 Type data in the first field.

The record selector at the left end of the row will change to show a pencil icon, indicating that you are editing the data. Press Tab to move to the next field. When you press Tab after the field on the far right of the Datasheet, Access moves the highlight to the next record.

4 Continue adding data as needed. Click any other record to save your changes.

5 The record selector will change when the record is saved.

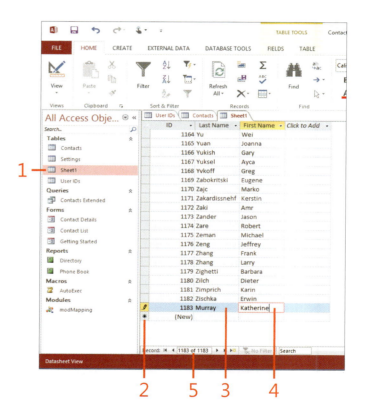

> **TIP** To change the format of the datasheet, on the Home tab, in the lower-right corner of the Text Formatting group, click the dialog launcher icon. The Datasheet Formatting dialog box opens, in which you can change whether you want the cells in the datasheet to look flat (the default), sunken, or raised; you can choose which gridlines you want to display; and you can change the background color of alternate rows by choosing new colors in the Background Color and Alternate Color options. Click OK after you've made your changes and the datasheet will reflect your new settings.

Importing data

If you've been collecting data in other places—perhaps in a text file or an Excel spreadsheet—you can easily import your data into Access 2013 so that you don't have to type it all again. You use the External Data tab to bring that information into your desktop database.

Import data

1 Click the External Data tab.

2 In the Import & Link group, click Access.

The Get External Database dialog box opens.

3 Click the Browse button. In the File Open dialog box, navigate to the file that you want to open, click it, and then select Open. The file name is added to the Get External Data dialog box.

4 Leave the Import Tables option selected.

5 Click OK.

The Import Objects dialog box opens.

6 Click Select All. Alternatively, select the name of the table that you want to import.

7 Click OK.

8 Click Close without choosing to save the import steps.

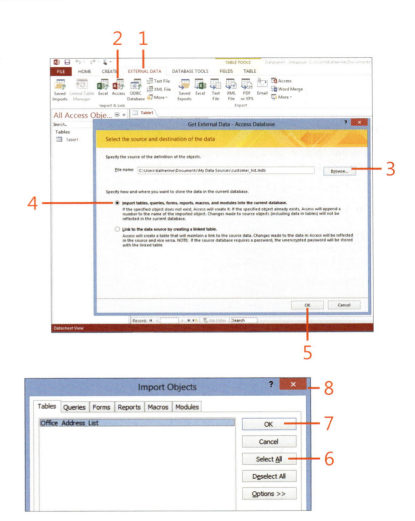

Creating table relationships

With Access 2013, you can easily connect the data tables you create so that you can look up information among all your connected tables. To create a relationship between tables, each table needs to have its own primary key field, which is the field that stores a unique identifier for each record in the table. That same field appears in the table with which you're creating a relationship, and in that table, the field is identified as the foreign key. For example, the User ID field in the User IDs table is a primary key. That same field in the Contacts table is the foreign key. You can create several types of table relationships with your data tables: one-to-one (which is what you'll learn about here); one-to-many, in which data from one table can be used in a number of different tables; and many-to-many, in which there are multiple ways the data can be used.

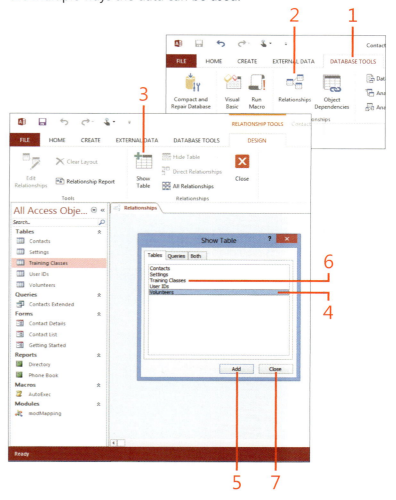

Define a relationship

1 Click the Database Tools tab.

2 Click Relationships.

The Relationship Tools Design contextual tab appears.

3 Click Show Table.

The Show Table dialog box opens.

4 Select the name of one table that you want to add to the relationship.

5 Click Add.

Access adds a table box listing that table's fields to the Relationships area.

6 Select the second table and then click Add.

That table's field list also appears.

7 Click Close.

8 Locate the primary key field in the first table and drag it to the field in the second table with which you want to create the relationship.

This field in the second table will become the foreign key field. The Edit Relationships dialog box opens.

9 Click Create to create the relationship and then click Close to close the dialog box.

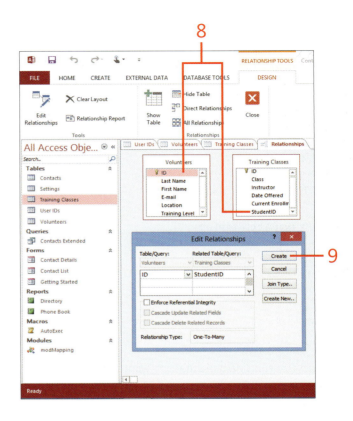

Creating a simple form

If you need to create a data-entry form so that others can add information to the database easily, Access has all the tools you need. The entire process is simple: just select the table you want to use to create the form and select the tool you need. Access does the rest.

Create a data form

1 In the Navigation pane, click the table that you want to use as the basis for the form.

2 Click the Create tab.

3 In the Forms group, click Form.

The Form opens in Layout View.

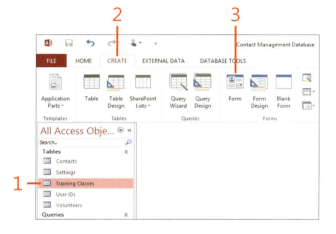

Modify a form

1 Click a form field and drag to resize it if needed.

2 Apply a theme to the form.

3 Change the form title.

4 Add a logo to the form.

5 Include other fields from the table on the form.

6 Click the Form Layout Tools Format contextual tab to format the text or background of the form.

7 On the Form Layout Tools Arrange contextual tab, choose tools to position the fields on the form the way you want them to appear.

8 Click Save to save the form.

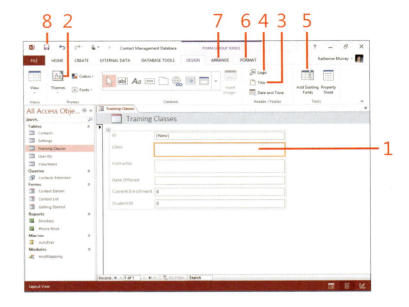

Creating reports

Reports in Access can help you to analyze your data in different ways. Perhaps you want to determine the current inventory levels of your ten top products. Or, maybe you need to check enrollment for a series of volunteer training classes that are coming up. If you've been entering and managing your data in Access, you can easily produce reports that give you just the information you're looking for.

Use the Report Wizard

1 Click the Create tab.

2 In the upper-right corner of the Reports group, click Report Wizard.

3 Choose the table that you want to use as the basis for the report.

4 Click a field that you want to include in the report.

5 Click the Add arrow. Repeat for additional fields.

6 Click Next.

The Report Wizard opens again, asking if you want to select a grouping level.

7 Click Next again, without selecting any grouping.

✓ **TIP** You can format your report by applying your favorite theme to the report; using the text formatting controls to change the look of headings and data; and even apply conditional formatting to data according to rules that you create. You'll find the tools you need in the Report Layout Tools available in Layout View.

✓ **TIP** You might find that you need to switch between Print Preview and Design View to make fine adjustments to column widths and the report width to fit the report on a single page width. Layout View is excellent for quickly removing fields and adjusting the width of fields, but Design View is needed for other adjustments.

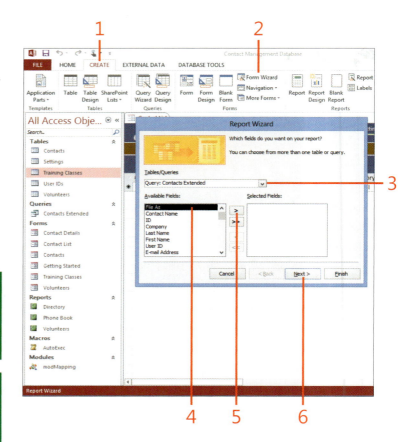

8 Click the first arrow to display the list of included fields.

9 Click the field on which you want to sort the report data. Include additional fields as needed.

10 Click Next.

11 Click whether you want to create a columnar, tabular, or justified report.

The preview changes to show you how each style will appear.

12 Click whether you want the report to appear in Portrait or Landscape orientation.

13 Click Next.

14 Enter a name for your report.

15 Click Finish.

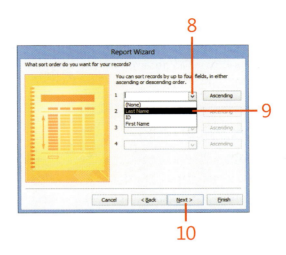

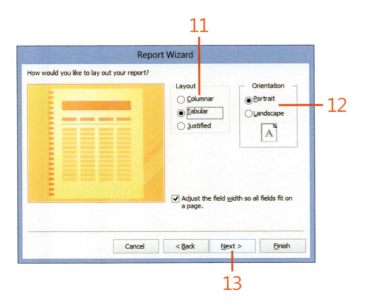

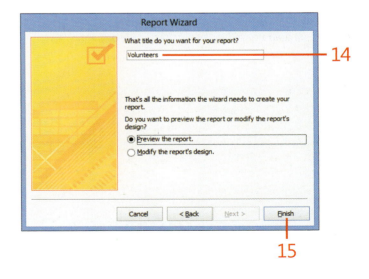

Creating a web app with Access 2013

21

The big story about Microsoft Access 2013 is its investment in the cloud. Now, Access includes tools that you can use to design your own custom web apps that share data in the cloud, using SharePoint and Office 365 technologies. Yes, this does mean you'll need an Office 365 subscription in order to use these web app features effectively. (You can find out more about the various subscription types at *www.office365.com*.) No matter which subscription you or your employer sign up for, you can add Office Professional Plus to your plan (which gives you access to SharePoint, so you can create your own custom web apps).

So, what is a custom web app and how does it benefit you to have these tools included in Access? Microsoft recognizes that much of what we do today is going to the cloud, and web apps that live online give you the option of gathering, managing, and sharing data in real time with people all over the world. You get to say who can access your data, of course, and you can customize the web apps you create to gather just what you need. But, the entire process is easier than you might think. And, Access 2013 includes a number of predesigned templates with web apps in mind.

In this section:

- Creating a new web app
- Adding tables
- Editing a data table
- Adding data
- Working with views
- Creating a new view
- Launching and using a web app
- Working with a team site

Creating a new web app

You can create your first Access web app based on a template designed to help you with the process, or you can go gung-ho and do it all from scratch. Either way, you'll have some simple choices to make about the type of information you want to gather and how you want to gather and work with it. Luckily, Access leads you through the steps, so getting started is fairly straightforward.

Start a web app from a template

1 Display the Access 2013 Start screen.

2 Scroll through the templates to find a web app template that you want to use.

Note that if a template name begins with the word desktop, it is not a web app template.

3 Click the web app template that you want to use.

4 Enter a name for the app that you're creating.

5 Click a location for the new app.

6 Click Create.

The web app opens in the Access window. The process takes a few minutes while Access creates the web app and adds tables and views for you to use. Your next step is to add the tables you'll use to store data in the web app.

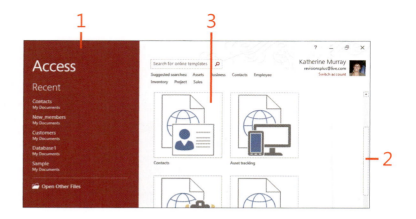

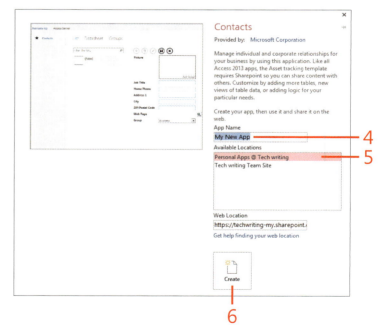

Create a blank web app

1 On the Access 2013 Start screen, click Custom Web App.

2 In the App Name field, type a name for the app.

3 Choose the SharePoint location where you want to create the web app.

4 Click Create. If prompted, sign in to Office 365 with your User ID and password.

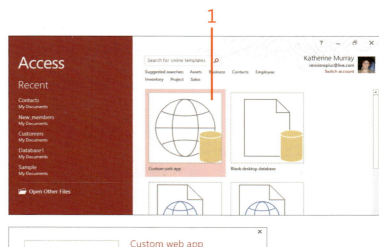

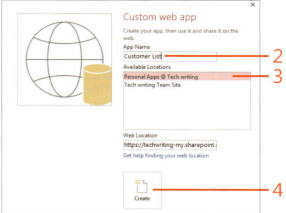

Adding tables

When you're working with an Access web app, the process of adding tables is streamlined so that you have only two options: you can search for a table style that you want to use for the data you need to manage, or you can open a table you've already saved in an existing file or list.

Search and find a table

1 Click in the Add Tables text box and type a word or phrase reflecting the type of information that you want to gather.

2 Click Search.

Results appear beneath the search box.

3 Scroll through the results list.

4 Click the table that you want to use.

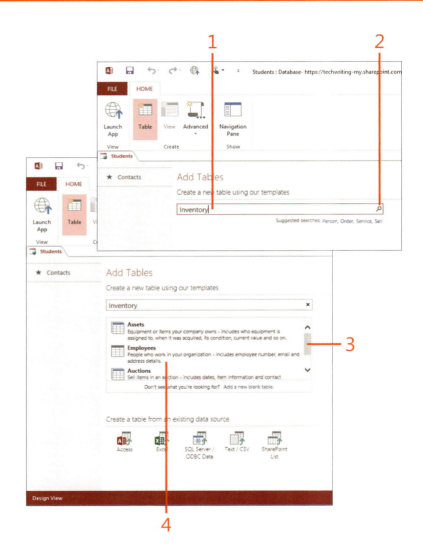

Add a blank table

1 On the Home tab, click Table.

2 Click to add a new blank table.

3 Click in a blank line in the Field Name column and type the name that you want to assign to the field.

4 In the Data Type column, select Short Text.

5 Click the Save icon.

6 Type a title for the Table name.

7 Click OK.

8 Click the View icon to display the table and enter data.

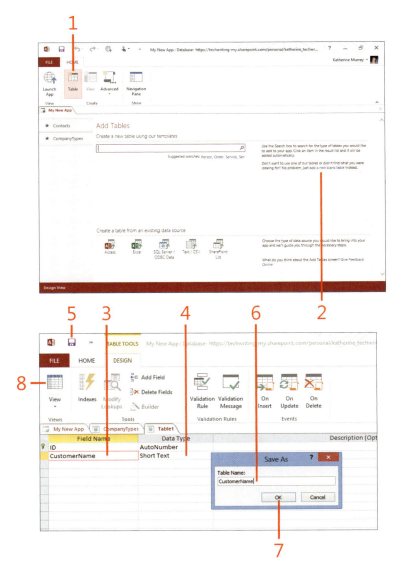

Editing a data table

You can easily change the data table you've added by modifying the content or the look of the fields. Especially if you've used the search tool to locate and open a ready-made table, you might have some tweaking to do.

Edit the table

1 Click the table that you want to edit.

2 Click Datasheet.

3 In the center of the web app window, click Edit.

Access displays the table in Design view.

4 Click the field that you want to change.

A series of three buttons appear, giving you the choice of changing Data, Formatting, or Actions. To change the name, source, or value of the data field (which is called a control in Access web apps), click Data. If you want to add a ToolTip, hide or display the control, or add a caption, click Formatting. If you want to change the action assigned to the control, click Actions.

5 Click Data.

A pop-up window appears, displaying your options.

6 Change the control name, if you'd like.

7 Click to display a list of other controls in the table and make a selection.

8 Enter a default value if you want to display one in the table.

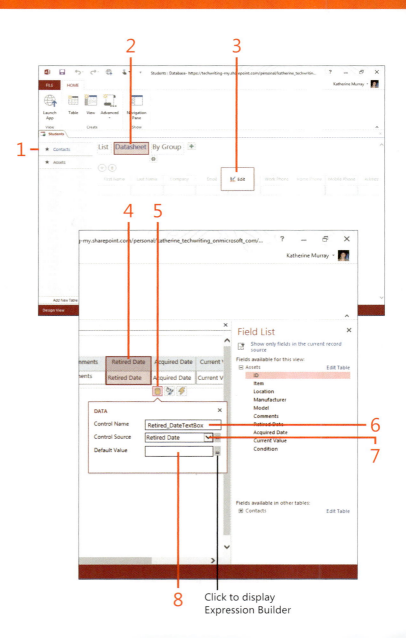

Click to display
Expression Builder

Adding data

You can add data easily while you're working with your Access web app. First, in Datasheet view, you display the table to which you want to add the information. Next, you click and type the new information, pressing Tab after each addition. Simple, right?

Add new data

1 Select the table that will store the new data.

2 Click the Settings/Actions button.

An options list appears.

3 Click View Data.

The table appears in Datasheet view.

4 Click the first available field and type the information that you want to add.

5 Press Tab to move to the next field.

6 When you're finished adding data, click the Close button.

TIP Once you get your table set up the way you want it, you can import table data by clicking Table in the Create group on the Home tab. This displays the initial tables page, where you can click the icon at the bottom of the screen that represents the type of data file you want to import. Access gives you the option of adding Access, Excel, SQL Server/ODBC Data, Text/CSV files, or SharePoint Lists.

Working with views

You can easily view the data from your Access web app in different ways. After you launch the web app, you can use both List and Datasheet view to review and update your information.

A list view provides two elements: the list and the associated details. As you click or search and filter the list, you will see a reduced set for records.

Work with a list view

1 Click a table that contains the information you want to view.

2 Click a line item to display the details for the order line.

The data record for that item appears.

3 Click the Edit tool to make the field available for editing.

4 Make the changes you want.

5 Click Save to save your changes.

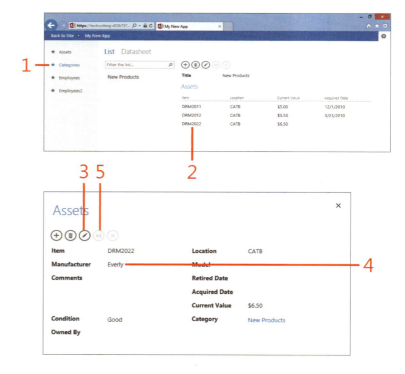

Work with a Datasheet view

1 Click Datasheet.

2 Click Add.

3 Enter data for a new record.

4 Click another record to save the new record.

5 To edit a record, click in the field and start typing.

6 To delete the record, click the Delete icon.

7 Click Yes to confirm deleting the record.

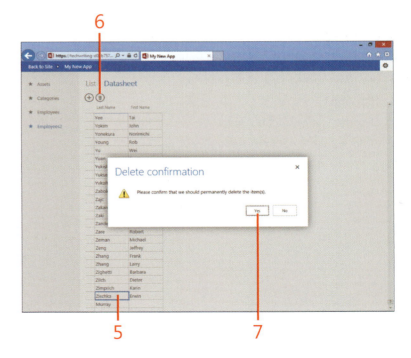

Creating a new view

In addition to viewing the data from your Access web app in List and Datasheet views, you can also use Access to create your own view so that you can analyze your data in the way that makes the most sense to you.

Create a new view

1 In the Navigation pane, click the table that you want to use.

2 Click the Add New View button.

3 Type a name for the new view.

4 Click the View Type down-arrow and choose the view you want from the list.

   You can choose from List Details, Datasheet, Summary, or Blank.

5 Leave the Record Source as it appears.

6 Click Add New View.

7 Click the Settings/Actions icon

8 Click Open In Browser to test the view.

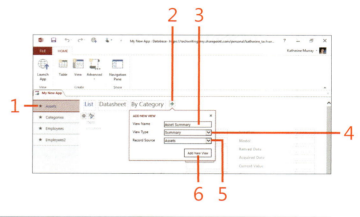

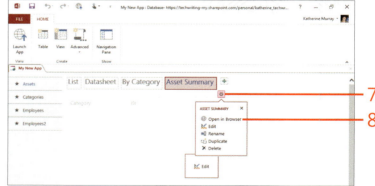

Launching and using a web application

After you've added the tables and tweaked them just the way you want them, you can launch the web app as a web application and test it out. You'll find the Launch App tool in the View group on the Home tab.

Launch and use a web app

1 On the Home tab, click Launch App. If you're prompted to log on, enter the user ID and password you use with Office 365.

2 Click Add to add a new record.

The data fields become available on the form.

3 Fill in the details for the new record.

4 Click the Save icon.

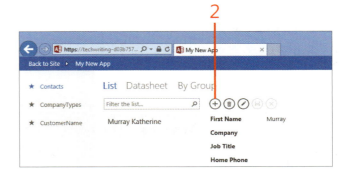

Working with a team site

While viewing any web page, you can click the Back To Site link in the far-left side of the navigation bar in the web browser to display your team site. From your team site, you have access to other files, blog posts, and more.

Open a web app in Access 2013 from a team site

1 Click Back To Site.

2 At the bottom of the navigation bar, click Site Content.

3 Click the ellipse to display options for the application.

4 Click the Web App icon once to open the Web App in a browser window.

5 Click Customize In Access to open the Web App in Access 2013.

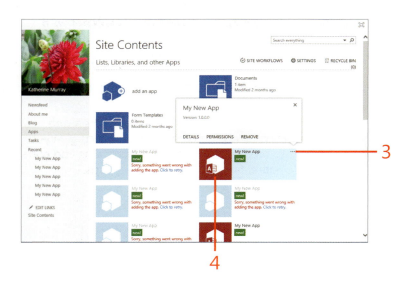

Appendix

Windows 8 brings an entirely new look and feel to your computer, offering bright color and fluid movement that makes it easy to work with apps, find and watch media, view and share photos, check email, and much more. If you're already a smartphone user, you are accustomed to tapping, flicking, and pinching your way through the operating system on your phone. Now, in Windows 8, if you have a touch-enabled device (which might mean you have a tablet or a touchscreen monitor), you can use touch to navigate your computer's operating system, too. If you don't have a touch device, don't worry: Windows 8 is just as natural to use with a keyboard and mouse as it is with touch. The choice of how you want to work with Windows 8 is entirely up to you.

Big features in Windows 8

After you first experience the brilliant color and smooth movement of Windows 8, you'll start to notice a number of new and unique features that Microsoft has included in the operating system. In fact, its developers say Windows 8 has been "reimagined from the chipset up through the user experience" (although as you will see there's quite a bit of familiar territory in the Windows 8 Desktop as well as the Control Panel). Here's a quick list of some of the big new features in Windows 8:

■ The new **Start screen** is optimized for touch but is great for mouse and keyboard input, too. You'll use the Start screen to launch the apps installed on your Windows 8 system. Some app tiles are known as live tiles, which update automatically to give you information, like the latest headlines on your favorite news app, the number of new email messages you've received, or what the weather is in your local area.

■ The **Charms** are a set of five icons that appears along the right edge of your Windows 8 screen, which give you quick access to the following common functions and controls: Search, Share, Start, Devices, and Settings.

- **App sharing** is a feature that makes it possible for your Windows 8 apps to share information easily, whether you're bringing together pictures from your favorite photo-sharing websites, all your contacts from various social-media accounts, or sharing a game through Xbox Live Games.

- The **Windows Store** is available as an app tile on the Windows 8 Start screen, and you can click it to browse, buy, and download apps available in a large collection of categories: Games, Social, Entertainment, Photo, Music & Video, Sports, Books & Reference, News & Weather, Health & Fitness, Food & Dining, Lifestyle, Shopping, Travel, Finance, Productivity, Tools, Security, Business, Education, and Government.

- **Internet Explorer 10** is the latest version of Microsoft's popular web browser. It represents a unique offering in the browser world because it actually has two personalities. On the Windows 8 Start screen, Internet Explorer 10 launches as a "modeless" browser, meaning there's no window that borders your browsing experience. The browser offers favorites as tabs that you can click and streamlines the search process to get you where you want to go quickly. If you open Internet Explorer 10 on the Windows 8 Desktop, however, you see a browser window and have an experience that is similar to what you experienced in Internet Explorer 9. Internet Explorer 10 for the Start screen doesn't allow plug-in utilities like Flash (because of the security risk they present), but you can still run plug-ins using the Internet Explorer 10 Desktop browser. (Don't worry—it's actually much more intuitive than it sounds.)

- **File Explorer** was formerly called Windows Explorer, and it's the tool you'll use on the Windows 8 Desktop to manage your files and folders in Windows 8. Now, File Explorer sports its own ribbon with tools for organizing, moving, sharing, copying, and managing the properties of your files and folders.

- You can use enhanced **Security features** to create a picture password, log on by using a PIN (instead of a password), and customize your Windows 8 lock screen with notifications (so you don't even need to unlock your computer to see the updates you need).

- **Xbox branding** for the Music and Video apps means that through Windows 8 you will have access to a world-class music library and a huge collection of TV series and movies, all through Xbox Live—and your Music and Video app tiles on the Windows 8 Start screen.

Learning about your Microsoft Account

Your Microsoft Account (formerly known as your Windows Live ID) keeps track of your program preferences, templates, program choices, and more as you work with Office 2013 on different computers and devices. Using Microsoft Account, your Office experience can travel with you because it keeps track of your settings and makes them available on whatever computer or device you use to log on next.

You first enter your Microsoft Account when you install Windows 8, but you can change it and modify your account settings at any time by displaying PC Settings through the Settings charm and then clicking Users. You can click Switch To A Local Account if you want to change your account settings so that they remain on your local computer only. This means your preferences, such as templates, color schemes, and more, won't be synced across the various devices you use. Additionally, your files won't be saved to SkyDrive by default.

To view other settings connected to your Microsoft Account, click More Account Settings Online. You can change your name, email address, personal information, and password. You can also add security information for the various devices you plan to use with your Microsoft Account. By choosing the categories on the left side of the Microsoft Account screen, you can also change the notifications you receive from Microsoft, change permissions and settings for various accounts linked to your Microsoft Account, and review and update your transactions and billing information.

Exploring the Start screen

The Windows 8 Start screen is the colorful, fluid place where you'll find the apps that you use most often. When you display Windows 8 for the first time, you'll find a collection of colorful app tiles, ready for you to begin working with photos, social media, your calendar, email, and more. You can use the Start screen as it is or add and remove tiles, customizing it to meet your own needs.

Use the Start screen

1 Start your computer, and then on the lock screen, swipe up with your finger or drag up by using the mouse.

   Windows 8 displays your logon screen.

2 Click in the text box and type your password.

3 Click Go.

   The Windows 8 Start screen appears.

4 Explore the Windows 8 Start screen elements by moving the screen to the left and right. You can drag the screen to display more app tiles.

Windows Store app

This notification shows the number of unread email messages

Click to change profile or log off

Small app tile

Find your files in SkyDrive

Large app tile

Launching an app

You can launch an app on the Windows 8 Start screen, whether you're using a mouse or touch. You begin by scrolling the screen to display the app that you want to use. Then, click the tile to launch the associated app.

Launch an app

1 On the Windows 8 Start screen, scroll or swipe to the left to display additional app tiles that are beyond the right edge of the screen.

2 Click the tile for the app that you want to launch

The app opens on the screen.

TIP You can start multiple apps in Windows 8 and you virtually never have to worry about running out of memory to store them all. This is because in Windows 8, apps are now suspended whenever they are not the full focus on the screen. This reduces the amount of energy your computer uses while simultaneously making it possible for you to keep multiple apps at the ready as you work. And, the best thing is that there's no wait time while the app wakes up from its suspended state—the app is instantly back in business, as soon as you display it on the screen.

Using the Windows 8 charms

In addition to launching and working with programs, Windows 8 makes it easy for you to take care of a number of other important tasks, like finding the files and programs you need, sharing your computer with other devices, and personalizing all kinds of settings that control how your computer works.

You might want to customize the look and feel of your operating system, set up additional user accounts, manage whether your settings are synchronized among all your computers, and change your privacy settings. You can take care of all these tasks in Windows 8 by using the charms.

Use the charms

1 If you're working on a touchscreen device, on the Windows 8 Start screen, swipe in from the right edge of the screen.

2 If you're working with a mouse, move the mouse pointer to the lower-right corner of the screen. When the charms begin to appear, move the mouse pointer and click the one you want.

3 Click the charm that you want to use. Here's what the various charms do:

- **Search** provides a means to search for apps, settings, or files. Additionally, you can search within specific apps for information by clicking the app you want to search.

- **Share** gives you the ability to share content from within specific apps. You might, for example, share photos, music, or a game you really like.

- **Start** returns you to the Windows 8 Start screen no matter where you might be in Windows 8.

- **Devices** makes it possible for you to connect Windows 8 to a second screen. Additionally, you can connect to other devices that are part of your HomeGroup or connected to your computer.

- **Settings** displays various items that control your Windows 8 experience. For example, you can choose your Internet connection, change the volume or brightness of your computer, change the way notifications appear on your Start screen, change your screen language, or turn your computer off.

Working with the Windows 8 desktop

Many of the programs you'll use with Windows 8 weren't designed specifically for this new, modern operating system. And, even some new programs, like Office 2013, need a more traditional interface, as well. The Windows 8 desktop will look familiar to you if you have previously used Windows 7, and you'll find that you can launch programs, use jump lists, and add shortcuts easily.

Work with the desktop

1 On the Windows 8 Start screen, click the Desktop tile.

2 Click and drag to move the taskbar to another side of the screen, if you'd like.

3 Click to open File Explorer.

4 Click to display the Windows 8 touch keyboard.

5 Click to change system settings.

> ✓ **TIP** To return to the Windows 8 Start screen, click your Windows button or swipe in from the right to display the charms and click Start.

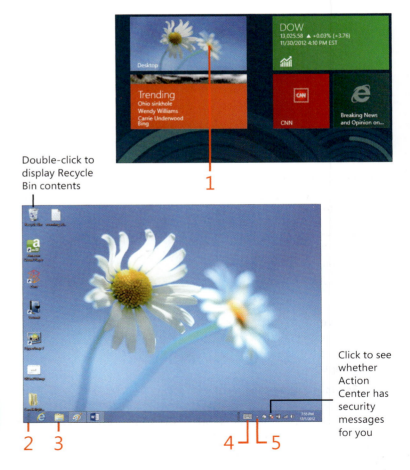

Double-click to display Recycle Bin contents

Click to see whether Action Center has security messages for you

Changing app options

The word "apps" is short for applications, and it's the name Microsoft has adopted for the programs you launch on the Windows 8 Start screen. By default, your Windows 8 computer comes equipped with a large collection of apps, and you can find, download, and purchase any number of new apps from the Windows Store (which itself is an app on your Windows 8 Start screen). You can leave your apps on the Start screen as they are if you like them the way they appear, but you can also change the way apps appear by moving them, grouping them, naming groups, changing them from small to large (and vice versa), and changing other app settings.

Change app options

1 Swipe down or right-click the tile of the app that you want to change.

The apps bar appears along the bottom of the screen.

2 Click the app option that you want to apply.

> ✓ **TIP** What you can change about an app depends in part on what the app developer enables it to do. Not all small apps can become large apps; and not all apps can be added to the Windows 8 taskbar. To see which options are available for a particular app, swipe down on the app tile or right-click it. The apps bar appears along the bottom of the Windows 8 Start screen, showing all options that are available for that app.

> → **TRY THIS!** To see all the apps installed on your computer, swipe up or right-click along the bottom of the screen to display the apps bar. Click All Apps to see a list of all the apps currently installed on your computer. If you see an app that you want to add to the Windows 8 Start screen, swipe down on it or right-click it. The apps bar appears, showing options for that app. To add the app to the Start screen, on the far left of the apps bar, simply click Pin To Start. The app is added to the far right of the Start screen where you can launch it by clicking the tile.

Moving from app to app in Windows 8

Even though when you're working with Windows 8 apps you don't see the same traditional windows you were accustomed to in Windows 7, you can easily move from app to app in

Windows 8. The process is as easy as dragging your finger in from the left side of the screen, and the next open application appears on your screen.

Move from app to app

1 Launch all of the apps with which you want to work.

2 Swipe in from the left edge of the screen and drag the app to the center of the screen and release it. If you're using the mouse, you can click at the edge of the screen and drag inward to replicate the swipe motion.

TRY THIS! You can also dock open apps to view more than one app on the screen at a time. To dock an app, swipe in from the left side of the screen to display the next app and flick it toward the top of the screen. You can continue to cycle through other apps, if you'd like, or work with the two open apps as long as needed. When you're ready to return to normal display, click the bar that divides the apps on the screen and drag it to the right.

TIP You can also move from app to app in Windows 8 by pressing Alt+Tab. A small pop-up window appears and you can press Tab to move the highlight to the app that you want to view. When you release the key combination, the highlighted app is the one the opens on your screen.

Rearranging app tiles

Windows 8 arranges your tiles by default but the tiles don't have to stay that way. You can rearrange the app tiles so that the ones you use most often appear in an area you can reach easily.

Rearrange app tiles

1 Drag the app tile that you want to move.

Other tiles on the Start screen move to make room for the tile.

2 When the tile is positioned where you want it to appear, release the tile.

Index

About the Author

Katherine Murray has been writing about Microsoft Office since the earliest version was available, way back in the dark ages of DOS. She loves the new minimalist design in Office 2013 and is a faithful cloud enthusiast, sharing folders and files with editors, friends, and family all over the globe. She's also a "tech-everywhere" kind of person who enjoys the flexibility of being able to work on her desktop, laptop, tablet, or phone—no matter where she may be. In addition to her long-time tech writing, Katherine is the publications coordinator for Quaker Earthcare Witness (*www.quakerearthcare.org*), where she uses Microsoft Office and Adobe technologies to create, publish, and share print and online communications. Additionally, Katherine is a contributor to Windows Secrets (*www.windowsecrets.com*) and CNET's TechRepublic, and she is also the author of *Microsoft Office Professional 2013 for Touch Devices Plain & Simple*, *Microsoft Word 2013 Inside Out*, and many other technical books.

What do you think of this book?

We want to hear from you!

To participate in a brief online survey, please visit:

microsoft.com/learning/booksurvey

Tell us how well this book meets your needs—what works effectively, and what we can do better.
Your feedback will help us continually improve our books and learning resources for you.

Thank you in advance for your input!

Microsoft® Press